Secret Strategies from North America's Top Whitetail Hunters

Nick Sisley

Published by

**krause
publications**

700 E. State Street • Iola, WI 54990-0001
Telephone: 715/445-2214

Please call or write for our free catalog of outdoor publications. Our toll-free number to
place an order or obtain a free catalog is 800-258-0929 or please use our regular business
telephone 715-445-2214 for editorial comment
and further information.

Library of Congress Catalog Number: 95-77311
ISBN: 0-87341-342-3
Printed in the United States of America

Contents

Foreword

As an editor who has eagerly read and published Nick Sisley's work for almost 30 years, the news that he was preparing a new book based on the experiences of record-rack deer hunters was like being handed a present I've always wanted. Now that I have opened that present, and devoured every word with great relish, I can report that here is a gift for all active buck hunters—a gift you will not only savor as a great reading experience but one that will undoubtedly improve your success and enjoyment in the field.

Nick Sisley's prose has been a mainstay in my editorial agenda throughout my career as editor-in-chief of *Sports Afield* and *Outdoor Life*, and today as editorial director of the Outdoor Magazine Group of Harris Publications. The same qualities I have always appreciated in Nick's writing—that it is both engaging and illuminating—have made his work eagerly anticipated by readers.

As a respected authority whose field experience and knowledge range from grouse hunting to bass fishing, Nick could fill an entire bookshelf with volumes based on sharing his own knowledge. However, distinguished journalist that he is, he does not neglect turning his considerable talents to reporting on the experiences of other sportsmen and women who have a worthy story to tell.

This book is the ultimate reflection of Nick's unfailing dedication to unearthing the details of actual hunting experiences too interesting not to be shared, too inspirational not to be reflected upon for improving our own skills.

The big one that got away! The big one that didn't get away! The theme is classic wherever sportsmen hoist a rod or gun or a glass, be it on a southern bass lake or a deer camp in the rock-ribbed hills of New England. We especially love to hear about those big bucks with huge racks—the kind that run through our dreams but are seldom encountered in the places we actually hunt.

When I was a teenager growing up in Georgia, experiencing acne, voice break and unrequited love, bagging a buck was so rare it could get your picture in the local weekly paper. (The game management efforts that have brought soaring whitetail numbers to that region since then is one of the great conservation stories.)

My first real chance at a wall rack came one dawn that found me settled against the trunk of an enormous white oak in the hills near Hanover, Pennsylvania.

Buck hunters pray for such a morning. At first light, the horizon was cut from steel—black humps of white pines, the knife-like rim of a distant ridge looming above the forest. Without wind, the stillness seemed almost electric as I shivered in the cold, nervous to the raw edge at the thought of the buck I hoped would be mine.

When the crows began to patrol, their raucous cries announcing that it was time for things to get moving, I detected the rustle of squirrels in the branches overhead. As the light came on, I began to hear occasional gunshots, echoing from the distant ridge.

Suddenly the sound of a limb breaking jerked my attention toward the trees to my left. I strained to see. Nothing! The sound came again, louder still, and was followed this time by the dry rustle of leaves being shuffled. Another hunter, I thought, bitterly. Perhaps if he sees me, he'll move on.

I stood up, and in that instant an enormous buck exploded away, his head adorned with what William Faulkner once described as, "...that rocking chair he toted."

I had blown it! I sat down, numbed, shocked. Certainly such an opportunity might never come my way again. For the next couple of hours, my mind seethed with bitterness over my inadequacy.

Gradually, though, the poison inside seemed to drain away. The forest came back to me—the sights and sounds of the birds, the feeling that possibilities still existed here. At noon I noticed that the squirrels were moving about just as industriously as they had at dawn. Strange, I thought. There must be some dirty weather knocking about. I can't see it coming, but they can *feel* it coming.

I knew I was back in the groove then, focused on nature instead of myself.

The next day it snowed, but I was at work, hunting errant commas and semicolons on manuscripts instead of bucks in the tracking snow.

As much as we love the tales of big bucks and continue to fantasize about them, for most of us *any* buck is a good buck. But someday...yes, someday...our chance might come. If and when it does, and a buck for the book becomes a reality, we'll be joining some mighty good company.

Turn the pages, and you can start meeting the best of the best right now.

Lamar Underwood

Acknowledgments

Thank you so much, everyone of you who contributed to this book; Brian Damery, Denny Stiner, Bob Wozniak, Bill Jordan, Bill Winke, Herb Scrip, Jim Hill, Rick Frame, Walter Hatcher, Will Primos, Rick Bagley, Toxey Haas, Don Warren, Dick Kirby, Bill Cole, Jim Massett, Jim Strelec, David Blanton, Joe Drake, Greg Olson, Blackie Lightfoot, and Roger Syrstad.

Introduction

The idea behind this book is simple: find out how some of the continent's biggest white-tailed bucks have been taken, then present that how-to to readers, so they can incorporate some of the ideas that have worked for others into their own quest for whitetails with out-size racks. I believe that's exactly what you'll find as you read and study this book.

Some readers are going to have minimal experience and big buck knowledge. These are the ones who are going to learn the most from these pages. But even those with extensive knowledge of big-buck how-to are going to glean a great deal from what these successful hunters have so generously shared. Most readers are going to be somewhere in between; plenty of experience, but they simply haven't had the time to spend literally hundreds of hours a year pitting themselves against the biggest of big bucks. While this book has been written for all deer hunters, it's this latter group that has been targeted first and foremost.

You sportsmen are going to learn a great deal here, so have a scratch pad close by for making notes. Frequently you may want to highlight specific lines, phrases, sentences, even entire paragraphs. So have a highlight pen handy, too.

As you learn more and more about the how-to of big-buck taking, be willing to share what you have learned, as the fellows who have contributed here have done. I assure you, when you share, you not only learn more, but the practice comes back to reward you many times over.

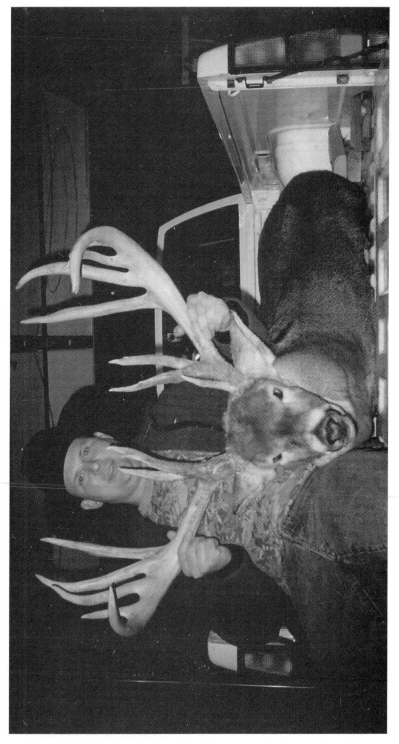

Note the double brow tines on Damery's buck. Though these tines are beautiful, they're a deduction in Boone & Crockett points. Without these deductions, this would have been the biggest whitetail ever.

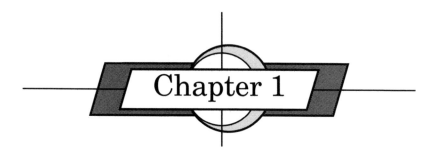

Brian Damery's Huge Illinois Buck: Almost A World Record

The minutes had ticked on endlessly. Now Brian Damery had been at this for hours, belly crawling in and around Illinois harvested fields, keeping low in the water courses since the terrain was near pool-table flat. Once he had to belly and knee right through the creek itself. Now it appeared he would have to reverse his course, somehow crawling through the creek again, somehow keeping his 870 pump slug gun dry for the second time. Brian took a moment to gather his bearings and reflect a little. "How did all this start?" he asked himself.

So let's go back to the beginning of Brian's saga, a saga involving one of the biggest bucks ever taken. Damery is the assistant manager at a fertilizer plant in Moweaqua, Illinois. He first began hunting at age 16, but then had a hunting hiatus for several years. Probably discovered girls big time. At 16 he hunted solely with a bow. Illinois does not permit rifle hunting. He'd hunt bucks maybe three to four times a year then, but it was in 1990 that he began hunting in earnest. Bow hunting was and is his favorite way to seek out whitetails, even though he took the huge buck pictured here with a shotgun. Since getting back into deer hunting in 1990, Damery has become dead serious about it. He's been averaging 20 days per year in the field, an eye out for the biggest of bucks. He does a lot of pre-season scouting, as well.

Brian's hunting adventure mentioned earlier began when a friend brought in one side of a pair of shed antlers to the fertilizer plant where Brian works. A dog dragged in what appears to be the other side of those shed antlers. Brian knows where both these sheds are today, but can't talk either of the current owners out of them. He roughly scored the right shed at 100 points, with a beam length of 29 inches. Brian took a photo of the two sheds. All of this occurred in March of 1993, so there was plenty of time to get mentally geared up to hunt this buck.

Brian obtained permission to hunt the property of his friend who had brought in the shed rack. He also secured permission from the adjoining landowner who was his cousin. However, another person had previous permission to hunt on his cousin's property, and Brian was worried about fouling up that fellow's hunting. More about that aspect shortly.

It was Brian's initial objective to take this brute buck with a bow. All summer long he kept his ear alert for information on the deer, of course, hoping the giant wouldn't meet death on the grillwork of some farm pickup truck. Through August and into early September Brian used his lunch hour to scout for the buck in question. The land was only three miles from the fertilizer plant, so he could be there in minutes. He saw plenty of sign that indicated the object of his quest was around, but he could never put an eyeball on this deer.

During some lunch breaks he'd scout new territory where he had not hunted before and found several spots he really liked. The opening day of bow season Damery selected a different area because he didn't want to foul up the hunting for the other fellow who had permission to hunt on his cousin's land. Also, he told me, "I was sort of saving that big buck for gun season." I get the impression that Brian had discovered from his pre-season scouting and patterning of this big deer that the lay of the land was not conducive to taking this buck from a bow stand. The deer simply didn't have any places he frequented where a close shot from a treestand was probable.

Brian had been doing plenty of pre-season homework, for this guy had six treestands in place before opening morning. He had been seeing a lot of deer approximately 6 miles away from where the big buck in question resided. He spent the first week and a half of bow season hunting the place where he had found so much good sign, again, maybe 6 miles from the area where he was at the opening of this chapter. No cigar, despite the worthy effort. Sound familiar?

As bow season was drawing to a close, Brian managed to hunt his cousin's property three times. All three were those typical, non-eventful stays in a treestand, and you know how doubt can creep into your mind during those long hours—doubts about why you selected this particular place, thoughts about how another treestand spot might be somewhere between slightly and infinitely better.

Two nights before the opening of shotgun season Brian made a monumental move, in more ways than one. He moved one of his treestands from one area to a new area on his cousin's property. The move eventually put him in a position so he could put an eyeball on the huge buck, but, as he did this in the gathering darkness, he didn't see the poison oak. The maddening itching began the day before shotgun season was to start. When the opening day for shotgunning deer in Illinois arrived, Brian was in the doctor's office, one eye shut with swelling due to the poison oak infection, much of the rest of his body writhing from the uncontrollable itch. I've suffered from severe cases of poison ivy more times than I care to remember in my life, so I can sympathize with Brian. What horrible luck to have to be in a doctor's office come opening morning, rather than out there seeking the buck that has filled your waking hours with never-ending thoughts for months.

But by noon Brian had de-scented himself and donned his clothing, which had also been de-scented. He was wearing an orange sweatshirt with cut-out sleeves, a Realtree light jacket underneath, and an orange hat, meeting the blaze requirements of his state. Soon he was in the treestand that he had repositioned two nights before. The wind was gusting up to 30 mph, so the opening day conditions left a lot to be desired. He had a 10X Tasco binocular around his neck. With them he spotted a hunter about 1/4 mile away, seated along a fencerow. This was the fellow Brian had been trying not to foul up, the guy who had previous permission to hunt his cousin's property. Brian was glad to see him because he knew his own hunting was not going to interfere.

With further glassing Damery found a group of deer. They were in a harvested cornfield that had been disked, then run over with a chisel blade. These deer were about 700 yards away when Brian first spotted them. Instantly, Brian sensed, despite the extreme distance, that this was the buck that had worn the shed antlers he had handled the previous March. "I remember feeling dizzy almost immediately after putting the binoculars on that buck," Brian told me. "The tree was swaying in the wind, plus I had been looking through the glasses for quite a while, but the sweep of emotional elation upon seeing that buck, I think, had the most to do with the wave of dizziness I felt."

There were four deer in the group: two does, a very nice 8-point, and, of course, the deer that this chapter is centering around. Both patiently and excitedly, Damery watched this quartet for a lengthy hour and a half. Then he heard a shot. It was the fellow who was a 1/4 mile away. The guy had shot another buck. That hunter wasn't in a position to see the buck of Damery's dreams. Maybe because the wind was blowing so hard, the four deer Damery was watching gave no indication that they had heard the shot.

A bean field and hay field separated Brian from the bucks in that harvested cornfield. In the hay field were a number of big round bales of hay. After assessing his position and that of the deer, he decided his only chance would be to move toward them. Using the hay bales to cover his initial stalk, he narrowed the distance from about 700 to about 400 yards, not even close to being in range for his slug-shooting 870.

From this new position Brian again assessed his possibilities. He had to get closer. A lot closer. That's when the first of his belly crawling began. Grazing along now, the deer started inching their way in the direction of a waterway. Damery felt, "If I can get into that waterway and start crawling, and those deer come to the waterway, that's my only chance."

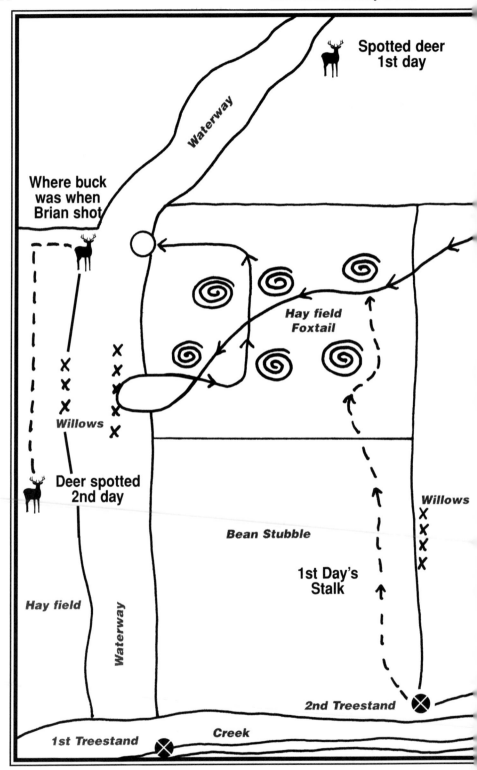

Spotted deer
1st day

Waterway

Where buck
was when
Brian shot

Hay field
Foxtail

Willows

Deer spotted
2nd day

Willows

Bean Stubble

1st Day's
Stalk

Hay field

Waterway

2nd Treestand

1st Treestand   Creek

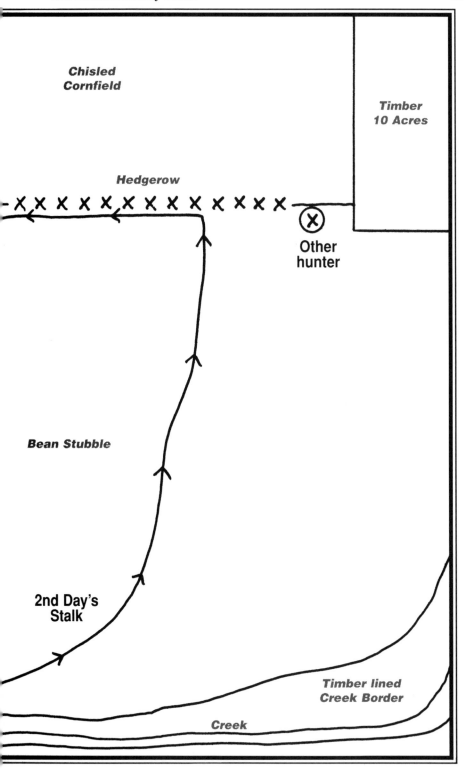

He inched his way along for a while into the creek bottom. There he'd be only a little lower than the surrounding flatland, but where the deer wouldn't be able to see his approach. It was a good plan, but it didn't work. The deer didn't move toward the watercourse as fast as Brian had hoped. He ran out of time! Daylight time! In the gathering dusk he belly crawled through the water course to stay out of sight, but this time back toward his pickup rather than toward the deer. He arrived home worn out, still itching from the poison oak, excited about all the time he'd spent looking at and trying to outwit the biggest buck he'd probably ever lay eyes on, hoping that the deer wouldn't go far overnight.

He was back at his hunting haunt before sunup the next morning. I didn't ask him how well he slept that night. Probably not at all. He told me his poison oak had improved a little, but maybe the deer prospects had his mind on matters other than itching. "Sunrise was at 6:30, and I didn't have to wait long before the excitement of the previous day picked right up where it had left off. At 6:40 I spotted a huge set of antlers near one of those big hay bales. Next I discovered a doe nearby. I watched the buck come to his feet, knowing all along that it was the same one. I sized up the situation. Here's what I figured. The deer were going to return to the same harvested cornfield. The buck had everything he wanted there; the does, the food, the protection of wide-open spaces. That's when I got down out of my treestand. Before the previous day I had never stalked a deer in my life, but I sensed that stalking was the only way I was going to get within shotgun range of this buck."

So again Brian Damery snuck and crawled his way, first through bean stubble, then along a hedgerow, next through a hay field with tall foxtail, all in an effort to reach the willows in a little creek bed. Note the sketch—and note how Brian crawled for hundreds of yards parallel to the deer before starting in their direction. After belly crawling through the bean field, next it was 250-300 yards of crawling along a hedge row, using the vegetation there to hide his movements from the deer he was stalking. Every few minutes he'd take time to peak at where the deer were, for now he knew it was a timing thing. He had to reach the part of the watercourse where the deer would cross, but before the whitetails got there.

To prevent the deer from seeing him, Brian crawled right through the watercourse. He got soaked for his trouble, but managed to keep his 870 shotgun high and dry. He paused to catch his breath. He knew he was getting close enough now, and the suspense was getting to him. Then he heard noise in the nearby willows. Something was coming. It had to be the deer. "My heart is pounding so fast, I'm never going to be able to pull the trigger, let alone hit the deer," Brian was thinking to himself. Just when he was wondering about how he might get control of his shaking body the 8-point buck that had been palling around with the two does and the big buck crossed the watercourse—exactly where Brian had just bellied through it.

"He's going to smell me. He's going to smell me," Brian lamented to himself. "This hunt's over. He's going to whiff my scent any moment, snort, and they'll all skedaddle. Darn."

But the 8-point never gave a hint of smelling danger. Just kept on moving slowly away. Now we're to the point where this chapter opened, with Brian soaked pretty well through and through, and facing the necessity of bellying through the little creek again.

"This was about the time that I got my wits back, quit shaking so horribly, and my heartbeat returned closer to normal. I steeled myself to what I had to do. I had already been on my belly for close to two hours, but I had to stick with what I was doing. Bellying along hadn't produced a suitable shot yet, but my tactics hadn't spooked these deer either."

So he crawled back through the watercourse, then carefully peeked above. The surrounding grass was sparse but about two feet high, so it offered a little protection from being seen. Getting to this position had taken some time since he'd seen the 8-point cross the creek, and now the four deer were 100-125 yards away, and they had bedded down.

Again Brian had the good sense to carefully assess the possibilities. He could use the watercourse and willows a second time to hide his movements and belly crawl closer. He crept back out of the willows into the tall foxtail of the hay field. Again note sketch—and how Brian crawled away from the deer, then turned left, then made another left back toward the little creek bottom. A savvy piece of stalking work here! Slowly, he eventually got to the place where he wanted to be, assuming the deer were still bedded down. Ever so cautiously, he took a look and found them resting.

Now what for a game plan? Should he stay put and be patient, hoping the deer would work toward him when they did get up? Or should he attempt to move even closer? He mulled it over briefly, then decided on the latter. Again, he slowly crawled 25 yards closer yet. He figured the range now to be 75 yards, but judging range can be fickle, especially when you've been crawling around the ground for two hours, never having once stood up. I wonder if he yearned for a scope sight on that 870, for 75 yards can be pushing it for open sights and a shotgun. The deer got up, milled around a bit, then lay back down.

It was now about 8:30. He waited some more. Finally, the deer got up and started to move. It became obvious that they were going to move on, move out of that bedding area, head for wherever they were going to spend the rest of the morning. It was rug-cutting time for Brian Damery. Would his pre-season practice shooting pay off? Had he done enough of it?

The 870 came up smoothly. In less time than it takes to tell it, Brian had the sights aligned with the big buck's chest. He sent a 1-1/8 ounce Brenneke slug on its way. The buck whirled at the shot. Brian's first thought was that he had missed. The buck ran directly at him though. Damery told me he was so rattled at that point that he short shucked the pump's action. When the deer got within 20 yards he spotted Brian and turned. Now Brian's second shot was a clean miss. The deer looked

***Brian Damery's huge Illinois whitetail. It was officially scored at
200-2/8 B&C points.***

like it was going to get away. Was all that work of belly crawling for
hours to be wasted? Was the buck of a lifetime going to escape him?

No. Brian's third Brenneke slammed home low in the neck, breaking the
spine. The deer was running away from him at the time. Later Brian paced
that third shot off: 80 yards. As with all spine shots, the huge buck dropped
in his tracks. The hooker is that Brian's first shot had been a telling one, for
that Brenneke had taken out both lungs. Also, after standing up Brian
decided the 75 yard range he had suspected when he had been lying prone,
didn't look that long. So he paced it off: just over 50 yards instead of 75.

So the saga was finally over. Or was it? The buck had to be shown all
over town to friends at surrounding farms and nearby workplaces.
Shortly, the magnitude of this prize really began to assert itself in
Brian's life. His phone was ringing with magazine and TV inquiries.
Bill Jordan of Realtree camouflage brought his television show crew to
Illinois. They did a partial reenactment of the hunt. It has been an
exciting several months for Brian Damery, but he admits he'll probably never experience the excitement of those two hours, belly crawling
down and around one of central Illinois' little watercourses.

One interesting aspect about this buck's rack is its double brow
tines. Boone & Crockett looks at double brow tines as a negative, not a
positive. Consequently, B&C uses a deduction for those extra tines.
Brian's deer had been officially measured shortly before our interview,
since the 60-day waiting period had elapsed. His typical scored 200-2/8

B&C points. However, if Boone & Crockett had recognized the double brow tines as a positive his buck would have measured 214-7/8, beating even Milo Hanson's whitetail record of 213-1/8. The longest tine on this buck measures 13 inches, while the spread is 28-3/8.

Brian Damery's Equipment

Shotgun - *Remington 870 express with rifled barrel and rifle sights.*
Load - *Brenneke 2-3/4-inch slug at 1-1/8 ounce.*
Binocular - *10X Tasco.*
Clothing - *Realtree camo jacket, in conjunction with required blaze orange clothing.*

Scoresheet

Final Score: $200^{2/8}$

Scorable Points: 17
Right Antler 9 Inside Spread: $28^{3/8}$
Left Antler 8 Greatest Spread: $30^{6/8}$
Abnormal Points: $22^{5/8}$ Tip-to-Tip Spread: 26

Area	Right	Left	Difference
Length of Main Beam	32	$32^{4/8}$	$4/8$
Length of First Point	$9^{1/8}$	$8^{6/8}$	$3/8$
Length of Second Point	$12^{1/8}$	13	$7/8$
Length of Third Point	$11^{5/8}$	$11^{2/8}$	$3/8$
Length of Fourth Point	$9^{4/8}$	$7^{4/8}$	2
Length of Fifth Point	$5^{6/8}$	$4^{5/8}$	$1^{1/8}$
Circumference Between Burr and First Point	$5^{4/8}$	$5^{3/8}$	$1/8$
Circumference Between First and Second Points	$4^{4/8}$	$4^{4/8}$	—
Circumference Between Second and Third Points	$8^{2/8}$	6	$2^{2/8}$
Circumference Between Third and Fourth Points	$5^{4/8}$	$5^{1/8}$	$5/8$
Totals	$104^{1/8}$	$98^{5/8}$	$8^{2/8}$

Exact Location of Kill:
Macon County, IL
Taken By:
    Brian Damery
Measured by:

Spread: $28^{3/8}$
Column 1: $104^{1/8}$
Column 2: $98^{5/8}$
Subtotal: $231^{1/8}$
minus Column 4: $8^{2/8}$
minus Abnormal: $22^{5/8}$

Final Score:
$200^{2/8}$

Brian Damery's Boone & Crockett scoring form.

The timing was November 20th. The rut was over in Jim's part of Minnesota. His grunt calling was a major positive with this "metro" buck.

Chapter 2

Minnesota's The Setting For Two Big Bucks Taken By Jim Hill

Jim Hill sort of blew Gary Sesselmann's mind. Gary heads up the company that makes and markets Scent-Lok clothing, the hunting apparel that contains activated charcoal for odor elimination. It appears Jim was the first hunter to use one of Gary's Sent-Lok suits to successfully take a big white-tailed buck. That was in Montana, early during the 1992 season when the Scent-Lok stuff was brand new. Weeks later Hill also took bragging-size bucks in both Minnesota and South Dakota. Thus the Scent-Lok outfits, marketed via Sesselmann's company, called ALS Enterprises, received an excellent initial shot in the arm. Hill's bucks didn't receive much publicity, but Sesselmann knew right away that his product was a winner.

When Jim was only 10 years old, his Dad took him squirrel hunting in Wisconsin. He has been an avid woodsman ever since. At age 15 he first took up deer hunting, and he hunted that season with a bow, before rifle season started. He bought a .270 and hunted bucks that fall. In those formative years rifle hunting was the "real" hunting. Days afield during bow season were then traditionally looked upon as "....scouting for rifle season!"

That was in the early 1960s. Jim's 47 now, and he concentrated on rifle hunting for many years, but always bow hunted prior to the rifle stuff every season. He was living in Michigan during the mid-1970s where the bow hunting was exceptional. Jim was beginning to learn more and more about bow how-to, in addition to becoming more intrigued with that type of hunting. Since the mid-1970s he has hunted whitetails exclusively with a bow. For a number of years he hunted both Wisconsin and Minnesota every season. These days he has branched out even farther, adding quite an impressive list of states where he has taken good bucks. Yet Minnesota is where he lives, where Jim does the bulk of his hunting, and where he's been fortunate to take several exceptional specimens. We're going to cover his interesting how-to on two of those Minnesota bucks here.

One of those Minnesota bucks became sort of a passion with Jim Hill. That's because he first saw the deer in 1990. Hunted him hard, too. The buck survived to grow even bigger horns in 1991, when Jim again pitted outdoor skills against that buck, only to come up empty for the second year in a row. "The landowner who first spotted this buck for me is sharp," Jim began. "He knows a great rack when he sees one and doesn't get excited about racks that aren't of trophy quality."

Here's the hooker. The buck Jim chased hard in 1990 and 1991, then eventually bagged in 1992, wasn't as big as another buck that the same landowner/friend had seen on his property, but we'll get to that later.

In 1990 Jim saw the deer he was after between the state's two gun seasons. The buck had taken up bedding residence on an island in a tag alder swamp. The island was fairly clear in the center, but it was rimmed with trees. Jim felt that nobody was hunting this deer, and further, no one had probably ever hunted the island tag alder swamp. Such swamps are always miserable places, and this one was especially nasty. The whole of the territory was small, just a couple of acres.

Hill did have one good chance for the buck in 1990. He snuck in as quietly as possible, downwind, got into a tree and waited. In due time he tickled his rattling antlers slightly. That's all it took to get that big buck interested. "One glimpse and I knew he was a definite shooter," was the way Jim told it. "Immediately I saw good mass—and a lot of points. I wasn't able to scrutinize the rack because of the intervening foliage, but I did see seven points on one side. There wasn't a lot of height to the rack, but I knew he was a dandy anyway. He stopped at 25 yards. I had an opening, but the shot wasn't right since it was a face-on angle; from my position in the tree his face presented the biggest target. Naturally, I didn't take it.

"What I needed right there was a decoy. The buck eventually came closer, within 20 yards, but there was no clear shot this time. Too much vegetation between me and the deer. I tickled the rattling horns one more time. The buck grunted in reply, then just angled off. I never saw him again that season."

In the summer of 1991 the landowner saw that buck again, and reported the sighting to Hill. I guess the tip here is to work on your landowner relationships. Wouldn't it be great if you had several landowners who not only allowed you to hunt their property, but also kept an eye out for trophy deer, then told you when and where they were seen?

Hill spotted the buck again while walking in to try to set up a stand during the 1991 season. This time it was two bucks, standing in a ditch, but skylined against the pale yellow of a breaking dawn. Jim froze. The two bucks eventually melted into a CRP (Conservation

On October 28, 1992 the landowner called Jim. He had seen the buck crossing into land Hill could hunt. It was on October 30, 1992 that Jim was finally successful—after three years!

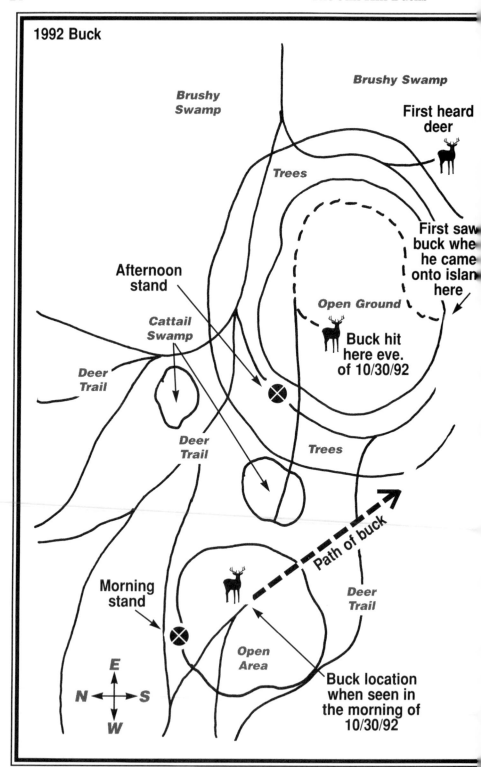

1992 Buck

Brushy Swamp

Brushy Swamp

First heard deer

Trees

First saw buck when he came onto island here

Afternoon stand

Open Ground

Cattail Swamp

Buck hit here eve. of 10/30/92

Deer Trail

Deer Trail

Trees

Path of buck

Morning stand

Deer Trail

Open Area

Buck location when seen in the morning of 10/30/92

E

N ← → S

W

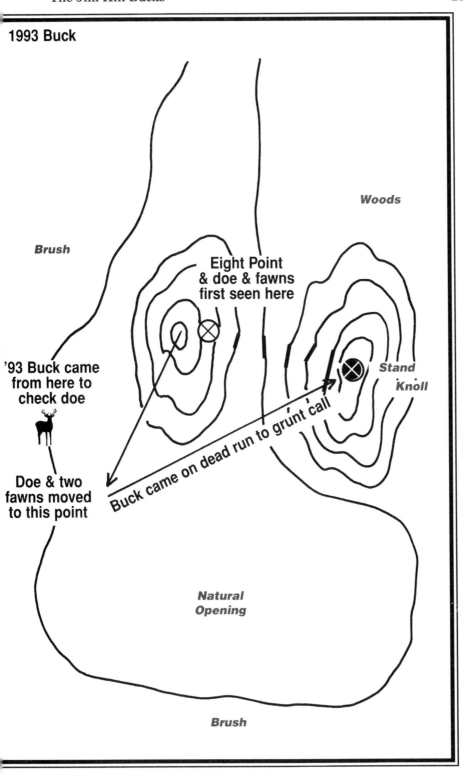

1993 Buck

Woods

Brush

Eight Point & doe & fawns first seen here

'93 Buck came from here to check doe

Doe & two fawns moved to this point

Buck came on dead run to grunt call

Stand
Knoll

Natural Opening

Brush

Reserve Program) field, where Jim figured they bedded down for the morning. Hill hunted that big buck a great deal the rest of the season, but he never saw him again.

Due to the type of terrain and vegetation in a lot of the other areas where Jim hunted, he made some changes prior to the 1992 season, philosophical changes. He reasoned that when hunting open spots he'd have to shoot farther. Consequently, he went for a fast bow and faster, flatter-shooting arrows. Prior to the archery opener he had selected several spots to adapt this "more open terrain" hunting philosophy. Mostly, however, those spots didn't produce any action with big deer, so as the season progressed, Jim began to gravitate to the aforementioned alder swamp island.

The farmer saw that buck again. So did others, who told the landowner, who, in turn reported the sightings to Jim Hill. Others hunted the deer. Jim speculated about their non-success, "Maybe they weren't experienced at hunting really wary bucks. Or maybe they spooked the buck off the island. At any rate, the others never scored."

The landowner called on October 28th. He had seen the buck, and it had crossed to the south where Jim could hunt. Jim couldn't get away from his business on the 29th, so he had his fingers crossed as his hunt began October 30, 1992. There's a square grove at the corner of the woods that leads to the swampy island. That's where Jim set up his stand. (See '92 Buck sketch.) It was cold, and there was reasonable deer activity. Jim described how two smaller bucks, ones most any hunter would love to hang on the wall, fought and sparred in front of his stand. Toward maybe 9:30 he began to hear a lot of farm machinery, as harvest activity shifted into high gear. The machinery noise made it difficult to hear deer sounds, but soon Jim thought he heard a grunt. Shortly, he was certain he heard another grunt. Slowly, he turned in his stand. There was the trophy standing in the distance.

Not only was the distance far, even for his high-tech new bow, the shot angle was also wrong. Jim's hopes sank as the buck turned and walked back toward the island. (Again, note sketch.) Slowly and silently Jim hung his bow up and grasped the rattling horns around his neck. Another tickle. Not only did the buck turn, it came racing back. He stopped at 40 yards, a perfect broadside shot. Jim had one hand on his still-hanging bow, but he was frozen. Flick one eyelash and the buck would have seen him. "If only this deer would have walked back, instead of run, after that last antler rattling," Jim was saying to himself. "I'd have been ready to shoot and not been caught flat-footed, my figurative 'pants' down like this." Soon the buck melted away.

Jim had placed a couple of Burnett decoys in the landowner's barn earlier in the season. He figured they would be just what he needed to take the deer's attention away from himself so he could draw his bow, maybe make another necessary movement or two at rug-cutting time. Jim's plan banked on the wind blowing to the southeast, for he moved his afternoon stand to the edge of the trees that surrounded the swamp. It would be good unless the deer took the only trail that was downwind from him. (See sketch.) The stand had to be positioned lower than normal, the island being slightly higher than the tree he hunted from. Since he knew he could be seen more easily by the deer at the minimal elevation, Jim went with thin, lightweight clothing, so he'd present a smaller silhouette.

Jim is in position now, as is a deer decoy. He knows the deer are still on the island. After more than an hour's wait he hears deer. The sounds of their movement indicate they're coming in directly downwind from him. He grumbles, "Dern, they're bound to scent me. They're moving in the only direction I didn't want them to take."

He senses that the deer do, in fact, smell him, for they begin running. As quickly as they bolt, they stop. Shortly, they're milling about, indicating they're a little spooked but not overly so. Searching and searching, Jim can't locate the big buck. So he chances tickling his rattling horns one more time. This is immediately followed by the sound of deer running in the water. Dejected, Jim figured he spooked all the deer.

That's when an 8-point buck decided to come on the scene. He drove the does back toward Jim. Here they milled about briefly. The 8-point made a bolt toward one of the does. Then Jim saw the big buck at the far edge of the cedar swamp. All this last part happened in less time than it takes to tell it. The does were within 30 yards, but it took the big buck a heart-thumping 15 minutes to skirt around them to a point where Jim could have his shot. Again, he was impressed by the antler mass, but, again, he was only getting glimpses of the rack. One doe made a move toward the big buck. He then moved to her. Now Hill had a 30-yard broadside shot, the deer angling slightly forward. Jim took him the last rib back, the arrow angling forward from there.

He heard the buck splashing out through the water again. He checked his watch. Sixty minutes later he came down out of his tree and took up the spoor, but it was already twilight. The tracking was easy, with lots of blood. He heard the buck walking, however, so he sat down for 30 more minutes. Taking up the blood trail, he started again, but soon heard walking once more. He abandoned his search right there.

He was up at 3:00 the next morning. Snow was coming down, but he easily found the brute. He started the drag at 5:30 A.M. The swamp, the alders, the thickness, the water—all were awful. Exhausted, Jim found he couldn't budge the deer another inch. It was then 1:30 in the afternoon, and it was extremely cold. He returned to the farmhouse. He had a change of warm, dry clothes in his car. On return he obtained help from the landowner and two high school lads. All of them were dressed in waders and hip boots. It was another 2-1/2 hours before the four of them could get the buck to where they could handle him more easily. He field dressed at 245 pounds, but getting him out of the island swamp is what made that drag so torturous. He grossed 173, netted 146 P&Y. Inside spread: 20 inches.

Jim Hill spent three years chasing this swamp buck before taking him in 1992.

What's the most important part on this one? Maybe the Scent-Lok suit!! The wind blowing to the southeast was great—until the deer elected to come in directly downwind from Jim!! If one of the does had bolted severely (as in smelling Hill's body scent) that doe would probably have bolted, snorted, or done something worse than the rather calm shuffling off that she did. Had that happened, as Jim says, "It would have been all over. I'd never have had a chance to see the big buck."

Also, if the does hadn't run off, the big buck would never have smelled (or maybe heard) them. Had the smaller 8-point been alerted by the does shuffling off, it would also have changed things; but the smaller buck was able to herd the little band of does back the way they had come. That, in turn, enabled Jim to put his orbs on the monster.

His bow is a Hoyt Super Slam, with overdraw for more arrow speed and flatter trajectory. His release is from HHA, and his sights have micro adjustments. Jim shoots five to six days a week all summer long. He uses no cover scents with his Scent-Lok suit, but he does go for attractor scents, using those from James Valley Scents. He changes high-tech camo clothing patterns, depending upon where he's hunting, the surrounding foliage, and the time of the year.

Now to that big 1993 buck that's pictured at the opening of this chapter. He grossed 170-1/8, netted 154+. This was one of those "metro bucks" that had spent its lifetime not far from million dollar homes, considerable blacktop, school kids with loud radios, and other suburban development. Bucks grow old and sport big antlers in such an environment because they have plenty to eat, and they're sometimes never hunted because no one has access to where they live. But a friend of Jim's had access, and Jim had heard about a buck of outlandish proportions that lived there. Jim hunted the spot a couple of times, but he could only hunt the heavily populated area when his friend hunted. The particular woods in question was sort of surrounded by the expensive homes.

Several times Jim hunted a stand that was in a "hole" or depression. The stand was already erected, and though it wasn't a sight Hill would have selected himself, there was a tremendous amount of the right sign around it.

One evening around eleven o'clock Jim's friend called. Hill was already in bed. "Can you hunt tomorrow?" the question was posed.

Jim could always rearrange his schedule to hunt that area. "Where would you hunt that cover if you were alone?" his next day's partner posed.

Jim was being set up, perhaps. He answered honestly, "The ridges."

"Good," his buddy came back. "I'll hunt the ridges tomorrow. You take the lower ground."

Thus both their fates were set in stone. There was a clearing near a knoll where Jim's cohort had seen a mammoth 14-point, and that's where Jim decided to put in his vigil. (See '93 buck sketch.) That morning an 8-point came right to his stand. Jim's scent was blowing

100 percent right at the deer; but the buck never showed any sign of smelling him. Chalk up another plus for Hill's Scent-Lok suit. Jim had some James Valley doe lure out, and the buck did smell it. "He was in the 125 point Pope & Young class," Hill told me later.

Broadside, that buck stopped at 15 yards. Piece of cake. It was getting on in the season, so Jim would have been tempted to shoot had he not known about the huge deer that was also calling this bailiwick his home. Shortly, a doe and fawns came straight in, also downwind. They too showed no indication of smelling Hill. Again, if any of these deer had smelled him, then bolted, spooked, snorted, or whatever, Jim would never have laid eyes on the monster.

Finally, the big buck jumped into view. He was about 150 yards away, but Jim knew where the deer would go, probably because of having just witnessed where the 8-point had walked. Jim grunted twice. The big buck didn't hear him, or at least he showed no signs of hearing Jim's grunt calls.

So Jim grunted into his call a third time, this time louder. The big buck picked up his head in response. Jim grunted a fourth time. The huge buck came running. Jim got rid of his binoculars and readied his bow. He didn't want to get caught like he did with that 1992 buck running out of the swamp and freezing Jim so he couldn't move. When the running deer was still 100 yards out, Jim drew his bow. For a time he couldn't see the deer. When he came into view there was only a face-on shot. It was a long one. Jim knew he could make that shot if the deer would turn broadside, so he didn't take it. The deer came closer.

When Hill has his bow drawn on a big buck, the question he continually asks himself is, "....is the pin there?" On that November day he said the sight pin "....looked as big as a tomato." The deer moved 20 yards, traveling in sort of a half circle, and stopped. Jim saw him clearly, but only briefly. Shortly, the buck started to walk off. That's when Jim grunted again. Now the buck eased toward Jim's stand a little. Soon he had the shot he had been waiting for.

Without the cape and entrails that 13-point went 165 pounds. What's the most important part here? Again, Hill goes back to the Scent-Lok suit. Without using it Jim feels he would have been had by the other deer in the area. In turn, their spooking would have prevented him from ever seeing that big "metro buck."

Further, Jim had the savvy not to even tickle his rattle horns. The timing was November 20, so the rut was over in his part of Minnesota. The grunt calls worked, but tickling horns would probably have been a negative. Also, he had to grunt loudly to get the far-off buck's attention. The grunt call he used was a Larry Jones model. Jim thinks very highly of it because of its authentic sound. He had misplaced that call, but spent an inordinate amount of time searching for it. Since it worked so well that November 20, it"s obvious his search time was well spent.

Jim Hill's Equipment

Bow - *Hoyt super slam*
Release - *HHA*
Sight - *With micro adjustments*
Camo - *Goes high tech and changes with differing conditions, foliage, and where and when he's hunting*
Scents - *James Valley doe lure*
Clothing - *Scent-Lok suit with activated charcoal to eliminate human odor*
Call - *Larry Jones grunt call*

This 131 point Pope & Young buck came from the Perlitz Ranch in South Texas in the middle of October, 1993.

Bill Jordan Takes Five Great Bucks In One Season

At the 1986 Shooting, Hunting and Outdoor Trade Show (S.H.O.T.) I saw Harold Knight of Knight & Hale Game Calls early the first morning of the show. "Nick, you gotta come with me. There's a booth not far away, and you're not gonna believe what's there. I'm tellin' ya, it's the biggest thing at this show, and it's gonna be big news for years to come." I followed Harold Knight for I intuitively knew he had something.

Shortly we arrived at Bill Jordan's S.H.O.T. Show booth where Bill was introducing his Realtree camouflage pattern for the first time. I was certainly impressed with what I saw, and Harold Knight had made a great prediction because Realtree camo soon became a part of most every deer, turkey, and duck hunter's vocabulary, and established itself as probably the biggest selling camo pattern of the 1990s.

Since 1986 I have hunted with Bill Jordan plenty, mostly in and around his local haunts of Harris County, Georgia, but also in Texas and other far-flung places, chasing bucks and gobblers. I've been with better duck callers, maybe better woodsmen, but Jordan has a scientific sense about him that few outdoorsmen possess. He goes to great efforts figuring out the habits of the local game whether he's close to home, ten states away from home, or in his beloved Canada.

Last year Bill took not only one buck all of us would be proud to put on the wall—he bagged five of them; two with a gun, three with a bow. All of the latter qualify for Pope & Young. Bill's television show is called "Realtree Outdoors," plus he markets his own line of videos, all of which means every whitetail he attempts to take must be on film, and, yes, all five of his '93 season monsters were captured by one or more video cameras. In case you weren't aware, it's much more difficult to shoot a big buck, bow or gun, and have the event captured with camera than it is to merely shoot the deer.

Jordan was introduced to the outdoors early. His Dad was an avid quail and deer hunter, and equally enthusiastic about bass and crappie fishing. Luckily for Bill, since a smaller and smaller percentage of fathers do it any more, his Dad started taking him hunting and fishing from age seven, long before Bill could even think about carrying a gun.

While he was bitten by the hunting bug early on, Bill was a top athlete and won a football scholarship to Ole Miss. "One of the reasons I decided on that school, Nick, was because of the great hunting and fishing close to campus." He was a successful wide receiver at Ole Miss, catching a significant number of his passes from none other than Archie Manning of New Orleans Saints' fame in the NFL.

As Bill found himself getting more deeply immersed in the taking of big white-tailed bucks, he was bitten by another bug, that of spring gobblers. Turkey hunting was becoming better and better in his parcel of west central Georgia during this time. As mentioned in my opening paragraph, Bill has a scientific approach to the outdoors, and before he was 20 years old he was thinking about more effective ways to hide himself from his quarry, first white-tailed bucks, later those long beards in the spring. It was this type of innovative thinking that produced his first Realtree camo pattern, and it's Bill's scientific mind that keeps new and better Realtree patterns in front of the public every season or so.

Big bucks are the reason Bill Jordan has fallen in love with Canada. So many record whitetails have come from Saskatchewan and Alberta that these provinces hold a mystique, no doubt the hope and wonder of taking the biggest buck ever. This is the place where deer have the genes, food, minerals, even the tradition of growing outsize antlers. So Jordan returns every year, and it's my guess he'll revisit Canada during every future deer season. Perhaps more of us should consider doing that.

"In every previous year," Bill was talking early in our interview, "I had gone to Saskatchewan either during the peak of the rut, which is usually around the middle of November, or during that often equally excellent period, the pre-rut, which usually occurs from late October to early November. But in 1993 I wanted to try something different, so I hunted September 7-10, very early, during the opening of the province's archery season. By scouting during the peak rut or pre-rut period, it's only a matter of time before a hunter comes across the type of scrape and rub activity he's looking for. But this wouldn't be the case when bow season opened 'up there.' Most every archer I know begins his bow hunting that very first day of the season, just as I always have here in Georgia. This is when there's little or no sign of the rut, and there's not a heck of a lot of how-to offered in books, magazines, or videos on being successful." For Bill Jordan it was another challenge.

"When you hunt away from home you have to depend upon your outfitter," he advised. Bill counted on Brian Hoffart to put him in an area that held big deer. "The key ingredient Brian discovered while scouting before our arrival was a natural salt lick," Bill explained. "This Saskatchewan area is dotted with woodlots, many of them thick, having been timbered recently, plus there are grain and alfalfa fields." Hoffart had purposely not put any stands up in the area he had reserved for Jordan's first several days of hunting since Bill wanted to scout further and erect the stands himself.

Interestingly, Hoffart took Bill and his video cameraman, David Blanton, on a 10-12-mile ride on Green Lake to reach their hunting area with the natural salt lick. Bill and Blanton began their scouting immediately after Hoffart cranked the outboard back up to depart. Most of that day and the next Bill and David hunted a little and scouted a lot. "Even in the peak rut or pre-rut, I keep reminding myself, food source, food source, food source," tells Bill Jordan. "Where you find the concentrations of scrapes and rubs, you'll also locate the prime food source. When I give seminars about hunting during the early archery season, I keep harping on food sources and their importance. Here I was in Canada hunting the early archery season, so I took my own advice, continually reminding myself to think food source."

In addition to the already-mentioned alfalfa, Bill discovered these early season Saskatchewan bucks were also feeding on river alder in the creek bottoms; saskatoon, a browse in the emerging timber; pin cherry, also in the new growth; and chokecherry growing in the little openings. Thinking of these food sources, Bill wrote off the one most of us might gravitate to first: the alfalfa. Why? While does and lesser bucks might show up in the open alfalfa before sundown, Jordan reasoned that the bruiser bucks wouldn't leave the heavier woods until well after dark, plus they'd probably leave the alfalfa before daylight in the morning.

Another habitat feature Bill and David Blanton sought during their scouting was deer trails. "Where deer trails converge has long been known as a likely place for a stand. David and I kept scouting until we came up with a spot where three trails converged, plus a convergence of two more trails was close by (see Sketch A), and all this was in close proximity to the key food sources: the river alder in the creek bottoms, the saskatoon browse, pin cherry, and the chokecherries."

They also found two ideal trees, one for Bill's stand, plus one for Blanton's stand where he'd have a good view of both Bill and where they expected to first see deer. While scouting they were careful to be silent and always wore freshly laundered camo clothing and high rubber boots. When they decided on where to put up their stands they did it quickly and quietly, since both are so experienced. They also took time to prune out shooting lanes for bow and camera.

The next morning both were full of anticipation as they climbed softly into their stands long before daylight. For more than two hours they didn't see a thing. While Bill didn't say so, I wonder if it was one of those mornings with dew when the alfalfa tasted so good, so the

In September of 1993 Bill wanted to try a new challenge in Saskatchewan: a hunt very early in the season—long before scrape activity. His idea paid off with this 147 Pope & Young buck.

deer, especially the does and yearlings, stayed in the field longer than usual. By eight o'clock that morning the activity picked up, a doe here, a doe and yearling there, then more.

By ten o'clock they had seen and filmed eight deer, all "baldies." That's when Bill looked back toward where these deer had come from. A very big buck was following the does. Bill glanced over to see that David already had the video camera on this prize. Aren't we all lucky that videos are so silent, that we can video so much wildlife, and they are never aware of our presence?

"I watched that buck come all the way in, arrow knocked, arms ready to draw, eyes fixed, heart thumping," Jordan later revealed. "The shot, when I finally took it, as we'd observed this deer coming from such a long distance, was 32 yards."

The arrow was perfectly placed, so the big buck, a 147 Pope & Young, didn't go far. Soon there were congratulations between these two hunters, then the after-kill video interview.

What's the most important part here? It's relatively easy for an expert hunter who does plenty of scouting to (1) learn whether or not a big buck is using his area, (2) determine ideal places to put up a stand or stands by focusing on rubs and scrapes, and (3) thus be successful. But take most experts out of their local bailiwick and their success ratios are likely to plummet. These days more deer hunters are traveling farther afield in pursuit of their passion. Those who travel out-of-state to hunt usually do so at a time when their own state's seasons haven't started or have already closed. Such hunters may also have already bagged a local buck.

For your best out-of-state chances for success, seek an outfitter who you believe has an excellent buck or bucks scouted out. Most will tell you what you want to hear with your first several questions, so keep probing with additional questions until you're satisfied that the outfitter has what you're looking for, or start questioning another outfitter. When you hunt non-local places well before or well after the rut, concentrate on finding out the deer's favorite foods since these foods could be quite different than those in your locality.

Last autumn Bill took a 131 P&Y buck at the Perlitz Ranch in South Texas and his experiences there will add more to this scenario of not hunting during the rut. In that part of South Texas the pre-rut usually occurs around the 5th to the 9th of December. The peak rut is mid-December, and some years that peak rut can last to well after Christmas, even the end of the Texas season, which is usually after the first of the new year. Jordan's hunt took place in the middle of October, when the weatherman had programmed conditions to be hot (temperature-wise) and they were!

A key to Bill's success at the Perlitz Ranch was not only the food, but in this normally arid area of the country, water, as well. Bill knew the Perlitz Ranch had some big bucks, so he knew the outfitter could get him into the thick of some dandies. Before even starting to scout he had the outfit-

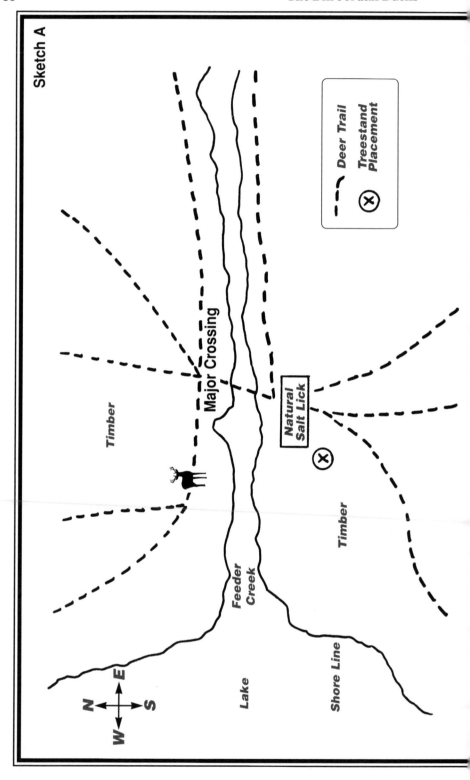

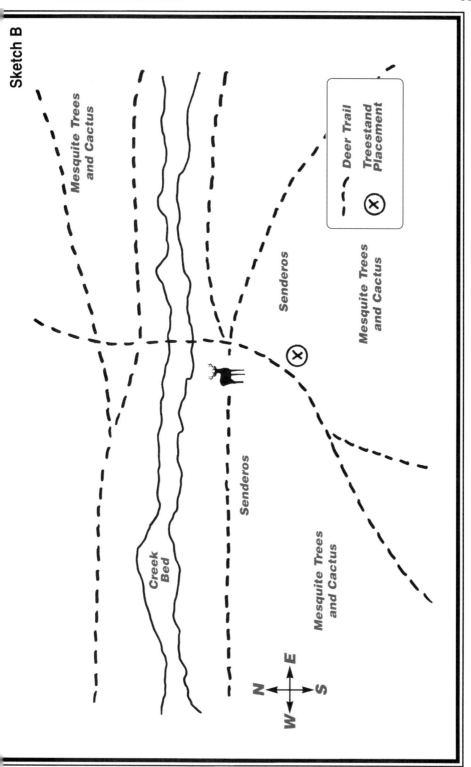

Sketch B

ter take him to several of the prime food sources. "I like to see the food and the tree, bush, or cactus that produces it. I want to touch it, feel it, be certain I know what it is. The food sources in South Texas are totally different than the food sources of my home grounds in west central Georgia. I recommend to all deer hunters who travel that they have local experts identify the preferred deer food sources. Keep in mind that those food sources will likely change over the course of the long bow seasons."

When Bill was hunting the Perlitz Ranch, the deer were feeding on tasajilla, a succulent cactus. So during his scouting Bill looked for concentrations of this cactus in conjunction with water. Fortunately, South Texas had some significant rains prior to his arrival, so water was fairly easy to find. They discovered a few rubs and scrapes during this early part of the season, but all of them were in proximity to the cactus food source. Texas isn't the only prime whitetail part of the country where water is critical to your buck success.

Bill also had the outfitter help him learn to distinguish between the similar tracks of the deer, the javelina, and the wild hogs. David Blanton was with him again. Within hours they had found the concentration of tasajilla cactus they were looking for, water, and two convergence-of-trails areas. (See Sketch B.) Now the problem was how to set up. In the low mesquite trees there was no way to get off the ground 18 or more feet as he and David are prone to do in Georgia and other states where deer gravitate to hardwoods like college students gravitate to beer.

The two Georgians tried the typical tripod stands, for which Texas is so famous, but they're weren't right for bow hunting. "I saw a great buck at 70 yards from a tripod, Nick, but I was hunting with my Jennings Carbon Extreme, not my .280 Remington." The inference here was that the tripod stands were too open, leaving the hunter too exposed, so big bucks weren't likely to come within satisfactory bow range.

So Bill and David experimented next with a couple of ladder stands, pushing them back tight into 10 to 14 foot mesquites, then judiciously pruning shooting lanes, but keeping plenty of the tree-top vegetation around their bodies for added protection against being seen. "Despite the best camouflage clothing and plenty of greenery around, it was still essential to sit very still since we weren't very far off the ground," Bill explained. "Hunting at home or in another state, I suggest carrying pruning shears and a small hand saw. Work slowly and silently when sawing. Pruning allows you to act with more stealth, but some limbs that need to be cut are too big for hand shears. That's where the little hand saw comes in."

On their morning of Texas destiny David and Bill were in their stand 30-40 minutes before shooting light. (Note Sketch B.) They knew that the deer had been moving early. They parked the vehicle a long way off so it wouldn't spook their quarry, another important tip. This 131 P&Y buck came in to their stand at 8:30 that morning. Bill drilled him through the heart at 22 yards, and the buck died within sight of the stand. It was all captured on video, the same as the other four great bucks he shot in the fall of 1993. Bill and his crew also videoed bucks other fellows shot while hunting the same areas with them. You'll find all these big buck kills in *Monster Bucks II*, the video available from Spartan Realtree Products, 1390 Box Circle, Columbus, GA 31907. Phone 800-992-9968.

Bill's 11-point, taken in Nuevo Leon province in Mexico, and measuring 160 Boone and Crockett, was taken with a .280 Rem. model 700 Mountain Rifle. Bill saw this buck the very first day of hunting. The deer wasn't spooked on that initial encounter, so Bill kept concentrating his efforts each day thereafter to try to take him. A key here was moving his stand. Often each time he'd move his stand (Blanton's video stand had to be moved each time as well) Bill would see either more or less deer activity. Naturally, he kept moving in the direction of the concentrated activity. As he and David moved they saw more scrapes and rubs. Their timing was the pre-rut period. As they moved into the prime use area, with all the rubs and scrapes, they also moved into a prime food source area.

So, never quit thinking food sources when deer hunting or deer scouting. Most of us are well familiar with rubs and scrapes and how to use them to our best advantage during pre-rut and peak-rut periods. Trouble is, we spend a lot of our time hunting deer before the pre-rut and after the peak-rut, especially archers, and particularly with the continually lengthened and liberalized deer seasons. While hunting the rut can be great, as well as perhaps the most effective time period, hunting only the rut is definitely restrictive when seasons are now so liberal. This is when identifying and finding food sources can go such a long way toward deer success. Finally, those who travel out-of-state to hunt don't enjoy the luxury of time. They're often restricted to days rather than weeks or months (as they have when hunting at home). When you have a limited amount of time to hunt or you have to hunt before or after the rut, do what Bill Jordan does: think food sources, food sources, food sources!

Bill Jordan's Equipment

Bow - *Jennings Carbon Extreme*

Arrow - *Easton Aluminum 2216*

Broadhead - *Game Tracker Tri-Lok*

Clothing - *Realtree Gray All-Purpose Pants - Polarfleece jackets in cool weather*

Rifle - *Remington Mountain Rifle in .280 Rem*

Ammo - *Federal Premium 140 Grain*

Scope - *Simmons Whitetail 3x-9x*

Herb was briefly mesmerized when first watching this buck. Who wouldn't be?

Chapter 4

Herb Scrip Takes Two Huge Pennsylvania Bucks, Each On The Last Day Of The Season!!

Herb Scrip is proof that perseverance pays off. On the last day of muzzleloader season, January of 1989, Herb took a Boone & Crockett 175+ buck. In late October of that same year, this time on the very last day of the archery season, he took what is perhaps the biggest 8-point ever arrowed in Pennsylvania, rough scoring 178, with full score just shy of 165 B&C points. Scrip's success should spur us all on to positive thinking, despite how late in the season it is and how hard we've been hunting without any success.

I've heard many a muzzleloader hunter lament that all the bucks have lost their antlers by the time black powder season comes around, traditionally the day after Christmas in Pennsylvania. But Herb's big Boone-ee still had its rack right to that last day of the season, where in the Keystone State it's flintlock only. How long bucks go before shedding their racks probably has a lot to do with their overall virility and health. The more virile the buck, the more likely he'll be able to keep his rack in place longer. So, no matter where you're hunting in the late season—stay positive. While the lesser bucks may have already shed their horns (you're probably not interested in them anyway), the brute bucks tend to carry their racks well into the winter, sometimes even beyond.

Herb Scrip is a 55-year-old school teacher and lives in Baden, PA. He began hunting with his father and three brothers when he was 12 years old. His Dad's first hunting camp was near Warren, PA. As the woods grew too high for ideal whitetail habitat there, they acquired a new camp, this time closer to north central Pennsylvania, near Emporium. Herb confided, "The deer populations are increasing around Warren now, probably decreasing around Emporium, so my brothers and I are ready to switch back."

Herb's last day success in both muzzleloader and archery seasons should spur us all on to positive thinking.

Maybe because of his teaching background, Herb approached deer hunting as a scholar might approach his studies. "I read everything I could get my hands on, books and magazines both," Herb confided. Back in the 1960s there wasn't much high-tech stuff written. Today's buck trophy hunters who are on the youthful side will have a tough time appreciating how much great whitetail information has been dispensed over the past 10 or 15 years. In the 1960s there was little, if any, information about even scrapes and rubs. The "licking branch!" Forget it.

But Herb Scrip learned about deer scrapes early, so he's been hunting them for many more years than it's been fashionable to do so. He also took up archery hunting very early in life. Those formative bow and arrow years were pretty much uneventful as far as any shooting went. Herb postulated, "Of course, we have a lot more deer today in the counties where I now do my archery hunting, far more than we did when I began with the bow."

Eventually Herb got that first shot. However, his arrow missed, and that experience resulted in new resolve. He muttered to himself, "This isn't the way to do it." The outcome was practice, practice, practice with the bow until Herb became an expert. Of course, these days every serious archer shoots maybe thousands of practice arrows a year. Yet Scrip began doing this way back in the 1960s, when few, if any, considered such dedication. He shot his first buck with a bow in 1967.

Fifteen years ago Herb started hunting out-of-state. No extremely far-flung trips, but so far he has hunted in West Virginia, Virginia, Maryland, Michigan, and Ohio. Last year he killed four bucks in four states. Pretty impressive for a fellow who teaches school fulltime, so his out-of-state hunts are limited to weekends or vacation days.

It was five or six days before the end of archery season in 1989 that Herb Scrip discovered a huge scrape and rub. Put the timing into late October. Normally the archery season runs about four weeks, so Herb found this sign while he was scouting. Like most of us, he likes to spend plenty of hours in a tree, but he also knows it's essential to big-buck success that he move around a bit, scouting the territory for something special. In this case his discovery was extra special.

"The size of this scrape meant maybe this buck was in a class by itself," Scrip told me. "Abnormal, it was nearly eight feet square. The center part of that scrape had been worked, worked, and re-worked. No doubt my mouth was agape as I looked at it the first time. Next to the scrape was a tree all rubbed raw on one side. The tree trunk was as big around as my thigh. The tracks in the scrape measured 3-1/2-inches long! I remember noting that the rub on the tree was extremely high, which indicated this was a big-bodied deer. That the rub was on one side of the tree trunk suggested what direction I might expect this buck to come from. The over-hanging branch, the licking branch above the scrape, was also high, higher than any I've seen before or since."

Herb found this scrape on a Saturday afternoon. Again, the timing was late October, so this was no doubt the pre-rut period. Since Pennsylvania does not allow Sunday hunting, it was back to school with his teaching Monday through Thursday of the next week. He asked for a personal day on Friday and got it. Pennsylvania's archery season would end at sunset that evening. Herb had purposely avoided the area all week, though he might have been able to hunt it briefly each morning or evening, before or after school. His philosophy, however, was to rest the area. Though he had spent only minutes around that huge scrape, and he had taken his normal precautionary measures regarding his own scent, Herb simply felt not hunting that scrape for as long as possible was the best game plan. He waited as long as he could: until the final day of the season!

The spot was a difficult one to hunt, for there was no tree where Herb could use his self-climber stand. At that time he didn't have a lock-on type stand, though now he has several. Instead, he lashed a couple of boards to a pine tree near the scrape, got as comfortable as he could, then took up the vigil. His position was well back near the pine's trunk, so he wasn't very visible. The longer the day went, the more he worried about his scent. Repeatedly, he scraped pine sap from the tree with his fingers, then wiped it on his clothing and exposed parts of his skin. Scrip considers pine sap as one of nature's best cover scents. He never got down out of his tree. A urine can went up with him before daybreak that morning.

Herb had some good how-to advice. "Don't touch anything. Don't even taint the ground by laying your bow down on it so you can later pull it up. Instead, hang the bow high, then, when you're in your stand, pull it on up. How you approach the stand area is almost always critical to your success. Most hunters approach a stand site by taking the easiest route in. Almost invariably, the easiest route to the stand is the wrong one, often the worst possible one. So, once your stand sight is selected, give a great deal of thought to which entry route is best. Also, the most obvious-looking trees are often poor choices for your stand, sometimes downright lousy choices.

"Again, don't let anything touch the ground around your stand site; bow, quiver, gloves, rattling horns, any of your clothing or equipment. Rubber boots are the only type of footwear to consider for serious big-buck hunting," Herb Scrip finished up.

In October of 1989 Scrip took this magnificent buck, rough scoring 178.

Herb took this buck on the very last day of the January, 1989 muzzleloader season—a buck that scores 175+.

Herb had an old pair of rattling horns with him. Late in the afternoon, when most of us are growing weary, and when pessimism would tend to creep into our minds, Herb was still positive. He tickled the horns very lightly, and just a few times. He had also put out some Tink's Buck Lure by uncovering a 35mm film canister, the cotton inside soaked with the mentioned scent. Plus he had added a few drops to the mammoth scrape.

It wasn't long after he had tickled the rattling horns again that he heard a "snap" noise. Was the buck coming? Had the deer mistakenly stepped on a twig that would telegraph his approach? Indeed, he was, and the buck was making his approach with the wind at his back. Another mistake on the buck's part? Aside from the twig snap, the buck's approach was in total silence. Herb sensed from the deer's demeanor that he was coming to the sound of those antlers being tickled softly.

The shot was anticlimactic to the long four-week season, only 18 yards. The buck went directly to his huge 8 x 8 scrape, stretched his neck out, nostrils pulsating. Was he scenting the Tink's that Herb had put there? The deer then walked to his tree rub. The deer turned, then started walking away. All this while Herb hadn't done one thing. Apparently, he had been mesmerized by the buck. Maybe the deer's rack size was a hypnotizing factor.

As Herb drew the bow he also whistled softly when the deer stepped into one of his shooting lanes. The shot angle was near broadside, but angling slightly away. At the arrow's impact the huge Pope & Young buck bolted. Herb listened. Soon he heard this magnificent creature crash to the ground. When he paced it off he found the buck had run about 75 yards.

What does Herb think the most important part is here?

"You have to be willing to put in the time scouting. Scout, scout, scout. Then, if you're lucky, you'll find the sign of a really big deer. If you don't work at scouting, you'll never come across scrapes and rubs that make you tingle with excitement at first glance." Sage advice offered by Herb Scrip.

In January, prior to the bow kill just described, Herb shot an even bigger buck. As mentioned, this one happened on the last day of muzzleloader season. In Pennsylvania he went through the entire 1988 archery season without drawing his bow. Not that he didn't have ample opportunities. At the season's beginning, however, he vowed he wouldn't shoot unless he could draw on a bigger buck than he had taken previously. That was a tall order for himself, because in 1987 he had arrowed a Pope & Young buck of 145 points. Herb revealed, "Despite not shooting, 1988 was one of the best archery seasons I've ever enjoyed. I hunted 15-20 excellent bucks, plus had shot opportunities on many of those. None of them, however, could match the 145-class buck I'd taken in 1987, so I gladly let those bucks walk."

Rifle season came and went similarly, good bucks seen, but no star-
tling ones. Then came the flintlock season after Christmas. For several days it was hunt hard and scout hard, for school was out on
holiday break. At the end of that period Herb got his "break," for a
friend told him about a near-collision between his car and a huge
buck. Herb was back at his job, teaching then, so there was precious
little time left; but he persevered and found the buck's big tracks.
Later he discovered what he figured was this deer's bedding area on
some very high ground. Back home that evening he postulated on how
to hunt this deer. The next day was Saturday, so he could hunt all day,
but it was also the last day of black powder hunting for the year, in
fact, the last day of Pennsylvania deer hunting for the season.

Drive-type hunting is very common and highly traditional in Pennsylvania during the flintlock period, and Herb Scrip had done plenty of
it over the course of his hunting life. And that's the game plan Herb
came up with for the next morning. He called a close friend and laid
out the plan over the phone. The friend elected to be the driver, while
Herb would be the stander. The idea was to wait for the buck to bed
down for the day (where Herb had found his bedding area), then make
a one-man push, hopefully to ease the buck to the area where Herb
was standing in wait.

Herb's friend wasn't familiar with the hunting area, while Herb was.
As often happens on deer drives, the friend didn't come through the
bedding area. Of course, communications sometimes fail. A word
description of where to start, where to move through, and so forth,
usually gets confused once the person doing the driving actually gets
to the area(s) in question. This resulted in no bucks for Herb.

In whispers the two hunters talked it over. They decided to try the
mini-drive again. The friend wanted to do the driving a second time.
Understand, theirs was silent stuff. No whooping and hollering or
whistling. Just sneak hunting that would hopefully result in the buck
trying to sneak off, not skedaddle at top speed for a half mile or more.

This time Scrip's hunting buddy came through, not only at the right
pace, but also the right place. Herb's heart must have been pounding
and skipping when he heard the first shuffling noises. Soon a herd of
does appeared. (Note sketch.) Would the buck be behind? Yes he was!
But Herb was disappointed. "Nick, it was a beautiful 8-point with
probably a 16-inch spread, maybe a 110-115 Pope & Young count, a
buck anybody would love to shoot."

But Herb had already passed up many a buck that size and bigger in
archery season. Here it is, the tail end of the last day, and he's passing
up yet another, this time with the flintlock rifle. Herb mused, "To col-
lect the biggest bucks, you have to be able to allow some very good
bucks to walk!"

Shortly, through several backward glances, the 8-point indicated
that there might be another deer behind him. This smaller buck's body

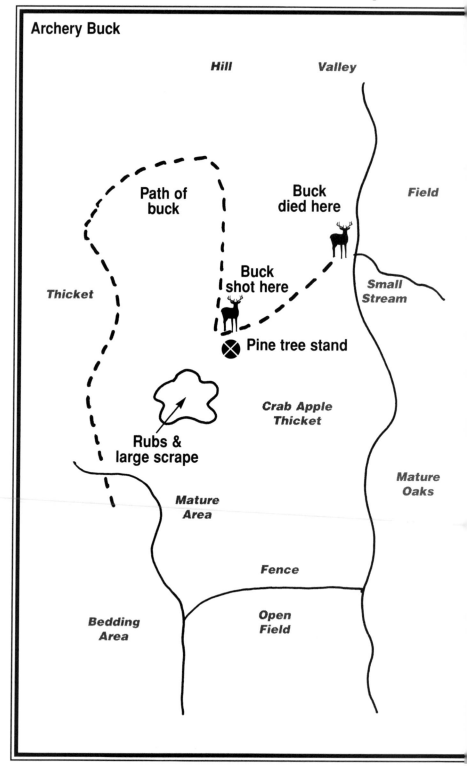

Muzzleloader Buck

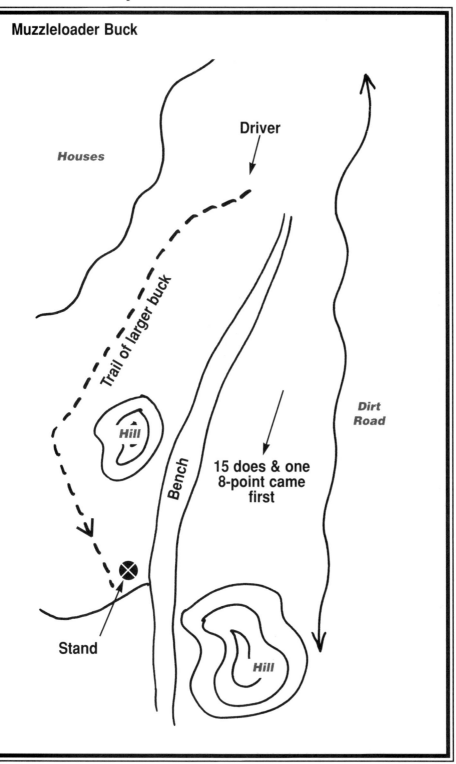

language also suggested that a big fellow might be bringing up the rear. Soon that big buck did come through, but on a different course. (Again, note sketch.) He probably thought he was smart, not to follow exactly where the others had fled. One of the does was lagging behind, and Herb wondered if she might be interested in breeding, for now the big buck was showing interest in her, despite the early January date.

The flintlock shot was within archery range: 16 yards. "There was a tremendous cloud of black smoke at the shot. I waited awhile after he ran off. When I got down out of my tree and started looking for blood my heart sank. For 30 yards I couldn't find a speck. But then my elation level jumped into high gear when I saw a bright red smear. Seventy yards farther, there he was."

What a magnificent buck. Of course, both Herb's bucks are pictured in this chapter. His archery Pope & Young 8-point at nearly 165 points could be the largest 8-point ever taken in Pennsylvania. Then there's his 13-point flintlock buck at over 175 points. It's amazing that both were taken in the same year, January and October respectively; but what's even more amazing is that both were taken on the last days of their respective seasons. Put perseverance to work for you, and never let pessimism creep into your thinking.

Herb Scrip's Equipment

Herb's Bow - *Hoyt Easton*
Arrow - *Easton XX75*
Broadhead - *Zewickey*
Sight - *Pins*
Clothing - *Woodland Brown Camo*
Muzzleloader - *.50 Caliber Thompson / Center Flintlock*

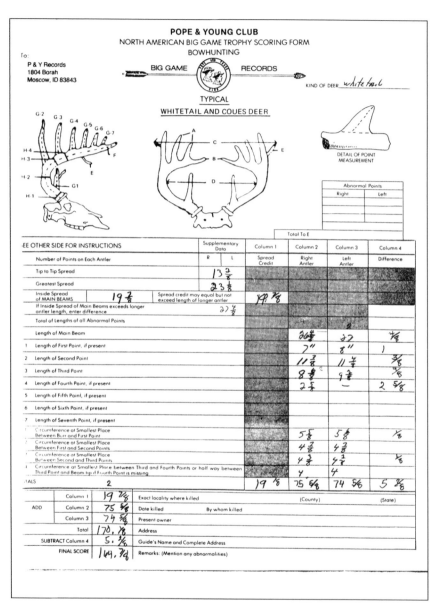

POPE & YOUNG CLUB
NORTH AMERICAN BIG GAME TROPHY SCORING FORM
BOWHUNTING

To:
P & Y Records
1804 Borah
Moscow, ID 83843

BIG GAME   RECORDS

KIND OF DEER _whitetail_

TYPICAL
WHITETAIL AND COUES DEER

DETAIL OF POINT
MEASUREMENT

	Abnormal Points	
	Right	Left
Total To E		

SEE OTHER SIDE FOR INSTRUCTIONS	Supplementary Data		Column 1	Column 2	Column 3	Column 4
	R	L	Spread Credit	Right Antler	Left Antler	Difference
Number of Points on Each Antler						
Tip to Tip Spread	$13\frac{2}{8}$					
Greatest Spread	$23\frac{3}{8}$					
Inside Spread of MAIN BEAMS	$19\frac{7}{8}$		Spread credit may not equal but not exceed length of longer antler	$19\frac{7}{8}$		
If Inside Spread of Main Beams exceeds longer antler length, enter difference		$27\frac{4}{8}$				
Total of Lengths of all Abnormal Points				4	2	
Length of Main Beam				$26\frac{4}{8}$	27	$\frac{4}{8}$
1 Length of First Point, if present				$7''$	$8''$	1
2 Length of Second Point				$11\frac{3}{8}$	$11\frac{4}{8}$	$\frac{3}{8}$
3 Length of Third Point				$8\frac{8}{8}$	$9\frac{3}{8}$	$\frac{4}{8}$
4 Length of Fourth Point, if present				$2\frac{5}{8}$	$-$	$2\frac{5}{8}$
5 Length of Fifth Point, if present						
6 Length of Sixth Point, if present						
7 Length of Seventh Point, if present						
1 Circumference at Smallest Place Between Burr and First Point				$5\frac{5}{8}$	$5\frac{6}{8}$	$\frac{1}{8}$
2 Circumference at Smallest Place Between First and Second Points				$4\frac{3}{8}$	$4\frac{3}{8}$	
3 Circumference at Smallest Place Between Second and Third Points				$4\frac{3}{8}$	$4\frac{2}{8}$	$\frac{1}{8}$
4 Circumference at Smallest Place between Third and Fourth Points or half way between Third Point and Beam tip if Fourth Point is missing				4	4	
TOTALS		2	$19\frac{7}{8}$	$75\frac{5}{8}$	$74\frac{5}{8}$	$5\frac{2}{8}$

ADD	Column 1	$19\frac{7}{8}$	Exact locality where killed	(County)	(State)
	Column 2	$75\frac{5}{8}$	Date killed	By whom killed	
	Column 3	$74\frac{5}{8}$	Present owner		
	Total	$170.\frac{1}{8}$	Address		
SUBTRACT Column 4		$5.\frac{2}{8}$	Guide's Name and Complete Address		
FINAL SCORE		$164.\frac{7}{8}$	Remarks: (Mention any abnormalities)		

Herb Scrip's Pope & Young scoring form for his October 1989 buck.

Denny Stiner with the biggest non-typical buck taken in Illinois during the 1993 season. Note his life-like decoy in the background. The decoy played an integral part in Denny's success.

Don D. Stiner's Huge 27-Point #1 Non-Typical Buck Taken In Illinois In 1993

The D, Don's middle initial, is for Dennis, and Stiner goes by his middle name, or Denny. Check out his huge buck in the photo on the previous page. Obviously, this was a trophy worth a lifetime's wait. However, Denny's basement is full of big buck mounts, hard evidence that he knows what he's doing when it comes to scouting, finding, and bagging brute deer. The magnificent buck he took in November of 1993 was the culmination of all the hours and efforts he has put into his bow hunting. Further, Stiner took a second excellent buck later that same season, a very nice 9-point. Its photograph also accompanies this chapter (see page 61).

But it's the buck photographed here that you're interested in, so let's find out more about Denny Stiner and that 27-point that has made your eyes pop. Stiner (pronounced like Steiner) is 44 years old. He started deer hunting when he was 19. He currently lives in Owaneco, Illinois and works as a heavy-equipment operator. This state has an extremely long bow season and a much shorter shotgun slug-only season that usually lasts about 10 days spanning two weekends. Denny's consuming interest is bow hunting.

The area he hunts is a relatively small one, and it's not very close to home. It's a 50-mile drive one way, but Denny told me, "Even if I only have two hours to hunt, I'll make that 50-mile drive. The area is unique with its woodlots and open fields. I've hunted it for so long that I now know exactly what a deer is going to do if pushed."

Another reason Denny likes this hunting area is that it has been loaded with big bucks historically. He told me, "I expect to see about five bucks every trip that will be in the trophy class. I mean 120 Boone & Crockett points or better!"

Agreed, that's one heck of a lot of big bucks to see during a full day's hunt, but keep in mind that Illinois is famous for its many huge, open fields, and many of its woodlots are small. So when a buck is pushed out of a small woodlot, there's no place to go except the next woodlot. That one's likely to be a mile or more away, so the deer will have to cross the wide open spaces to get there. The hooker is that there's no rifle season in Illinois. When you're hunting with a bow, or even a shotgun, seeing a buck at 250-800 yards might get your adrenaline pumping, but the buck is as safe as you were as a babe in your Mother's arms.

A little description of Stiner's hunting area will be helpful. He says there's a big hill (though I can't imagine a big hill in Illinois—but then I'm no flatlander) with 600-700 acres of timber. Some of it is thick, some maturing, and there are rolling humps on this timbered hillside. "Deer use this timber stand heavily for bedding," Denny Stiner explained.

Of course, there are lots of open fields all around this timber section, which I assume is quite large for that area of Illinois. Further, there are many hedgerows that lead to and join the fields and meandering watercourses and creeks. In the creek bottoms you'll find smatterings of woodlots, often 40-50 acres in size. Study the accompanying sketch of Stiner's hunting area so you might understand it better, as well as grasp the paragraphs which follow.

The key to Denny's success with all the big bucks he has taken in this area, including the 27-point upon which this chapter is centered, is this hunter's knowledge of how the bucks move from one woodlot to another woodlot, or from that big patch of timber to smaller woodlots. When hunting with only two or three of his buddies they can make a plan—have one guy move through a woodlot or the big 600-700 acre patch—to get the deer on the move. But the two or three hunters on stand might be an unbelievable four or five miles away. Denny has patterned the deer movements so well that he can actually get a buck to move that far, and have the deer end up so close as to be within bow range of the stander five miles away!!! No wonder he likes to hunt this area. Not only does it have big bucks, it looks like Denny Stiner and his cohorts can move the big-racked critters around as surely as if they had them tied to a string.

One example Denny told me about was this: "I posted two of my buddies where I thought bucks would run if I was able to jump them out of one particular woodlot. Once I was certain the standers were in position I started walking through that woodlot, wind at my back. Sure enough, I jumped a very good buck. He went right to where I thought he would. Buddy Number One missed him with his bow. The buck kept on trucking for three more miles, where he ran right into Buddy Number Two. He, too, misdirected his arrow."

This buck was a huge 10-point, and Denny had his heart set on bagging it during the 1994 season. No wonder he'll drive 50 miles for a two-hour hunt!

The first time Denny saw the 27-point pictured at the chapter's beginning the buck was 15 yards away, 35 yards from his decoy. But that's getting too far ahead of this story. Denny had illusions about going into the decoy-making business. He even had a mold made. But he discovered there was too much time and expense involved. He had to sell his full-size deer decoys for well over $300, just to make a $20 profit. However, he has been using a decoy very successfully the last several years, and his foam decoy could have been a most critical factor in bringing the huge 27-point buck in so close November 13, 1993.

Here's some how-to about Denny's use of a decoy. He turns it into a buck decoy using a commercial set of rattling horns topside, and suggests using this buck decoy before and after the rut. However, during the rut he prefers to go without the antlers on the decoy. Because he often has to move considerable distances to change hunting stands during any given day, and he has the decoy to transport as well, Denny relies heavily on a 3-wheeler.

Now to the day of reckoning, November 13, 1993. Stiner was programmed for an all-day hunt. He made the 50-mile drive early in the morning. The wind was up, and it was blowing from the wrong direction. Consequently, he had to walk, circling about a half mile, carrying the decoy, to get to a spot where he had a makeshift blind that he'd used previously. He thought he was alone, looking over a good edge of the big 600-700 acre timber stand I referred to before. Though Denny was upwind of this stand, he figured he'd be able to get off a shot at any deer that came past before that deer scented him. From the timber's edge blind he soon saw another hunter. What happened next wasn't to Denny's liking. "I couldn't believe it. This guy walked right through the big stand of timber, wind at his back. Every deer in the place had to run out the opposite side." That ruined Denny's carefully planned hunting day.

A road cuts through the center of this big timber stand. Denny's makeshift blind was on the north half of it. He was disgusted, and it was still early in the morning. He walked to his 3-wheeler and headed out. On the way he saw some does. He made a calculated stalk but never found them again. Returning to the 3-wheeler, he discovered the does were close by. He gave a bleat on his Woodswise Buck & Doe call. One doe was so interested she jumped a fence to get to him. She walked right up. Denny had one doe tag as well as two buck tags. "That doe was pretty small," Stiner mused. "I passed it up because I knew how much flack my buddies would give me if I returned to camp with it."

He was back at his friend Ron's house, who was one of the landowners in this area, at about 11:30 that morning. Shortly, Ron and another of Denny's friends, Jim (also his taxidermist), returned from hunting and they all went to town, had lunch, and Denny was considering returning home. He was still demoralized over the hunter who had walked through the big area of timber and thus ruined his well-

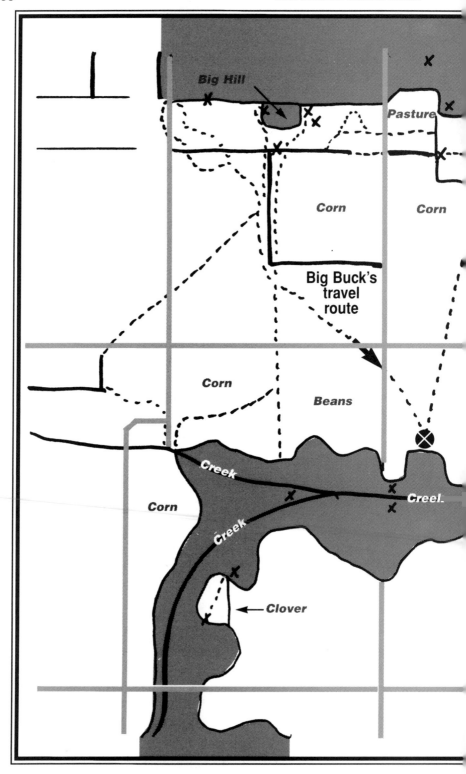

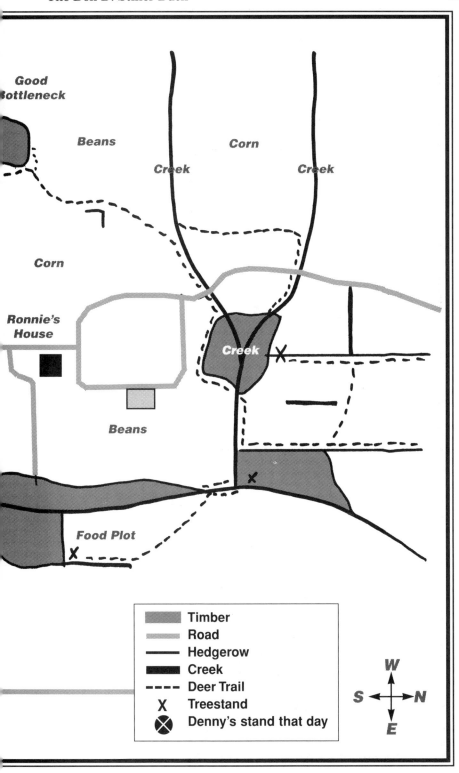

Good
Bottleneck

Beans

Corn

Creek

Creek

Corn

Ronnie's
House

Creek

Beans

Food Plot

Timber
Road
Hedgerow
Creek
Deer Trail
X   Treestand
Denny's stand that day

W
S — N
E

***Denny likes to use a Jennings Carbon Extreme Bow shooting a
Beman Carbon Arrow with 100 grain Thunderhead Broadhead.***

planned hunting day. The landowner buddy, Ron, however, wanted to
move one of his bow stands, in anticipation of the next shotgun season.
Denny decided to help. As it turned out, this was a fatefully good decision. In moving the stand, Denny discovered a mass of brand new
scrapes and rubs in a little creekside woodlot where Denny had not
seen a great deal of big buck sign previously. The landowner friend
told Denny he had seen a big 10-point in that woodlot not long ago,
while performing farm chores. Denny wondered about the size of the
10-point. To his friend, Ron, a 10-point was a 10-point, with tine
length and beam spread maybe of little consequence to him. Turned
out that the 10-point the landowner had seen here was not the buck
Denny bagged later that day.

After the stand-moving chore was finished, it made more sense to
hunt again rather than drive 50 miles home, since the slack mid-part
of the day was gone. Around 2:00 that afternoon Denny went down
into the bottom where he'd found all the new buck sign. It was a half
mile down a lane, then three quarters of a mile along the creek. His
deer decoy was lashed to the back of his 3-wheeler. He stopped 200
yards away from the woodlot in question, then hid the 3-wheeler
behind a levee. The wind was now out of the west, changed from its

Here is a 9-point that Denny took later in the same season as his monster 27-point.

southerly direction that morning. Denny was facing to the west, the levee at his back. (Note sketch.) He placed the decoy 35 yards southwest of his position, just out into a field. He was sitting on the ground. Brush was behind him and on his right.

"When deer come to the decoy, they typically circle downwind," Denny explained. "That's what I wanted to happen, then the deer would be directly in front of me, and still not have my scent when it was time for me to shoot."

It didn't happen that way. Someone had evidently jumped the deer from a distant woodlot. It came to him after running across two and a half miles of open fields. And the giant buck came right for the decoy. Stopping to eye the decoy, tongue hanging out from its long run, the buck was only 15 yards from Denny. While the huge deer watched the decoy, Stiner calmly picked up his bow, which had been laying at his side, the arrow nocked and ready. It was a Beman Carbon arrow with 100 grain Thunderhead Broadhead, shot out of a Jennings Carbon Extreme bow. Denny hit the buck, which was standing broadside, just behind the shoulder. The arrow exited behind the shoulder on the opposite side, though Denny wasn't positive of the shot placement at the time, only pretty certain.

No newcomer to the taking of big bucks, here are some of the super whitetails Denny has taken over the years.

The deer took off upon being hit. He passed the decoy, then stopped. Denny said, "It was as if he was waiting for the decoy to come run with him."

Stiner's quiver was behind him, and he didn't want to move if the deer had been hit well, as Denny suspected. "Just give him a few more moments and it'll be all over," he was thinking, but at the same time he was wondering if another arrow to a critical area might also be a good idea. While the buck was still trying to figure the decoy out, Denny saw its backside drop down significantly. Then the deer walked slowly to the decoy, where it fell over dead!

After he got his shaking under control he thought, "I've got to get back to the 3-wheeler, go to the house and get some pictures of this buck while there's still enough light."

So he did. He hoped his friends would be there, for one of them had a video camera, but both buddies were still out hunting. He returned to the deer with his one still camera. He set up for a photo, tried to snap the shutter, but found to his disgust that the battery was dead. What is it they say about the best laid plans of mice and men???

He had brought a two-wheeled trailer behind the 3-wheeler. "When I finally got that big buck up on the trailer," Denny proclaimed, "I couldn't believe how the antlers stuck out beyond both sides of the rig. I had some maneuvering to do as I drove out, so the antlers didn't catch on brush and pull the buck off the trailer."

In actuality, this is a 10-point, but obviously with a great many "stickers." Check page 65 for the actual measurements on the Pope & Young score sheet.

Denny eventually got back to the landowner friend's house. He took the 3-wheeler with trailer and buck around to the back, out of sight for the time being. It was then about four o'clock. He cleaned up, had a cool one, then called home to tell his wife he wouldn't be home for dinner, since there was some celebrating to do. He also talked to his daughter, who is an enthusiastic bow hunter herself. When Denny told her that the buck he had just bagged was a lot bigger than any of the taxidermy specimens he had in their basement, his daughter's retort was, "No way!"

In reply, Denny's comeback was one word and quite to the point, "Way!"

When the landowner friend, Ron, and Denny's other buddy, Jim, returned to the house, Denny didn't say anything about his big deer. Just listened to their stories of how the afternoon hunt went. They both had stories to tell, about seeing this or that, getting fouled up by another hunter, whatever. Finally, one of them asked Denny what he'd seen. He came back nonchalantly, "Oh I got one, but it's not all THAT big."

"Well, where is he?

"Round the back of the house," Denny told them.

During our interview Denny told me, "When they saw that buck they went nuts, absolutely crazy."

Denny Stiner's Equipment

Bow - *Jennings Carbon Extreme*
Arrow - *Beman Carbon*
Broadhead - *100 Grain Thunderhead*
Clothing - *Original Realtree Pattern Pants And Coat*
Later that season, when Denny Stiner took the 9-point buck (alluded to in the text with photographs provided as a part of this chapter), he wore the new All-Purpose Realtree.
Binoculars - *7 X 35 Jason Empire*
3-Wheeler - *Yamaha*
Decoy - *His Own*
Rest - *Golden Key Super Star*
Sight- *T-Dot Sight Pins*
Boots - *Knee-High La Crosse*

Denny feels these knee-high rubber boots are an important part of his hunting apparel. "I tuck my pants inside these higher boots," Denny instructs. "Rubber definitely helps keep your scent down. Deer can smell leather or at least human odor on leather. Also, if your pants brush against vegetation while you're walking, the scent will be transmitted, increasing the chances of deer smelling that scent while walking toward or near your stand." Denny plans to wear Scent-Lok charcoal activated suits in the future.

He's also a big believer in washing his hunting clothes in detergent that eliminates ultra-violet (UV) rays. "Last year I had a raccoon walk right across my feet while wearing camo clothing that had been washed in detergent that was UV protected. Also, I now see a big difference in deer NOT seeing me, compared to the days before I never worried about UV protection for my bow hunting clothing."

The clothing he wore on the day this 27-point was taken had been stored in clean plastic bags with H.S. Scent earth-scented wafers.

POPE & YOUNG CLUB
NORTH AMERICAN BIG GAME TROPHY SCORING FORM
BOWHUNTING

BIG GAME **RECORDS**

KIND OF DEER _Whitetail_

NON-TYPICAL WHITETAIL AND COUES' DEER

DETAIL OF POINT MEASUREMENT

ABNORMAL		
Points Line E		
	R	L
3 R		4 L
	5/8	6/8
1 7/8	1 1/8	
2 5/8	5 1/8	
3 3/8	3 6/8	
3 2/8	6 6/8	
8 6/8	5 0/8	
1 2/8	1 4/8	
	5 5/8	
	1 7/8	
1 2/8		
22 6/8	33 6/8	
Total To E	56 4/8	

SEE OTHER SIDE FOR INSTRUCTIONS

		Supplementary Data	Column 1 Spread Credit	Column 2 Right Antler	Column 3 Left Antler	Column 4 Difference
A.	Number of Points on Each Antler	R 11 L 14				
B.	Tip to Tip Spread	25 7/8				
C.	Greatest Spread	35 1/8				
D.	Inside Spread of MAIN BEAMS	27 3/8	Spread credit may equal but not exceed length of longer antler 26 4/8			
E.	Total of Lengths of all Abnormal Points	56 4/8				
F.	Length of Main Beam			25 7/8	26 4/8	0 5/8
G-1	Length of First Point, if present			7 0/8	6 1/8	0 7/8
G-2	Length of Second Point			12 1/8	12 4/8	0 3/8
G-3	Length of Third Point			9 3/8	9 5/8	0 3/8
G-4	Length of Fourth Point, if present			—	—	—
G-5	Length of Fifth Point, if present			—	—	—
G-6	Length of Sixth Point, if present			—	—	—
G-7	Length of Seventh Point, if present			—	—	—
H-1	Circumference at Smallest Place Between Burr and First Point			6 1/8	6 3/8	0 1/8
H-2	Circumference at Smallest Place Between First and Second Points			5 0/8	4 7/8	0 1/8
H-3	Circumference at Smallest Place Between Second and Third Points			5 5/8	5 3/8	0 2/8
H-4	Circumference at Smallest Place between Third and Fourth Points or half way between Third Point and Beam tip if Fourth Point is missing			6 3/8	5 0/8	1 2/8
	TOTALS		56 4/8	26 4/8	77 2/8	76 3/8	4 4/8

ADD	Column 1	26 4/8	
	Column 2	77 2/8	
	Column 3	26 4/8	
	TOTAL	180 0/8	
SUBTRACT Column 4		4 0/8	
Result		176 0/8	
Add Line E Total		56 4/8	
FINAL SCORE		232 4/8	

Exact locality where killed _Logan_ CO. (County) _IL_ (State)

Date killed _11-13-93_ By whom killed _Donald D. Stiner_

Present owner _Same_ Phone (217) 879-2305

Address _Box 121 ; Owaneco, IL 62555_

Guide's Name and Complete Address

REMARKS: (Mention any abnormalities)
Common base brow LT Side
Tip of Abnormal LT Side broken off measured to point of Abnir

Denny Stiner's Pope & Young scoring form.

On November 15, 1992 Bill took this 10-point that dressed at about 185 pounds.

"New-Place-Everyday" Theory From Bill Winke Leads To Bragging-Size Iowa Bucks

Bill Winke is 30 years old as this is being written. He's another one of those lucky outdoorsmen who, at age 12, was introduced to hunting early in life by his father. Most of that early outdoor fun with his Dad involved bird hunting, and it was excellent in Iowa as Winke was growing up. Deer hunting was a natural next step, shotgun hunting in Iowa, but when he was getting started the state's whitetail herd hadn't begun to blossom yet. After obtaining his engineering degree from the University of Iowa he went to work for a company in Michigan that built control systems for fighter aircraft. It was in Michigan that Bill was bitten by the deer-hunting bug.

He began with the rifle, then started to set his sights on bigger and bigger bucks. Eventually taking up bow hunting, he has become totally enamored with archery. He discovered early on that in the states where he hunted, the pre-rut and main rut periods coincided with the bow seasons; this factor helped him become an avid archer. During his travels he met Spencer Land, who owns High Country Archery. Bill went to work for him in Tennessee. In turn he met up with Greg Tinsley, who currently edits Petersen's Bow Hunting magazine, and now Winke is on the editorial staff at Petersen's.

Bill thinks one of his most interesting big bucks (from a how-to standpoint) was taken during the 1992 season. That was the second year he had been playing with a new hunting technique, one designed to take the big fellows with more consistency. As a writer who concentrated on bow hunting and bow hunting tactics and methods, Winke had a lot of research to do. One thing he discovered was that many beginner-type hunters were taking some magnificent whitetails. Luck is involved in most any great buck kill, but, as you already know from reading these pages, we're concentrating on hard-core how-to—how-to that you can hopefully put to work in your own whitetail search.

Delving deeper into why these tyro-type hunters were enjoying more success statistically than they had a right to, Winke came to the conclusion that a significant percentage of these new, successful hunters were hunting areas that they had never hunted before. These guys had never scouted, never even seen their hunting area previously. Getting the picture? Bill Winke began adding the figurative two and two together here, then decided to devote the next several years to "playing" with his theory. He began with this in 1991.

The basic idea is not to scout an area, but to go into it once for an afternoon hunt. If the spot didn't produce on the first try, Bill would leave it for good, never coming back. The next day or the next hunt he would seek out another new place. Occasionally, it might be close by. He theorized that when a hunter goes into an area and a really big buck detects his presence the first time, it's extremely unlikely that the brute buck will ever be seen by that hunter again. By hunting areas once and only once Winke was stacking the odds in his favor, the odds that the buck hadn't been hunted before, odds that Bill would have a well-placed arrow on its way before said big buck detected his

Bill, once he heard about a big buck, would scrutinize topo maps, looking for the perfect spot to set up on the bruiser.

presence. As most of you will agree, this is quite a departure in think-ing when it comes to whitetail hunting, for one of the main points we've been taught is to scout, scout, scout.

So how did Bill have a clue any big bucks might be in the areas he was going to hunt? This is where his "scouting" came in. First off, he knew he had to have many, many places to hunt since he was going to move to new hunting grounds virtually every day he hunted. One bonus was that he was hunting the area of Iowa where he grew up, thus he knew numerous landowners. So he talked with them, farmer after farmer. He was not only seeking permission, he was questioning them about big bucks, too. Once he came up with a likely area where a good deer had been sighted, he bought topography maps and started scrutinizing them. His part of Iowa is typified by vast farm fields, but it's rolling country and the draws are usually brush-filled fingers that lead down to smallish woodlots in the creek bottoms. It's the type of terrain that lends itself perfectly to planning hunts via topo maps. Natural game movement corridors often stick out like the proverbial sore thumb on these maps, at least to anyone with some experience in reading topo maps and guessing how game will probably move.

Because every one of these hunts was into a new area, Bill decided before the season began that he'd only utilize this new theory of hunt-ing during the afternoon. If he tried finding what he wanted in dark-ness (going in during the dark of pre-dawn) he'd greatly increase the chances of spooking the bucks he wanted to surprise with an arrow. For each morning hunt Winke would revert to the "old ways" of hunt-ing stands that had been strategically placed in areas which had been thoroughly scouted. Around ten o'clock each morning, he'd come out of that stand, then put into practice his "new-place-every-day" theory.

"I look at this way of hunting as having 'ultra low impact' on the deer. They never get spooked," Bill tells us. "So I'm always hunting an area where the deer don't have a clue that I'm around, and I think the theory has important success implications with big bucks."

During the 1992 season Bill passed up three Pope & Young bucks on his afternoon hunts with this new big-buck plan. This was through Novem-ber 14. On the morning of Sunday the 15th he botched a good spot by get-ting there too late. It was a classic, perfect day for big bucks, the figurative bottom having fallen out of the thermometer, the timing right in the middle of the Iowa rut. At church later that morning he met his friend Don. Don and his wife had seen a huge buck on their land on their way to church, and Bill received a hunt invitation then and there.

"I tend to see a great deal of deer movement from noon to three in the afternoon," Bill went on. "That's when most hunters have left the woods, of course."

Shortly after Sunday lunch he had checked out his topo map of Don's farm and was on his way. He had Don pinpoint exactly where the buck had been seen. Then Bill postulated where the buck would bed down

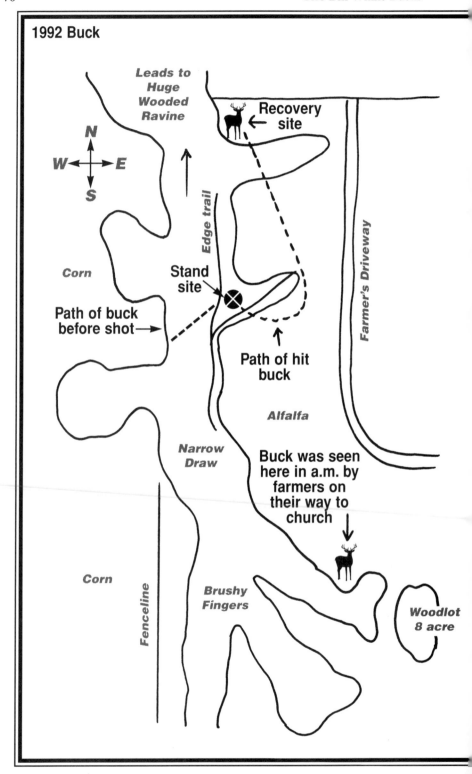

1992 Buck

Leads to
Huge
Wooded
Ravine

N
W ← → E
S

Recovery
site

Edge trail

Farmer's Driveway

Stand
site

Path of buck
before shot →

Corn

Path of hit
buck

Alfalfa

Narrow
Draw

Buck was seen
here in a.m. by
farmers on
their way to
church

Corn

Fenceline

Brushy
Fingers

Woodlot
8 acre

1991 Buck

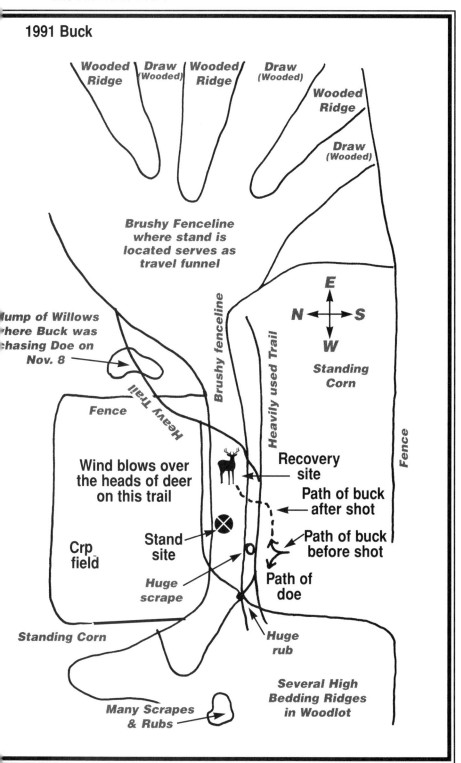

Wooded Ridge | Draw (Wooded) | Wooded Ridge | Draw (Wooded) | Wooded Ridge | Draw (Wooded)

Brushy Fenceline where stand is located serves as travel funnel

Clump of Willows where Buck was chasing Doe on Nov. 8

Brushy fenceline

Heavily used Trail

Standing Corn

E
N ← → S
W

Fence

Heavy Trail

Fence

Wind blows over the heads of deer on this trail

Recovery site

Path of buck after shot

Stand site

Path of buck before shot

Crp field

Huge scrape

Path of doe

Standing Corn

Huge rub

Several High Bedding Ridges in Woodlot

Many Scrapes & Rubs

for the rest of the daylight hours, in one of several brushy fingers that led to a wooded ravine. Bill reasoned that as evening approached the buck would make its way to the wooded ravine from where it was bedded down in the brushy finger. All Bill had to do was set up his stand at the right place to intercept him. Via the topo map he selected a narrow spot where three brushy fingers "gapped" into the wooded ravine. (Note sketch.) There were a couple of other narrow gaps Bill saw on the map, but he selected the one he felt offered the best opportunity. In the early afternoon daylight, the narrow corridor was easy to find.

A factor that led him to put up his stand where he did centered around a little thicket that was 30 to 40 yards away from an open field, a classic place from which deer love to watch the open field for danger, or other deer, from the safety of the thicket. All the while, of course, the day's light is waning.

A key in this situation? Don't walk and wander around. Know what you're looking for from the topo map. Go directly to where you want to put up the stand, then get it positioned, quickly and quietly. By two o'clock Bill was in position. Around four to four-thirty he saw a good buck, but it was going out of the wooded ravine, headed up one of the brushy fingers. A half hour later his buck appeared, this one coming toward him from one of the brushy fingers, as he'd theorized. That buck was headed Bill's way toward the wooded ravine. When he first saw it, Bill hadn't positively decided whether or not he was going to try for it. For a few seconds he was still sizing him up. It wasn't long before he had his estimate at about 140 P&Y points. He was a 10-point with good tine length, nearly 20 inches of inside spread. The buck stopped at 12 yards and began sniffing the ground. "I don't think he smelled me then," " Bill postulated. "But when he stopped and I got a good look at his rack, that's when I decided I'd take him. Of course, that's when everything changes, especially the level of adrenaline flow."

That year Bill was using a recurve bow, a Dan Quillian Patriot takedown, and shooting instinctively. Note the accompanying photo of that excellent whitetail on page 66. According to Bill he dressed at about 185 pounds. Winke is a trophy hunter, but is not interested in the actual measurements of the bucks he takes, and I can empathize with that.

Bill's idea of hunting totally new territory every afternoon obviously requires having a great deal of land to hunt. However, since I've lived in the same area of Pennsylvania for so long, I know it wouldn't be hard for me to adapt to Winke's method, for I have more places to hunt than I can get to in any given season. If you've lived in the same area for years, you could be in a similar situation. The problem for many people is the commitment to planning such a long series of individual hunts, then sitting down with the topo maps to zero in on the "perfect" stand spot at each hunt location. There's a lot of time and detail work here. But that's stuff most hunters won't commit to, so any of you who do want to adapt to Bill's theory aren't likely to encounter others with

Winke was working on a theory. Select a hunting area via topo maps and input from someone who had seen a great buck. Then he'd go in, select his treestand spot carefully, and hunt that area only one afternoon.

similar hunt philosophies. So it's sort of a way to beat the competition to the big bucks.

Bill says you also need to use a treestand that complements this type of hunting. For the hunt in question he used a Trailhawk Vantage Point. Once he became experienced with it, Bill says he could put it up without making much noise at all. Use screw-in steps to get up your tree, then use "pins" that come with this stand. These are silently screwed into place, then the Vantage Point hangs on those "pins." Some treestands are so noisy they can't help but spook the big bucks.

A key piece of equipment for Bill is a good range finder. When hunting out of a known stand, the hunter has usually paced off a number of distances in different directions, so he or she has an excellent perception of how far most any shot that's presented is going to be. But remember, with Bill's new technique you want to go directly to your stand site, not move around and "scent up" the area at all. Consequently, there's no pacing off distances. Let a good range finder do this for you. Bill has used the Ranging 50/2, as well as others.

Yet another key is to keep the pruning of shooting lanes to a minimum, and when you do prune, don't let the pruned limbs fall to the ground, for they could have your scent on them. Keep as much natural foliage around you as possible. Don't give the deer you're after something new and unusual to look at around your position in the tree. When you do prune a branch for a shooting lane or whatever, keep it in the tree with you, weaving it into place, maybe where there's a natural opening.

As to clothing, don't wear much to your stand. Bill often ties his outer clothing to his treestand. Wind chill factors are often around zero degrees in the midst of the Iowa rut, but he often walks into his stand in a T-shirt and light pants. Once you get to your stand, don't put all the clothes on right away. Get in your stand, maybe put one layer of topside clothing on, then add others only as needed. Bill is very big on insulated bib overalls for this cold-weather hunting. He has also found that a knit face mask keeps a significant amount of his body heat in. He also packs in food with high fat content, like sandwiches with lots of salami, pepperoni, and the like. Winke also gravitates to the so-called high-tech camo clothing patterns.

Let's revert back to 1991 and a second big Winke buck, one he took when he first began "playing" with his "new-spot-every-day" theory. Again, the buck was taken with a bow in Iowa. By the time the pre-rut was started, Winke had seen 20 bucks of Pope and Young quality. Of course, very few of these were within archery range. In talking with landowners and scrutinizing his topo maps, he had saved his best spots, avoiding them in the early season when rutting activity was nil or almost nil. Further, Bill told me, "I was not only saving my best spots for one-time hunts during the rut, I was saving my *very* best

Winke trying to rattle up a buck.

spots for the *very* best hunting days during the rut, which is often
when it's cold and clear."

On October 30, Bill put up a stand on one side of a 75-acre woodlot.
The stand overlooked a scrape. He saw a 130 class buck that evening
and decided he would take that deer. The distance was about 50 yards,
and Winke had it figured for that 8-point to come toward him. But the
buck kept at a tangent, never getting within bow range before disappearing. He rested that woodlot until November 8. He had another
stand location in mind from looking at his topo maps, on another portion of that 75-acre wooded tract.

He was screwing in his first step when he heard a deer grunt. There
were three funneling draws that led to a fenceline which connected to
the 75-acre woodlot with a standing cornfield nearby. (See sketch
regarding the 1991 buck.) Bill had approached this area by walking
through the standing corn, thus it was easy to keep out of sight. The
grunting buck was a good 140 class, chasing does. Bill knew the deer
would hear or see him, or both, if he put up his stand. More about that
stand shortly. Rather than take a chance at spooking this big buck,
Bill left his stand at the tree, backed out into the standing corn, and
went home. Although he had been to this stand spot only once, he
never hunted it.

On the morning of November 9th Bill hunted elsewhere, but he was
back to the previous afternoon's spot plenty early. He was using a
chain-on type stand, which he says isn't nearly as quiet to erect as his
previously mentioned Trailhawk Vantage Point that hangs on the
screwed-in pins. Bill spent a lot of extra effort and time getting the
chain-on stand in place on the 9th; he recalls that it took about 45
minutes to do that. Around two o'clock that afternoon Bill noted doe
activity in a CRP field behind his stand. The cornfield was in front of
him. His wind was blowing toward the CRP field. The does were milling about, maybe indicating some concern, but they weren't spooked.
"At three o'clock the buck activity started. I saw a great many Pope &
Young bucks, so many I'm not going to even say what I counted. It was
unbelievable, and I'll leave it at that. I passed up one good 8-point
because of the buck I'd seen the previous evening. The others didn't
offer a shot opportunity."

"Around 4:30 I heard a grunt from the cornfield. Shortly, a doe came
tearing out of the corn. The buck was right behind her. My first
thought was, 'This is a mule deer!' The buck was so big, so heavy. He
stopped 15 yards broadside."

When Bill had gotten into his stand he found no shooting lanes to
the south. He wanted to be able to see and shoot on both sides of the
fenceline in question. So he had gotten down out of his tree and, as
quietly as possible, cut down a tree of three inches in diameter. That's
the exact spot Bill's buck picked for stopping for the previously mentioned 15-yard broadside shot. Did the buck pause because he smelled

A great 8-point with excellent tine length and spread. Winke estimates this one at 140 Pope & Young points.

Bill's scent? Who knows. The arrow was on its way to destiny moments after the deer's pause. The buck swapped ends as Bill released, so maybe it was spooked. But the arrow cut a femoral artery.

Winke watched the deer walk away into the woodlot. There were 8 inches of snow on the ground, and Bill could see blood accumulating as the deer stopped and stood watching its backtrail. The hunter waited until full dark to come down out of his treestand. The buck's body size was unbelievable. Though never weighed on a scale, Bill took some body measurements, then referred to charts that indicated the buck had to weigh more than 300 pounds!!! It was an 8-point with 22 inches of inside spread, the brow tines not overly long, scoring in the 140 class. For that hunt Winke was using a High Country Supreme compound bow with a release.

This great buck was the second largest killed by a bow hunter in New York during the 1991 season.

Bob Wozniak's 1991 Buck: Second Largest Bow-Killed Deer In New York State

Bob Wozniak's 1991 buck measured 161-2/8, a trophy worthy for inclusion in this book, but further, Wozniak's a dedicated whitetail hunter, and through this account of his hunt, Bob reveals some excellent techniques that we can incorporate into our own hunting.

Wozniak, who works for the New York State Department of Conservation, first took his friend Dick Kirby hunting many years ago. He helped him call in his first gobbler and set him up on his first bow-killed whitetail. It was shortly after one of their early hunts that Dick suggested the two of them go into the call-making business. Wozniak declined way back then. "I was sort of a 'paid gun' at the time, Nick. My job with the Conservation Department was perfect for me. Of course, Dick has gone on to such great success that it's easy to see I didn't have the vision for the future that Dick had!" (Dick Kirby started Quaker Boy Calls which is based in Orchard Park, New York.)

Bob has been working for the Conservation Department for 27 years now. The last seven he has spent in the Environmental Section, keeping tabs on the transportation and disposal of hazardous waste. But let's get right to the nitty gritty: Bob Wozniak's how-to that resulted in the magnificent Pope & Young whitetail pictured here.

In the summer of 1991 he first discovered a 10-point buck that he figured had a 23-24-inch spread. That was the buck he had his heart set on. Wozniak has an interesting way of scouting in summer. He goes out in the evening after work with binoculars and a spotting scope. The area of New York where he hunts is blessed with huge valleys where vistas tend to be long. Dairy farms prevail in the valley bottoms and part way up each mountain slope, with timber on the

Bob, while summer scouting, had found a 10-point with a 23-24-inch spread. But that buck disappeared. While Wozniak was still searching for the 10-point, he came upon this one.

ridges, especially hardwoods. I believe there's considerable limestone in the soil, too, which adds to the area's potential for producing prodigious bucks.

Glassing and using a spotting scope might be an excellent way for you to locate brute bucks if you hunt in an area where you can get perched on one high vantage point, then be able to look over lots of country. Deer, of course, tend to come into the field edges late in the day. For Bob it's easy to glass fields that are 1000 yards, 1/2 mile, even over a mile away. The bucks don't have a clue they're being observed, so, by taking his time, it's possible to make very accurate estimates regarding rack size. Naturally, once a good buck has been spotted with binoculars, Bob unpacks his spotting scope to scrutinize the distant rack.

A key tip Bob passed along might be one you can use in your hunting area. In late summer, say from mid-July through mid-September (at least in New York where Wozniak is), the bucks tend to leave the valley bottoms and head for the highest ridges. This is probably to escape pestering flies, as well as to live in temperatures that might be a few degrees cooler. Bob calls it a migration, and he has found that bucks might move quite a distance to gain the comfort of a high ridge. This is also a time when bucks tend to bunch up. Often those that have recently had their first birthday band together, and the mature bucks, those that have had their second, third, and fourth birthdays, tend to bunch up with one another.

Bob is dedicated to his pre-season scouting, and he was really getting excited about trying to outwit the 10-point he had discovered, for he was seeing it several times a week prior to the archery season opener, traditionally October 15 where he hunts. The big buck had started making scrapes in late August. As the season approached, Bob began to see less and less fresh sign. Then, just before the season was ready to begin, the buck disappeared. This was very disappointing. He was hoping to hunt a huge ridge, owned by six different landowners, and he had taken the time to obtain permission from each of them.

Through the first two weeks of archery hunting, Bob stayed within the area where the 10-point had been seen all through late summer. But he struck out. After the first week he'd go to his stand at daybreak, spend an hour in it, then he'd start walking. He did more scouting, which is vital, and it's a good way for all of us to bow hunt. Naturally, many of you already do that. Each day he'd walk in a different direction, the idea being to find an area that was loaded with big buck sign. It took a week of this walking, after spending the first hour of light in his stand, before Bob found anything significant.

That's when he discovered a rub/scrape line 1-3/4 to 2 miles away from where he had been hunting. When he found the first rubbed tree he marveled at its size, over 6 inches in diameter. He looked farther up the trail, without moving, and could see another massive rub. This time it was an 8-inch tree the deer had rubbed. He followed the rub line for about half a mile, to where it lead into an old, overgrown orchard. The orchard was surrounded by a beautiful stand of hardwoods. Actually, Bob had scouted that same orchard two-and-a-half years earlier when he was scouting in March. Tracks were everywhere, but there's wasn't one apple the following autumn, nor a single smidgen of deer sign. But as Wozniak approached the orchard in late October of 1991 he found every tree limb bent nearly to the ground. "Nick, there wasn't room for one more apple on any of those trees," Bob told me.

Also, there was a field of weeds, a small one of maybe 50 yards by 40 yards. That field was surrounded by numerous trees that had been rubbed raw. The trees in and around the old orchard and field were rubbed completely around their circumference, whereas the trees on the rub line that led to this hub of deer activity were rubbed on one side only. Bob says the significance, when you find a similar situation, is that trees rubbed on one side are the ones the buck rubs as he's moving along a trail toward a desired destination. When you find an area of rubs where they completely encircle a tree, this is where the buck is spending a lot of his time, like a major feeding location or a major bedding grounds. Obviously, finding an orchard/old field situation in the middle of a stand of hardwoods on a ridge is the type of perfect spot most of us would love to find on any given hunting day or even any given hunting season. Usually, we don't, however. Also, big bucks might go through a lifetime and never find a spot where they can concentrate such time efforts as they did at the ideal spot Bob Wozniak discovered.

Deer trails led into the orchard from every direction. When Bob had first discovered the place two years before, he had taken the time to cut out some shooting lanes in strategic locations. He did more judicious pruning when he found the place loaded with apples in late October of '91. He also put some Doe-In-Heat in a scrape that was about 25 yards in front of his blind. Then he left. He came back the next morning. During the next several days he hunted his orchard spot four times, day or evening, whenever he could find time. Each time he returned, the scrape in front of his tree was bigger. On the fifth day he said he could lay down, stretch out, and he couldn't touch one leaf, the buck pawing it had been so thorough and ambitious with his work. It was bigger than a dining room table. Bob had also poured an entire bottle of buck urine next to the scrape a day or so after he'd used the previously mentioned Doe-In-Heat. Usually he prefers to pour these liquids outside already-made scrapes, not right in them, so you might muse over that idea a bit.

He could only hunt this orchard stand when the wind was out of the west, so that limited his days of going in there. It was also a long trek to reach this haven. He was hunting out of a Loc-On Limit stand.

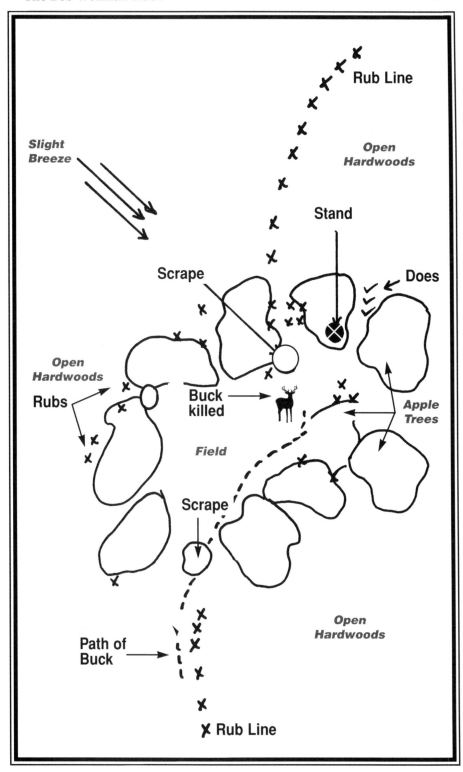

His fifth hunt to the orchard paid off. Normally, he's in his stand 15 minutes before it's light enough to see. This gives him time to rest up, quit breathing heavily, and get his senses tuned to his wild surroundings. But on the morning in question he arrived late. Why? He forgot his bow and had to return home. Sound familiar? Reminds me of the times when I've left the house to go grouse hunting and forgotten the dogs! Or my shotgun! I've actually done both. Several times! Bob's excuse was that he'd done a deer seminar for Quaker Boy the previous evening, so he had gotten home late.

As he reached his apple tree, while he was still on the ground he heard deer running, like a herd of them. This was very upsetting, for he figured his late arrival to his stand had spooked them. Soon he discovered that wasn't so. This deer herd wasn't spooked, they were running right at him. Several passed less than 10 feet away, all does. One doe stopped and looked at him eyeball to eyeball, only three feet separating their orbs. She was breathing heavily.

That's when the idea light bulb went off in Bob's head. "These deer are probably running because a buck is chasing them."

Thus he knew he had to get up in his tree. Otherwise he'd never be in a position to spot the buck that was hopefully chasing this herd of does. But what about this doe that was standing three feet away? Would she give the alarm snort and send every deer on the ridge skeedaddling from the prime orchard area? Slowly Bob got the two screw-in steps out (he takes those with him when he leaves his stand) and screwed them into place. Slowly again, Bob started up the tree. The doe ran off to maybe 10 feet, then just stood there, bewildered but not spooked. Carefully and quietly he pulled up his stand and locked it on, taking only seconds since he is so experienced at it. He saw the buck coming, but still hadn't pulled his bow up.

When the buck went behind some shielding vegetation, he got his bow up and notched an arrow. When he next came into view, the buck was 35 yards off. He was walking around the little field, headed toward one of the shooting lanes Bob had pruned out. As the deer was approaching he was grunting heavily, plus his nostrils kept flaring. When the deer got even with that huge dining-room-table-size scrape, he gave it his attention. Didn't go over to it and work it, just looked at it. Bob hadn't put anything in the scrape that morning, but he sensed that the buck could smell something in the scrape, and it took his attention briefly. The buck walked five to six yards to his left, which gave Bob the opportunity to draw his bow. It was a perfect 25-yard broadside shot, through one of the pruned openings Bob had carefully cut out.

In five days of hunting that orchard treestand, this was the sixth buck Bob had seen. In the previous four days he had already passed up four year-and-a-half-old bucks, plus a very good 8-point. But he was holding out for the huge 10-point he had discovered way back in July.

The one that disappeared just before archery season. Though Bob has made numerous inquiries about that deer, from the autumn of 1991 until the present, he hasn't heard one more thing about it. It's as if that buck simply vanished. As you've seen from the photo accompanying this chapter, the buck he shot was a 13-point that scored 161-2/8.

But back to the end of Bob's hunt. At the shot the buck bolted for the hardwoods. Shortly Bob heard a tremendous crack of antlers. It wasn't the sound of antlers hitting the ground. Within seconds after that there was deer chaos, a herd or herds of whitetails scattering. Bob told me that as the noise of their departing hoof beats were fading, "It sounded like someone had dropped a huge feed sack from an airplane—splat when it hit the ground. That was my buck caving in."

But the antler crash had come many seconds before that. What had happened? Bob just sat there in his Loc-On. A minute later another buck walked out of the hardwoods, coming toward Bob from exactly where the buck he had shot had run. Once down on the ground he found the blood trail was huge. It went for about 70 yards to where Wozniak found his trophy. Had the huge buck run into this second buck, and had they butted antlers? Did the trophy whack his horns into a tree or something? Bob's still trying to figure that one out.

What are some important factors in Bob's hunt? Bob Wozniak is a firm believer in rub lines. They usually tell an interesting story. Often it's a story that you can unravel to the point where your success ratio can soar. The chances of a buck coming to one rubbed tree are not great. But if you can locate a series of rubs that follow one direction you've probably found a travel corridor of a specific buck. This is usually when the rubs are on one side of a tree, as previously mentioned. The side of the tree that's rubbed indicates the direction the deer is headed, especially if you can match several trees rubbed on the same side that are in a line. Locate a series of rubs that completely encircle the trees, and you've found a high-use bedding or feeding area. The number of trees so rubbed probably indicates how heavily these bedding or feeding grounds are being used.

Further, the rub and scrape activity could increase as the period of the major rut comes closer. If that happens, it's further indication that hunting time should be concentrated at this spot. For example, when Wozniak found the orchard hotspot in late October, there were three active scrapes. When he shot his buck on November 5th there were 10 active scrapes, including the one that had been expanded to dining-room-table-size. While Wozniak has never been all that big on deer lures, he is wondering whether or not the Doe-In-Heat and the buck urine were a factor in getting the big buck to expand upon his scrapes in this apple orchard situation.

Chris Kirby, Dick Kirby's son, was called in to help drag this huge buck out. Not only was it a long drag, it was first down off the ridge where Bob was hunting, and it was a steep descent. But then it was a

Chris Kirby congratulates Bob Wozniak on his excellent 161-2/8 Pope & Young buck.

Dragging this buck out required considerable effort. The buck was not only a long way from any roads, the drag involved a long downhill, then a steep uphill effort.

very steep climb back up the other side before they could get to their vehicle. Paradoxically, Bob found when he gutted the deer that its stomach wasn't full of apples—but corn! Why? Further scouting for future bucks, this time involving talking with landowners and seeking permission to hunt, might have provided some insight to him. Wozniak found that the deer had been seen 1 to 1-1/2 miles north of where Bob had shot this buck. He was spending most of his time in a tiny patch of trees that would normally be overlooked by any hunter. That tiny woodlot was surrounded by corn and other fields, so that's probably where the buck had loaded his belly the night before he met his demise. It was the onset of the rut and the knowledge of does on the distant ridge (through scent or whatever sixth sense the deer had) that took him on a rather lengthy journey of doe chasing.

Prior to talking with the farmer who had seen Bob's 13-point, Wozniak had erroneously assumed that the buck was a resident of a nearby piece of New York state land that was closed to hunting. Not so. The buck was spending most of the daylight hours in that tiny woodlot already mentioned. What ever happened to that 10-point that eventually proved the undoing of Bob's 13-point? No one knows. Maybe that buck is still out there. If so, he has to be plenty long in the figurative tooth by now, and his days of wearing out-size headgear are probably over.

Bob Wozniak's Equipment

Bow - *Hoyt Spectra Fast-Flight*
Arrow - *Easton Aluminum 2213*
Binoculars - *Swift 7 X 42 - Bob says they're extremely good in low light conditions.*
Clothing - *Woolrich pants since it was very cold that morning. Treebark Polarfleece Coat.*
Stand - *Loc-On Limit*

OFFICIAL SCORING SYSTEM FOR NORTH AMERICAN BIG GAME TROPHIES

Records of North American
Big Game

BOONE AND CROCKETT CLUB

P.O. Box 547
Dumfries, VA 22026

Minimum Score:	Awards	All-time
whitetail	185	195
Coues'	105	120

NON-TYPICAL
WHITETAIL AND COUES' DEER

Kind of Deer Whitetail

Abnormal Points

Right Antler	Left Antler
2.6	5.4
6.4	

E. Total of Lengths of Abnormal Points	14.6

				Column 1	Column 2	Column 3	Column 4
SEE OTHER SIDE FOR INSTRUCTIONS				Spread Credit	Right Antler	Left Antler	Difference
A. No. Points on Right Antler	7	No. Points on Left Antler	6				
B. Tip to Tip Spread	9.1	C. Greatest Spread	18.7				
D. Inside Spread of Main Beams	17.0	(Credit May Equal But Not Exceed Longer Antler)	17.0				
F. Length of Main Beam					22.1	21.5	.4
G-1. Length of First Point, If Present					6.3	5.3	1.0
G-2. Length of Second Point					10.0	10.1	.1
G-3. Length of Third Point					7.6	8.3	.5
G-4. Length of Fourth Point, If Present					4.1	4.2	.1
G-5. Length of Fifth Point, If Present							
G-6. Length of Sixth Point, If Present							
G-7. Length of Seventh Point, If Present							
H-1. Circumference at Smallest Place Between Burr and First Point					4.5	4.3	.2
H-2. Circumference at Smallest Place Between First and Second Points					4.1	4.0	.1
H-3. Circumference at Smallest Place Between Second and Third Points					4.3	4.0	.3
H-4. Circumference at Smallest Place Between Third and Fourth Points					3.6	3.4	.2
			TOTALS	17.0	67.2	65.5	3.3

Enter Total of Columns 1, 2, and 3	149 7/8	Exact Locality Where Killed:	EMERSON FARM, TN of Ashford, CATT. Co.
Subtract Column 4	3 3/8	Date Killed: 11/5/91 By Whom Killed:	Bob Wozniak
Subtotal	146 4/8	Present Owner:	Bob Wozniak
Add (E) Total of Lengths of Abnormal Points	14 6/8	Guide Name and Address:	
FINAL SCORE	161 2/8	Remarks:	For Pope + Young Records

Taken w/Bow + arrow

Bob Wozniak's Boone & Crockett scoring form.

Decked out in his ASAT camouflage, Rick Frame poses with his treestand, Knight muzzleloader, and very big buck. Note how long and even each tine is, plus how the main beams almost come to touch in front.

Indiana's A Sleeper For Big Whitetails Like Rick Frame's Buck

Rick Frame owns and operates a gun/sport shop at Rt. 2, Box 202A in Liberty, Indiana. Though only 33 years old at this writing, he has already taken an impressive number of big bucks. One very good reason for Rick's early success with so many big-racked bucks is where he lives. Indiana has been coming on very strong as a big-buck state, and Rick's location in the east central section has been prime for several years now. Little woodlots adjoining farm fields have provided the escape habitat along with abundant feed. Minerals that white-tailed bucks thrive on, especially their racks, are obviously a positive factor in antler growth rates, as well.

In addition to operating his gun shop, Frame's Outdoor Sports, Rick works for Perfect Circle Products, a division of the larger Dana Corporation. Perfect Circle manufactures piston rings, pistons, cam shafts and other products for the auto and related industries. Frame, an engineering graduate of Tri-State (near Angola, Indiana), is a designer in the advanced engineering department of Perfect Circle. It's my bet that he applies his engineering background and experience to his whitetail hunting, and that's where we can all benefit.

His Dad was a coon hunter, and he first took Rick to the night woods when he was only five years old, so Frame comes by his love of the outdoors naturally. Before going off to Milligan College in Tennessee on a basketball scholarship, Rick trapped in Indiana. He also trapped while going through college. That's where, in 1982, he met Greg Wilson on a fur selling trip in Bristol, Tennessee. He returned to Indiana to attend Tri-State, work for Perfect Circle, and start his sporting goods store in 1989. It was in 1982, when he and Greg Wilson met, that Rick Frame became a dedicated whitetail hunter.

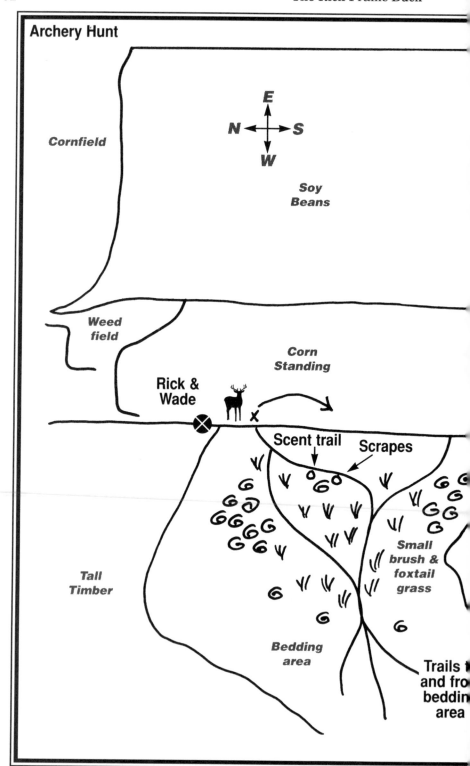

Archery Hunt

Cornfield

*Soy
Beans*

*Weed
field*

*Corn
Standing*

**Rick &
Wade**

Scent trail   **Scrapes**

**Tall
Timber**

*Small
brush &
foxtail
grass*

*Bedding
area*

Trails
and fro
beddin
area

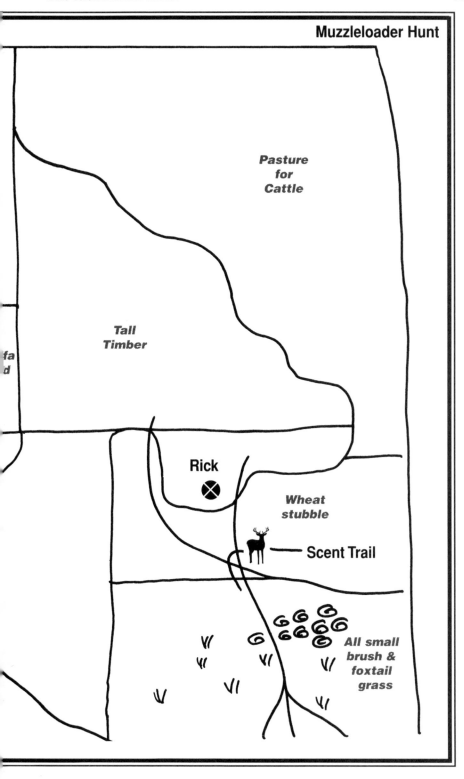

Muzzleloader Hunt

Pasture
for
Cattle

Tall
Timber

fa
d

Rick

Wheat
stubble

Scent Trail

All small
brush &
foxtail
grass

I'd like to take you through the scenarios of a couple of Rick Frame deer hunts so we can all take a hard look at the how-to he employed toward success. However, in this first case there was non-success. Let's see how this story unfolds.

Spotlighting at night is legal in Indiana, as long as there are no firearms in the vehicle. Most states which permit this practice require that spotlighting stop at midnight or some time. Penalties are very strict. If a firearm is in the vehicle, even if locked in the trunk, the truck or auto is apt to be confiscated. Where legal, spotlighting is an effective way of locating whitetails. Those who live in states where spotlighting is illegal may find fault with this method of locating big bucks, but it's a fact of life in many states. Obviously, one bonus of spotlighting after dark is that the biggest bucks don't come out of the woods and into the feed fields until well after sundown. This is especially true prior to the onset of the full rutting period.

Rick first saw this buck very late in the evening during the first part of October. Around the 15th of that same month, Frame came across him again. This time he was able to get a longer, better look at his rack. "I estimated that buck had a 20-22-inch spread. He was at least a 10-point, maybe even a 12-point. His tines were *very* long. I'd say he'd measure up to something like 160-170 Boone & Crocket points.

Rick had met a mutual friend of mine, Wade Nolan. Wade is one of the most successful outdoor video makers in the country. In fact, it was Wade who suggested I contact Rick Frame, for he thought Rick would be excellent subject material for a chapter in this book. Instead of concentrating on hunting this 160-170 point buck right from the start, Frame hunted another buck or two that he had seen. That's because he knew Wade would be arriving shortly, massive video camera in hand, and ready to shoot plenty of whitetail video footage.

Actually, Rick was hunting in the big buck's bailiwick, but from quite a distance so he wouldn't disturb this excellent buck before Wade's arrival. It was an "afternoon" hunting spot where this buck called home, and Frame didn't see him for four evenings straight. This was an afternoon (evening) spot because the deer were moving from their bedding grounds to a feed field. In the mornings (still dark) Rick couldn't get to the stand without alerting the deer to his intrusion. They would smell his entry too easily.

Wade and Rick were positioned at the west end of a partially harvested cornfield. (Note sketch.) There was a gate to their south. Beyond the gate was a big scrape area—scrapes Frame felt certain had been made by the buck they were after. But the closest tree for climbing was a good 70 yards away from the scrape area. How do you bring a buck 70 yards from his scrape to your tree? Here's one of the important how-to parts, and it's a key that Rick Frame has used to put his archery or muzzleloader tag on many an excellent buck.

Rick always wears high 17-inch rubber boots. There was a lot of fox-tail around the bedding area and the scrapes, as well as between the stand tree and the scrapes in the sketch. Wade was outfitted in hip boots, which feel like slippers to him since he spent better than a decade living in Alaska, where it's common to put on hip boots in the morning and take them off at bedtime. Of course, the even higher rubber hip boots insured that none of the scent from Wade's pants would touch the high foxtail. As Frame puts it, "Believe me, Nick, I've seen it. The big bucks, even the does, won't stand for any scent left on vegetation. Any buck I've ever seen wearing out-size headgear, when they whiff human scent, they're gone. Often they leave the area for days, even longer. You can't be careful enough with your own scent, and high rubber boots are one of the best and easiest ways to counteract this problem."

Further, Rick always wears an old jersey glove, not on his hand, but tied to a string to his boot. He continually soaks that glove with Buck Stop 200 Proof, then drags it everywhere he goes, but especially on his approach to his stand. This particular afternoon, however, Frame stayed at the climbing tree, while Wade, in the higher hip boots, walked to the scrape, tied the 200 Proof jersey glove to one boot, poured some of the Buck Stop into the scrape, then more on that old glove, and walked back slowly to the tree where Rick was waiting, dragging that ragged old glove the whole 70 yards. Would this be enough to convince a bragging-size buck to venture that far off his normal course?

Typically, three does were first to arrive at the feed field that afternoon. Wade caught them in living color and slow motion as they leaped the fence gracefully. Shortly, they were grinding corn with their molars. Rick's and Wade's hearts quickened as a 5-point buck walked up to a scrape and stuck his nose in it. Positively or negatively, he didn't show much reaction. Minutes ticked by. "I heard a 'hiss,' the unmistakable sound of a buck," Rick related. "He was still well back in the bedding area." Only about 20 minutes of shooting light remained.

"Finally, he came into view. Shortly, he went decisively to the scrape. One sniff and he began pawing and pawing. Next he stood up on his hind legs to reach and lick the branch that was very high above the scrape. All the while Wade's getting all this on his video camera. After that, nose to the ground, the big buck started down the scent trail Wade had left with that old jersey glove. Needless to say, we were both pretty excited with this spectacle so far.

"He stopped just shy of the gate, still 30 yards away. Up he came with a bound that easily put him over the fence. Now he was 20 yards, broadside. One limb obstructed my view. The sun had gone. Light was fading fast, for Wade's video camera as well as for my bow shot. The buck stayed right there for a seeming eternity. Finally, he took a step so the limb was no longer in my way, but the buck, in Wade's viewfinder, was against a dark green grass background. In the fading light there was no contrast, so the buck sort of melted into the grass. Wade wanted me to wait until the buck moved just a little more, so the background would be the cornfield, where the buck would stand out in front of it.

"At that critical moment one of the three does which had jumped the fence first whiffed our scent. We hadn't noticed that she had fed to a position behind us, and thus downwind. The buck vanished before we could think about reacting. He took off right after the spooked doe. I never saw that buck the rest of the season."

Frame says that hunting scrapes is a great idea. Nothing new, huh. However, he says that success in scrape hunting depends upon whether or not the buck making that scrape has found a doe or not. If a doe finds his scrape the buck might chase her a mile or more, and considerable time might be involved in doing so. All the while, you might be sitting anxiously over said scrape, and not coming up with a thing for your efforts. "I like to hunt scrapes early in the rut. After that any given scrape could be dead for a week." Sage advice.

Now to a buck that Rick was able to put on his wall. This was also a 1993 hunt, this one with a muzzleloader. Indiana has a shotgun or muzzleloader season that runs for slightly over two weeks, usually in mid-November, then a muzzleloader-only season that occurs later in December.

"I like to get on a well-used deer trail and follow it," Frame begins. "Sometimes I might have to follow such a trail for quite a distance. What I'm looking for is a concentration of 'big' rubs. By 'big' rubs I mean those that are made on tree trunks of some consequence, rather than thin, thumb-size saplings. Where you discover concentrations of big rubs it's safe to assume that (1) there's a big buck making them, and (2) that buck has probably spent a lot of time in the area, which has given him the opportunity to make all those rubs."

On the last day of the bow season, approaching the tail end of the rut, Rick was hunting such an area of concentrated "big" rubs. It was also a spot where does had been concentrating. "While the end of bow hunting season is great, because of the rutting activity, it's also a prime time for me to be scouting, as muzzleloader season immediately follows. That's the day I saw a very white-looking rack, a good one, spread of 19-20 inches, maybe a 10-point. Though the encounter was brief, so I didn't have time to fully study his rack, my impression was that both sides were very even, so there would be minimal deductions."

Muzzleloader season opened to the tune of rain pounding on the new-fallen leaves. Frame was in his stand just before the eastern sky began to lighten. It was still too dark when he heard a major raucous not far from his tree. Via shadowy forms he saw three bucks chasing one doe. One of those bucks stopped directly under his tree, and it offered a shot. Rick could only see one side of this buck's rack. It was a 5-point. Would there be 5-points on the other side? This was not the shimmering white rack he had spotted the previous day.

Seconds ticked by before he saw that unmistakable white rack, and it was coming his way. His heart pumped and his eyes scanned, but the white-racked prize simply disappeared. By then Rick had seen that the buck under his tree had indeed been a 10-point. Rick thought about the possibilities, crawled down out of his tree, then tried to slip up to this male/female pair. No luck, however.

He had been hunting a "morning spot," so Rick didn't return that afternoon. He was in his tree early the next morning, however. It was a Sunday. A 6-point was all he saw. Later that morning he returned to his gun shop, which is also a deer check station, so it stays plenty busy at that time of the year.

On Monday he was back in the stand again. The two-day rain was finished. Rick took the time to attach his old jersey glove to one boot, soaked it with the aforementioned Buck Stop 200 Proof, then walked about 100 yards to his stand, laying down a scent trail he hoped a sex-hungry buck would follow. His thinking was that two days of driving rain probably had all the local deer bedded down in heavy, protective cover. With the rain just finished they'd hopefully begin reacting to pent-up desires.

Again, Rick was comfortable in his tree well ahead of shooting light. As more light was gathering, he saw a flash out of the corner of his eye. It was the white-racked 10-point again. He *had* come back. That brute had his nose right on the ground, sniffing the trail a real doe had left for him. But that buck ran into the scent trail of the jersey glove drag. He stopped dead in his tracks. Rick Frame already had his muzzleloader to his shoulder. The buck had fallen for a pair of fakes: Buck Stop's 200 Proof and a lousy old jersey glove. The trigger went off, a puff of gray/blue smoke belched out of the gun's end. The bullet struck home in the boiler room. The distance was 60 yards. Rick had his taxidermist do this one in a full-body mount, leaping a fence.

Other than the scent drag, what is important here? Wind direction. Rick won't get into an afternoon stand if the wind is blowing from the stand toward the bedding area. Just the opposite for morning stands, plus there are other considerations here about travel routes—bedding to feeding areas and vice versa. Further, and this comes from Rick, "You have to be willing to pass up the smaller bucks. I call this patience. Sure, you have to have patience to stay on stand for hours at a time, but patience is also involved in passing up, say, an average buck after you've spent a lot of time on stand unsuccessfully."

Rick says you also have to have good equipment. Marginal equipment is apt to fail you at the critical time. Further yet, have a plan for each day. Plan on where you're going to hunt in the morning, and have good reasons for making that choice. Put yourself in a different stand location for the afternoon, again laying out good reasons why you want to be there as opposed to some other spot. Rick almost never hunts the same stand in the morning and in the afternoon.

The first two days of Indiana's 1994 season, Rick spent a lot of time scouting for that 1993 buck he and Wade didn't get, but he was in one location in the mornings, quite another in the afternoons. The second afternoon a 7-point buck, not a bad one either, offered an easy shot. But paying attention to his own advice, Rick passed him up.

Rick Frame's Equipment

Muzzleloader - *Knight MK-85 Thumbhole .50 Caliber*
Sabot-Knight/Hornady XTP 250 Grain .45 Caliber
Powder - *100 Grains FF*
Cap CCI #11
Scope - *Tasco 3x-9x Golden Antler*
Rubber Boots - *17-Inch Burley La Crosse*
Camo - *ASAT*

Walter holding his deer with shoulder mount. No wonder this buck made such deep gouges in the trees he rubbed. Look at all that rough-antler stuff around his brow tines.

Chapter 9

Walter Hatcher Bags The All-Time 2nd Largest Black Powder Buck Taken In Virginia

Walter Hatcher lives near Bedford, Virginia. He's 29 years old and does shift work in a paper mill for Georgia-Pacific. His hunting grounds are the steep, rugged mountains of Virginia's Blue Ridge chain. This is beautiful hunting country with wide vistas of near-magical scenes. While there's plenty of private land available where a sportsman can seek permission to hunt, there's also the massive George Washington National Forest with a figurative zillion acres open to public hunting; land that *we* own!

Walter began hunting at the tender age of 9 when his older sister's boyfriend first introduced Walter to the woods. By age 12 he had taken up deer hunting. Whitetail populations weren't all that high in his bailiwick in those days, but deer numbers have mushroomed over the last decade or so. "So has hunting pressure mushroomed," Walter told me. "I'm wondering if we're beginning to harvest too many deer in these parts. The last several years I certainly feel that I'm seeing fewer deer. Of course, I realize there's a natural trend for deer numbers to fall off from peak population levels."

During this period the Virginia Department of Game and Inland Fisheries significantly liberalized deer seasons. Not only were seasons lengthened, hunters were also permitted to take both a buck and a doe in archery, rifle, and muzzleloader seasons in several areas.

He started his whitetail love affair with a single barrel 12-gauge shotgun. At age 14 he bought himself a lever 30-30, and that was the year he bagged his first buck. At age 16 he took up bow hunting in earnest. During our phone conversations Walter was lamenting that he hadn't been able to hunt very much during the 1994 season since he was busy building a house. But in previous years, including the 1993 season, Hatcher had been able to get in the woods plenty. No wonder. Virginia has such long seasons. First there's archery that lasts about five weeks, beginning October 1st. Then there's approximately two weeks of muzzleloading, two weeks of the regular rifle/gun season, followed by two more weeks of the black powder stuff. For years Walter Hatcher has hunted *all* of these seasons, and in doing so has paid his dues for any Blue Ridge buck that might come his way.

Walter confided that for the 1993 season he had three extra-good spots, areas where he was almost certain to see deer any given day. The monster he ultimately bagged in 1993 (more about it shortly) did not come from one of those "prime" three spots, however. So you can easily deduce that Hatcher likes to move around a good bit, changing hunt locations as conditions of wind, weather, and other factors dictate.

"One of the keys to hunting these steep mountains," he begins, "is the wind. The predominant wind is out of the west or northwest, but there's also the natural inclination for the wind to blow *up* our mountains. It has to do with thermal updrafts, whatever. Knowing that, the deer hunter always has to strive to stay above where he thinks his quarry is hanging out, or where that buck might come from. I can't emphasize enough how important this wind draft factor is to hunting success in mountainous areas like ours."

In Hatcher's bailiwick, the rifle season, especially the early part, typically takes place in mid-November during the peak of the rut. However, Walter felt the onset of the rut was quite early in 1993. When the black powder season opened November 1st, rutting activity was already into high gear.

During the second week of archery season Walter was scouting some relatively new ground, an area that he had hunted before, but not often. There's an old logging road that traverses this tract, and it runs for quite some distance, making it an ideal place for bucks to make a scrape line. Despite it being only the second week of October, Walter wasn't disappointed. He found several smallish scrapes along the old tram, as well as a number of fresh tree rubs. It was the latter that particularly interested him.

"The several rubs I found that day were peculiar indeed. These weren't big trees, so I had no reason to initially assume the rub-maker wore headgear of outlandish proportions. But the bark wasn't scraped away in the typical smooth fashion. There were deep, deep gouges in these rubs. I remember thinking, 'These could have been made by a smallish buck with short, sharp brow tines.' I continued to follow that old logging road, and kept finding the same thing, more rubs, on smallish trees, and each rub had the unmistakable deep, deep gouges. I figured the buck making these unusual tree marks deserved further study," Hatcher told me.

Walter is the first to admit that it's not prudent to over-hunt an area. It's almost guaranteed that the hunter is going to leave some of his latent scent somewhere, and when a wary, mature buck discovers human scent, it's time for the figurative "fat lady" to sing, probably something like, "The Party's Over!" The buck vacates.

However, those deeply-gouged tree rubs had Hatcher intrigued. So he went back to this spot three or four more times during archery season. Of course, as October was bearing on, so was the rut. This was a morning area, one in which Walter could sneak in under the cover of darkness with the wind in his face. Not so in the afternoon. When his hunt was over at midday he could only move out as silently and quickly as possible, hoping the buck in question wouldn't spook.

What he found on these later trips into the area was that the buck was making more rubs, but now on bigger trees, and several of those trees were impressive in their diameter. The very deep gouging in these tree rubs was ample evidence that this was the same buck that had been marking those smaller trees earlier in the rut. Further, the deer was expanding on the size of his scrapes. Around the scrapes and rubs were signs of quite aggressive behavior. Walter also found some very big tracks. All these factors pointed to the possibility that this could be a very impressive buck. Never, however, did Hatcher lay eyes on the deer.

November 1st was the muzzleloader opening day of the first split. Walter was working the evening shift at the paper mill, 3-11 p.m. But he arose early and was on his stand at least a half hour early. He told me, "I prefer to hunt from the ground when rifle or muzzleloader hunting. This gives me the opportunity to move more quickly, and more silently, toward any buck that I might see in the distance. This can be a particularly important factor when hunting with a muzzleloader, for these black powder guns do have their distance restrictions."

There was a sugaring of snow for that first morning, crisp and cool; a whitetail sportsman couldn't ask for better opening day conditions. "That morning I saw a bobcat, and quickly leveled my sights on him, but missed," Walter Hatcher revealed. "The sound of the shot turned that bobcat nearly inside out with fright. It was a sure-enough flinch on my part. I thought to myself, 'Wonder if I'll flinch if I get a shot at this big buck.' In retrospect, what a catastrophe that would have been."

He had to quit hunting at noon on opening day to get back home and get ready for that 3-11 p.m. shift at the paper mill. In addition to getting the shot at the bobcat, he also saw a doe and a smallish buck, both of which offered good shots. But another key here. Walter has learned over the years that you have to allow those inferior bucks to "walk," and it's very difficult for most hunters to make themselves do this. If you're dead set on getting your bow or gun sights on a big buck, you have to get yourself into this mindset: allow inferior bucks to walk!

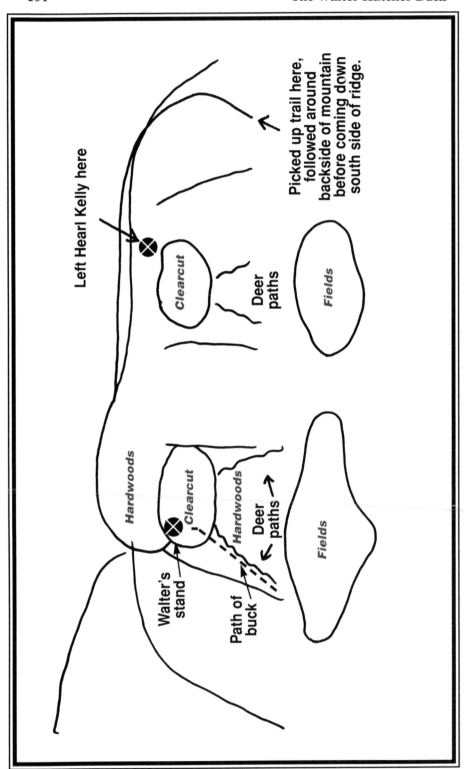

November 2nd was another perfect hunting day, but Georgia-Pacific had a "felt" change at the paper mill and Walter Hatcher had to work a "double," a dreaded 16 hours. A weather front was moving in. In Walter's experience, a front, especially during the rut, means deer are going to be on the move, either feeding or the bucks are anxious for doe encounters. So keep an eye on the weather forecast all throughout deer season. Arrange to be hunting when the weatherman predicts the onset of a front, especially when you know that rutting activity is high or peaking.

The morning of November 3rd, Walter took his friend Hearl Kelley with him. He and Hearl pair up for spring gobblers often, but they don't seek whitetails together very much. Walter returned to the same area he had hunted opening day. In the dark he walked with Hearl and put him on what Walter figured was the best stand. He then proceeded to another spot. "We weren't all that far away. I was trying to be the 'good guy,' so I put Hearl in what I felt was the prime spot, and took what I figured was second best for myself," Walter explained.

Despite having to get Hearl to his stand (Hearl had not hunted this area before), Walter was still plenty early, arriving at his stand 30 minutes before legal shooting time. The gun he carried with him was a Lyman Great Plains model in .54 caliber, shooting a round ball due to this percussion rifle's slow 1 in 66-inch twist. No fancy sights on this one, just a blade front and buckhorn rear. Hatcher had made this gun himself from a Lyman kit.

About nine o'clock that morning Walter heard something rustling in the leaves maybe 80 yards below him. He had heard some roosted turkeys yelping earlier that morning, and his initial thought was that maybe those turkeys were feeding, scratching away leaves. Shortly he discovered it was a doe that had made the rustling noise. She was moving slowly, feeding as she went. Her path was on an angle, not directly toward this camo-clad hunter. In time Walter figured she'd never get closer than maybe 60 yards before starting to increase her distance from him.

His hunting grounds in those Virginia mountains were near a couple of old cutovers. (Note sketch.) Once extremely thick, these cutovers were now growing up considerably. It's the type of habitat whitetails often like to seek. If oak trees are beginning to mature in and around such a spot, the younger trees can often produce bumper acorn crops. If there's thicker hiding/bedding cover nearby, these conditions make the habitat all the more ideal for whitetails.

As the doe was feeding, Walter glimpsed a flash of white behind her. Seconds later Walter confirmed those first suspicions, the bony shine of antler. "I knew immediately this one was a 'shooter.' However, the buck was still 80 yards or so off, with plenty of intervening vegetation, so I couldn't get a good look at him," Walter related. "But I knew there was a lot of spread and mass."

"The wind was gentle, but right in my face. My stand selection had been perfect—above where I figured this deer had been during the night. The doe paused briefly in an opening that was 60 yards away. Figuring the buck would probably step through that same place, I slowly raised the old Lyman, got the butt to my shoulder, and leveled the sights on that opening. When he stepped into it, I touched the Lyman off.

"The buck hit the ground immediately. Just as fast, I began to reload. I was hardly started with the reloading when the buck regained his feet and took off. I finished restuffing the muzzleloader in only about 20 seconds, then took off after him. Some say it might have been more prudent to wait, let the buck bleed out and die, but in this steep, rocky country I wanted to see if I could get a glimpse of him in the distance, which can be a big help in following a blood trail.

"I almost passed him up in my zeal. He was down again, definitely on his last legs. He raised his head and I put another round ball in his neck to not only put that big buck out of his misery, but to insure that he wouldn't regain his feet one more time and possibly escape."

Only then did Walter marvel at this buck's huge hat rack. And what a drop tine! This was the second largest buck ever taken by a black powder hunter in Virginia. His spread was 21-1/2-inches, 18-6/8-inches inside. Because of so many sticker points (remember those deeply gouged rub trees Walter had found while bow hunting in October?) the "greatest" spread was 26 inches, for a total of 40 points! There were 18 points on one side, 22 on the other. As you'll note from the accompanying photos, this is one impressive monster. Officially, this one goes 242-6/8 non-typical Boone & Crocket points.

During muzzleloader season, Virginia whitetail hunters aren't required to wear blaze orange, so Walter was decked out in Mossy Oak pants and a Realtree coat. However, he says, "I have reservations about using the 'green' shades of any high tech camo in the fall, especially in November when there's so little green left to the vegetation. I like the Kelly Cooper Trueleaf better for the autumn." Of course, Realtree and Mossy Oak both have new patterns with more drab brown overtones; All-Purpose from Realtree, Fall Foliage from Mossy Oak.

For that day's hunt Walter had donned Browning leather boots, but he almost always wears at least rubber bottom boots when archery hunting, due to the scent factor. He did advise, "I don't care how much trouble you go to in trying to cover your own scent, you're going to leave some of it in the woods. The idea should be to leave as little as possible, but a deer's scent powers are so good, it's just about impossible to prevent them from smelling you if you're upwind from them. That's the one thing I love about hunting these mountains. I'm continually trying to stay above the deer. That way I'm downwind and there's no way they're going to scent me."

The drop tine is a mammoth one! Also, antler points seem to go every which way.

Walter Hatcher's Equipment

Muzzleloader - Lyman Great Plains .54 Caliber - made from a kit
Sights - Open-Blade Front - Buckhorn Rear
Clothing - Mossy Oak Pants - Realtree Coat
Boots - Browning Leather - but prefers rubber or at least rubber bottom boots for most circumstances

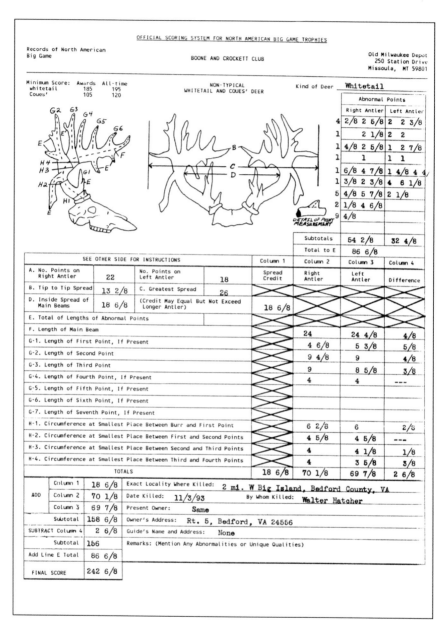

OFFICIAL SCORING SYSTEM FOR NORTH AMERICAN BIG GAME TROPHIES

Records of North American
Big Game

BOONE AND CROCKETT CLUB

Old Milwaukee Depot
250 Station Drive
Missoula, MT 59801

Minimum Score:	Awards	All-time
Whitetail	185	195
Coues'	105	120

NON-TYPICAL
WHITETAIL AND COUES' DEER

Kind of Deer **Whitetail**

Abnormal Points

	Right Antler	Left Antler
4	2/8 2 6/8	2 2 3/8
1	2 1/8	2 2
1	4/8 2 6/8	1 2 7/8
1	1	1 1
1	6/8 4 7/8	1 4/8 4 4/
1	3/8 2 3/8	4 6 1/8
5	4/8 5 7/8	2 1/8
2	1/8 4 6/8	
9	4/8	

DETAIL OF POINT MEASUREMENT

	Right Antler	Left Antler
Subtotals	54 2/8	32 4/8
Total to E	86 6/8	

SEE OTHER SIDE FOR INSTRUCTIONS

				Column 1	Column 2	Column 3	Column 4
				Spread Credit	Right Antler	Left Antler	Difference
A. No. Points on Right Antler	22	No. Points on Left Antler	18				
B. Tip to Tip Spread	13 2/8	C. Greatest Spread	26				
D. Inside Spread of Main Beams	18 6/8	(Credit May Equal But Not Exceed Longer Antler)		18 6/8			
E. Total of Lengths of Abnormal Points							
F. Length of Main Beam					24	24 4/8	4/8
G-1. Length of First Point, If Present					4 6/8	5 3/8	5/8
G-2. Length of Second Point					9 4/8	9	4/8
G-3. Length of Third Point					9	8 5/8	3/8
G-4. Length of Fourth Point, If Present					4	4	---
G-5. Length of Fifth Point, If Present							
G-6. Length of Sixth Point, If Present							
G-7. Length of Seventh Point, If Present							
H-1. Circumference at Smallest Place Between Burr and First Point					6 2/8	6	2/8
H-2. Circumference at Smallest Place Between First and Second Points					4 5/8	4 5/8	---
H-3. Circumference at Smallest Place Between Second and Third Points					4	4 1/8	1/8
H-4. Circumference at Smallest Place Between Third and Fourth Points					4	3 5/8	3/8
TOTALS				18 6/8	70 1/8	69 7/8	2 6/8

ADD	Column 1	18 6/8	Exact Locality Where Killed: 2 mi. W Big Island, Bedford County, VA
	Column 2	70 1/8	Date Killed: 11/3/93 By Whom Killed: Walter Hatcher
	Column 3	69 7/8	Present Owner: Same
	Subtotal	158 6/8	Owner's Address: Rt. 5, Bedford, VA 24556
SUBTRACT Column 4		2 6/8	Guide's Name and Address: None
	Subtotal	156	Remarks: (Mention Any Abnormalities or Unique Qualities)
Add Line E Total		86 6/8	
FINAL SCORE		242 6/8	

Walter Hatcher's Boone & Crockett scoring form.

This is the beautiful buck Will Primos took at Tara Plantation during the first few days of the 1993 archery season.

Rattling And Grunting Strategies From Will Primos

This chapter takes on a slightly different format than the others in this book. While we cover the how-to Will Primos used in the taking of two excellent bucks, another central theme concentrates on Will's input on several important subjects that can help us all get our sights on bragging-size deer more often and more consistently.

Will Primos is the guy behind Primos, Inc. His company specializes in the making of game calls, especially deer calls, and also in the making and marketing of deer videos. Based in Jackson, Mississippi, Will spent many of his formative deer-hunting years chasing bucks that wore headgear of marginal quality. Not that these bucks with inferior racks (by today's standards) did anything to dampen Will's enthusiasm for deer hunting.

However, for the last five years Primos has hunted only with a bow, exclusively with an expert video cameraman who has been charged with capturing all aspects of the hunts on film. It's very tough for the person with the video camera to do this, as anyone might expect. But the task might be even tougher on the hunter. He can't shoot unless the video is running. In many instances the hunter has a clear shot, but the cameraman doesn't. Or vice versa. Plus there are two people who can spook the deer before anything positive happens, doubling the odds in the whitetail's favor.

"Even though I was the main person, the one doing the hunting and the shooting in these videos, I've learned a tremendous amount by watching them over and over, being involved in the editing. By seeing these videos so many times, plus the slow motion and stop action that's easy to incorporate while editing, I continually see things that I failed to see during the stress of the hunting experience," Will explained.

Primos wasn't the only expert to discover how whitetails have a penchant for dipping down upon hearing the bow string send the arrow on its way, but this is one aspect of deer behavior that he has seen over and over as he edits and views the videos. Deer, especially when they have been alerted to even some minimal prospect of your presence, are capable of making you miss. Once their adrenaline trigger is set by this knowledge, their whole being begins to prepare them for escape. Their first move in their primary escape maneuver centers around their first bound. Physically, the only way deer can make that first, significant bound is by lowering their legs appreciably (loading the springs), which soon hurtles their body quite a few feet. But this lowering of the legs also lowers the back and whole body, Will says by as much as 14 to 16 inches, measured carefully by video stop action. So the tip here is, when you know a buck realizes something's awry, better hold appreciably low to prevent your arrow from going over the deer when he hears the bow string send the arrow on its way and he reacts with his initial bound, which lowers his whole body so much.

Primos was raised in a family whose central focus was hunting and fishing. His Dad was an avid sportsman, as were all his brothers. They lived on the outskirts of Jackson, Mississippi and wildlife abounded, especially doves, deer, and fish. Jackson's perimeter isn't as wildlife-plentiful these days as it was decades ago, for suburbia has sprawled there. Will started with a Crossman CO_2 pellet gun in 1958. He found starlings extremely challenging, so much so that he built a blind that helped him finally kill his first one. "At that time quail and doves were at the very top of my life list, maybe like a trophy bull elk is today," Primos offered. His mother rewarded him for bringing in a squirrel, but there was no songbird shooting, as she was an avid bird-watcher. He still has his first bow, which he was given in 1959. It had no rest, so young Will shot with the arrow resting on his hand. He made his arrows from scratch, usually odd limbs picked up around their house, and they were never perfectly straight. He plucked feathers from various birds to fletch those rough, handmade arrows himself. Later on he saw an older fellow's bow with a rest for the arrow, so young Will made a similar rest. "I knew so little that I ended up gluing the rest on the wrong side of the bow, but I could still shoot it," Primos told me.

His Dad had a wood lathe in the workshop. "I tinkered with that lathe to turn out my first duck call, and it was a pretty good one. When I first started hunting with real guns, I was absolutely possessed with duck hunting," Will reminisced.

His first gun was a Marlin 30-30, model 336 lever, and he killed his first deer with it when he was only eleven. "Back in those years deer hunting was all done with hounds in Mississippi. That first year with a gun I was on stand and the dogs ran a huge 10-point by me. I missed. The fellow in the adjoining stand shot it. Golly, I was dejected, in the throes of despair, but a little later a spike buck walked up, and I shot it. Talk about going from despair to elation in seconds."

He began bow hunting in earnest at age 15, with a Ben Pearson 45#
recurve. These were the early years of bow hunting when the sport
wasn't nearly as sophisticated as it is today. Will, like others of his
time, used the bow season to scout for the real season, the gun hunt
that always followed. Still, he learned plenty while bow hunting, but,
especially toward the last of bow season, his woodland tramps were
more with gun season in mind. Even at a young age he was able to
hunt in three states: Mississippi, Alabama, and Louisiana.

Already trophy whitetails were becoming an obsession with Primos.
Trouble was, all the deer had small racks everywhere he hunted.
There were none of today's modern deer management plans being
practiced anywhere. While attending Ole Miss, Will met Jim Humber.
Jim became involved with Dr. Skip Shelton at Ole Miss, and Primos
says that Shelton was responsible for putting the deer management
theory into practice, thereby insuring that some bucks would grow
older and develop more impressive headgear. Jim Humber eventually
began managing the Ward Lake Club, and it was there he instigated
Shelton's theories. "Nick, within three years there was a remarkable
difference in the Ward Lake Club's bucks. After only three years of
management, club members began shooting some great trophies."

In 1987 Will got to know Bill Walker. Bill owned a lot of land along
the Mississippi River, bordering both Mississippi and Louisiana. A
great deal of effort was expended by Bill Walker in properly managing
this land to grow big bucks. One key was to achieve a buck to doe ratio
of 1 to 3.5. Prior to the management plan, does were much more plentiful on this land.

I give you all this background so you can better know Will Primos.
He was born to hunt, especially born to hunt whitetails, and he has
devoted his life to learning more and more about them every day. He
has a great deal of experience with both rattling and grunt calls.
Before giving some of the background how-to on how Will took two of
his many excellent bucks, let's take a close look at what he has to say
about rattling and using grunt calls.

Some of you may not completely understand why a buck will
respond to rattling. The most obvious reason is that they're territorial,
or at least they become territorial as they mature. Current game management thinking is that this phenomenon occurs when a buck is two-
and-a-half years old. However, even 18 month-old bucks will come to
horn rattling. More about that shortly. Game managers have discovered that these territorial bucks settle into a home range that might
be as small as 200 acres, as large as 800 acres. Further, these bucks
spend a great deal of time in what managers are now calling "core"
areas, which might be only 20-50 acres. I assume the deer biologists
have discovered this through radio telemetry monitoring. Bucks spend
about 90 percent of their time in these favored core areas. Most bucks
are going to have more than one core area.

Will Primos trying to rattle up a trophy buck.

In the fall, core areas are typified by concentrated rubs and scrapes. So Primos suggests locating areas where scrapes and rubs are particularly plentiful. Find such a spot and you've located a core area, acres where a buck is going to spend a lot of his time. Once a buck becomes territorial he's ready to defend what he considers his, defend it against all intruders. Rattling is the auditory evidence that two mature bucks have invaded his territory and are fighting. Of course, an average buck might back down quickly if a super buck invades his territory, but at least he's going to give the fight a look-see before backing down. This is why rattling works.

Rattling can also bring in lesser bucks because of (1) simple curiosity ("Yell 'fight' in a school yard, and everyone's going to come running," is the way Will Primos put it to me), and (2) these lesser bucks "spar" naturally. No big out-and-out fights here. Two lesser bucks simply lock horns, softly in comparison to the real thing, and wiggle back and forth with one another for a bit.

Some hunters will use only real antlers to stage their mock fights in the woods. Most of these once-live antlers are discarded after a year or two. With a little age their sound tends to become unnatural. More and more though, man-made antlers are being very successfully used and marketed by companies like Primos, Inc. Will calls his "Fightin' Horns," and there's a good deal of science and engineering behind them. In addition to producing natural sounds, they're durable, work well even when it's wet or humid, and they have numerous contact points for realism.

Rattling works best during the rut. But this is not the only time to try rattling. The rut is when you should hunt as often as possible; stay in the woods as long as you can. When bucks are rutting, a trophy hunter's chances are greatly increased, particularly if the sportsman will rattle regularly during the rut. Here's how Primos says to do it most effectively.

First, there's no one way that's going to be better than any other. Obviously, sensible technique is a major benefit in rattling, but differing sounds and differing techniques do work. Here's what Primos suggests.

1) Set up for rattling in the previously described core areas, where you have lots of rubs and scrapes, indicating you're rattling in an area where a buck spends a great deal of time.

2) Set up near brush, cover, or a large tree (whatever will break your outline), on the downwind side if in the core area. Now you'll be rattling into the wind, the core area in front, and hopefully, the buck using it even farther in front.

3) Put out some buck scent and some doe scent. Give that scent a minimum of 10-15 minutes, to disperse a bit, but also to allow the area to calm down from the minimal noises you've made getting to the core area and doing the setup.

4) Use a grunt call before, after, and during your rattling sequence.

5) Holding the rattling horns about a foot apart, bring them together sharply. Next twist and intertwine the points, which entwines and grinds these points against one another. Continue this for 10-30 seconds. **Important**: Jerk the horns apart quickly.

6) No, you're far from done yet. Immediately thump the ground with both horns rapidly, from three to five times. Rake a nearby bush repeatedly with one horn, while still pounding the ground with the other. Watch, watch, watch. A super aggressive buck could be running toward you at full tilt.

7) If no buck comes in, repeat the battle, but don't slap the horns together as aggressively as you did the first time. Grind and click for 10-20 seconds. Now repeat the thumping, this time using the back side of the horns. Wait again.

8) End the sequence with a gentle ticking and grinding for another 5-10 seconds. Wait again.

9) After 5-10 minutes, repeat the whole sequence over.

10) If unsuccessful, move 100, 200, 300 yards, keeping the core area you have selected still in mind, or another core area, then go through the Primos-suggested sequence again.

Keep using the grunt call before, during, and after rattling. All through the rutting period, make it a point to stay in the woods. Your pre-rut scouting, hopefully, has helped you locate a number of these core high-buck-use areas. Keep hunting them as suggested.

To imitate light fights or sparring, the rattling horns are simply tickled together. Loud sounds are out, so minimal wind could be in your favor here. Also, don't be afraid to keep on tickling once you start—for up to five minutes, according to Will Primos. This sparring mimicry can be used from the onset of hard antlers right through to the last day of the season. Repeat every 10 minutes, or move to new core areas.

What about grunting? Primos first became interested in 1985. That's when he saw a grunt call while deer hunting in Georgia. This is also when Will became aware that whitetails acted more normally when not pursued by dogs. With no dogs involved, hunters in stands could hear whitetails communicate vocally. When he got home from that Georgia trip he contacted Mississippi State University and discovered a lot of research had already been done on deer vocalization. In 1987, while mowing a hayfield, Will accidentally hit a fawn. "It began bleating immediately," Will revealed. "Within seconds deer came from everywhere. My eyes were agape. It was unbelievable how many responded to that fawn's bleating—and how quickly."

But bucks have tended to run from the bleating call when Will has used it, except for younger bucks, which appear to be responding to their mother's bleat. "Grunt calls work best where deer are the least disturbed," Primos postulates. He also feels that bucks have a higher pitched grunt than does. "Deer are grunting at one another 365 days a year. It's how they communicate. Does grunt to fawns a lot. The time

Use a grunt call before, during, and after your rattling sequence

of the year and the body language has a lot to do with what whitetails are saying to one another with this grunting. Mostly, they're saying, 'Here I am. Where are you?' With their grunts deer will often snort and stomp. If you jump a deer and it hasn't smelled you, try grunting, snorting, and stomping. I think deer want to believe that another deer is the intruder. Often they'll come back. Of course, if they wind the hunter, that's the end of said story."

Aggressive grunts are rapid, in addition to sounding aggressive. Learn to make those. With experience, being able to see a deer and how its body language reacts to its grunting and yours will be most helpful. Deer want you to be another deer. As long as they haven't smelled or seen you, keep talking to them. A buck comes in curious when he's not certain of what he has heard, not so curious when he is certain.

When hunting the early season, remember that the deer's life centers around food. Locate those early season food sources. Grunt to add to your chances. Bucks are ready to breed as soon as their antlers harden. Most does aren't ready to breed until many weeks thereafter. Of course, the buck breeding intensity increases as does enter their estrous period. Also, when buck to doe ratios are closer to 1 to 1, grunt calls will tend to be more effective. For instance, a buck that's worn out servicing does won't be as easy to call as a buck that hasn't bred in days or longer.

Finally, before getting into the how-to of a couple of Will's whitetail buck successes, he made some interesting remarks on scents. First he told me about one of his favorite books, *Hunting with the Bow and Arrow*, by Pope and Young. In one chapter the authors told of a bear they came across that had its whole head inside the guts of a very ripe mule carcass. They observed the bear for a while from quite a distance. Suddenly the wind changed, blowing directly from them to the bear. Despite the bear's whole head being inside the very ripe mule carcass, the bear came out of there like a lightning bolt, indicating how a bear's scent powers are on such a significantly different level than ours. While trapping in earlier years, Primos discovered how beavers can smell human scent on castor bait, and the scent of a castor is overwhelming.

Will has been using Scent Shield of late, to try to cover his own scent. In addition to going overboard with cleanliness in both body and clothing, the Scent Shield gel causes a chemical reaction that keeps eliminating the formation of odor-forming bacteria. Will is not much on cover scents, but he does like to drip fresh deer urine in and around scrapes, plus use fresh tarsal glands there, even actual deer hooves in scrapes if the hooves are fresh.

Now to a couple of Will's big-buck successes. Both have one or two important tips that you can use. Back in 1986, Will was hunting the Port Gibson Club. While the club didn't have an ambitious deer management plan at the time, the grounds were unique for Mississippi in that there were numerous extra-thick areas that hunters couldn't get

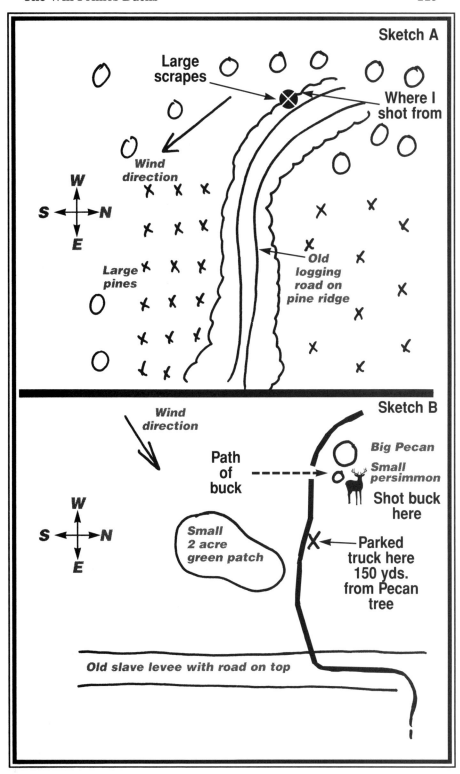

This great buck with long tines was taken at the Port Gibson Club in 1986. It scores 160-4/8 without deductions.

to and hunt effectively. The result was that some bucks here were able to grow older, plus live in a more natural deer environment since there was no dog hunting. Will found one particular scrape that he liked, a big one with lots of other scrapes nearby, plus plenty of tree-rub activity all around. Adding to this scrape's appeal was its location. (Note Sketch A. The heavily used scrape area is noted by the large scrape circles, which were below the higher ground on which there was an old logging road. Such a significant rise in the ground is unusual for flat Mississippi.) Will wouldn't even have to get in a tree. He waited for a day when the wind was right, then he approached the sight from downwind. Grunt calling on the way in, Will otherwise proceeded silently. He had no sooner arrived at his stand sight on the hill above the scrape when the buck came busting in from upwind. It was an easy shot with a .308 custom rifle by Brown Precision, and that buck measures 160-4/8 without deductions. (Note photo above.) So the tip here is when you locate a good, heavily used scrape that's adjacent to a hill, hunt that spot when the wind is perfect, approaching the sight into the wind, grunting as you get closer.

In 1993 Will hunted Willow Point South, a part of Tara Plantation, heavily managed for trophy whitetails and situated on the Mississippi/Louisiana border. It was very early in the bow season, so Primos was

Will Primos with a 132" 8-point that he took in November 1993.

thinking food sources. The entire first day of his stay he spent scouting. This meant he didn't see much in the way of deer, but it was deer sign he was after, and it was deer sign that he found. The season would open the following day.

The sign he found had to be difficult to see, as well as to interpret properly. Due to the early season, rubs were almost nonexistent, but one rub that he discovered was minuscule, a measly one inch top to bottom. Now who could get excited about that? Actually, any of us could, because of the tree the rub was on, a wild pecan with who knows how many winters showing in its growth rings. "Two grown men couldn't have reached around that pecan and touched hands," Will beamed while telling me.

He stayed away from that spot on opening day, probably wanted to rest it, or the wind was wrong. The second morning he also hunted another area on Tara Plantation. Here's the Primos key on this buck. While everyone else gathered at the plantation dining room for a heavy, sleep-inducing late breakfast, Will went hunting. He was the only one staying at Tara who did. Working his way up a logging road toward that huge pecan with the tiny rub (See Sketch B.) Will caught a flicker of movement. It was a buck (and a good one) that had crossed the tram, though he didn't get a good enough or long enough look to make an accurate estimate of trophy quality. The deer that had crossed the tram had been 200 yards away. With the wind in his face, Will was thinking ahead and already approaching that tiny one-inch rub on the massive wild pecan. He could see the deer begin to feed, so he started approaching from the ditch on one side of the road. Lots of heart-thumping time elapsed over the next several minutes, but the deer never knew Will was approaching. Will stopped at a mere 30 yards, which had to be a great sneak hunt. The big buck was loading up on persimmons from a tree next to the giant wild pecan. Seconds ticked by with agonizing slowness. Finally, the deer turned broadside. Will unleashed an arrow. Perfectly centered in the buck's chest, the critter didn't go far. This one was an 8-point with 20-7/8 spread, 4-5/8 bases and a 5-3/8 drop tine. (Note photo at beginning of chapter.)

Will's Equipment

Bow - *Gold Eagle Set At 74 Pounds*
Arrows - *26-1/2 inch 2213*
Broadhead - *Titan TNT*
Clothing - *Mossy Oak Camo*

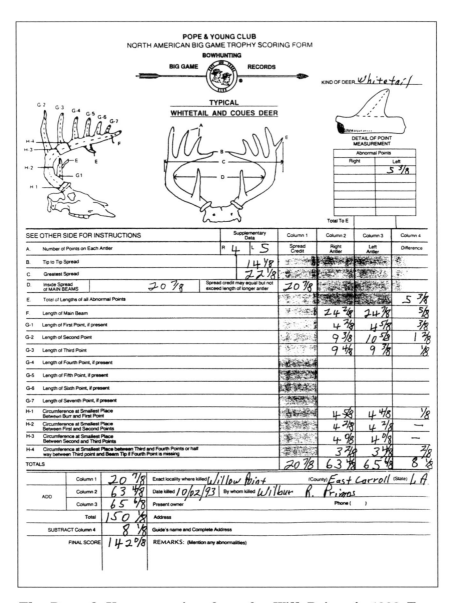

POPE & YOUNG CLUB
NORTH AMERICAN BIG GAME TROPHY SCORING FORM

BOWHUNTING

BIG GAME   **RECORDS**

KIND OF DEER *Whitetail*

TYPICAL
WHITETAIL AND COUES DEER

DETAIL OF POINT MEASUREMENT

	Abnormal Points	
	Right	Left
		5 3/8

Total To E

SEE OTHER SIDE FOR INSTRUCTIONS

		Supplementary Data		Column 1 Spread Credit	Column 2 Right Antler	Column 3 Left Antler	Column 4 Difference
A.	Number of Points on Each Antler	R 4	L 5				
B.	Tip to Tip Spread		14 4/8				
C.	Greatest Spread		22 1/8				
D.	Inside Spread of MAIN BEAMS	20 7/8	Spread credit may equal but not exceed length of longer antler	20 7/8			
E.	Total of Lengths of all Abnormal Points						5 3/8
F.	Length of Main Beam				24 2/8	24 7/8	5/8
G-1	Length of First Point, if present				4 7/8	4 5/8	3/8
G-2	Length of Second Point				9 3/8	10 5/8	1 2/8
G-3	Length of Third Point				9 4/8	9 3/8	1/8
G-4	Length of Fourth Point, if present						
G-5	Length of Fifth Point, if present						
G-6	Length of Sixth Point, if present						
G-7	Length of Seventh Point, if present						
H-1	Circumference at Smallest Place Between Burr and First Point				4 5/8	4 4/8	1/8
H-2	Circumference at Smallest Place Between First and Second Points				4 7/8	4 7/8	—
H-3	Circumference at Smallest Place Between Second and Third Points				4 0/8	4 0/8	—
H-4	Circumference at Smallest Place between Third and Fourth Points or half way between Third point and Beam Tip if Fourth Point is missing				3 7/8	3 4/8	2/8
TOTALS				20 7/8	63 4/8	65 4/8	8 2/8

ADD	Column 1	20 7/8	Exact locality where killed *Willow Point* (County) *East Carroll* (State) *LA*
	Column 2	63 4/8	Date killed *10/02/93* By whom killed *Wilbur R. Primos*
	Column 3	65 4/8	Present owner Phone ( )
	Total	150 0/8	Address
	SUBTRACT Column 4	8 2/8	Guide's name and Complete Address
	FINAL SCORE	142 0/8	REMARKS: (Mention any abnormalities)

The Pope & Young scoring form for Will Primos's 1993 Tara Plantation buck.

The 83 degree afternoon might have discouraged most of us, but not Rick Bagley. What a buck, huh!

Chapter 11

Rick Bagley Kentucky Bucks: Bow And Black Powder Strategies

Rick Bagley is Vice President at one of the biggest archery distributorships in the world, Pape's Archery in Louisville, Kentucky. Pape's ships archery equipment to virtually every state, as well as worldwide. So it's common sense to assume that Rick is a serious bow hunter. While he has taken numerous bucks of excellent quality, he took a dandy in early October of 1994, one that will gross at 177, net at 165. He has been bow hunting since 1969, so he has plenty of longevity as a serious bow hunter.

At an early age, Rick was introduced to hunting whitetails by his uncle. The uncle lived in Texas, and his area already had plenty of deer when Rick got started hunting in 1959, at the tender age of 12. Rick was living in Nashville at that time, and whitetail populations were slim to none in that area. But Texas was blessed with untold numbers of whitetails, and Rick learned about these animals' cunning ways from that dedicated uncle.

His Mother had been born in Australia, and Rick spent one early year of school in the land of the Aussies. After serving a tour of duty in the US Air Force he attended Cumberland College near Nashville, and that's where he started bow hunting. Over the years he has hunted bucks in Georgia, Tennessee, Alabama, Kentucky, and the already-mentioned Texas. He confided during one of our interviews, "Nick, honestly, I've seen many more bucks of trophy quality while bow hunting than I have while rifle or muzzleloader hunting, and, believe me, I've done plenty of the latter two. Obviously, I didn't bag a high percentage of the big bucks I saw while bow hunting, but that's not unusual."

Rick shot this excellent buck in 1975 in the Land Between the Lakes.

Mainly it's distance—between the hunter and the big buck—that results in bow hunters scoring on a relatively small percentage of the deer they see. But archers who spend plenty of time in the woods have the odds in their favor of seeing more big bucks than the average gun hunter. The latter sportsman is often afield when numerous other riflemen are out. The result tends to be that deer don't move in their normal patterns since so many orange coats have invaded their bailiwick and sent them scurrying, having taken them out of their normal daily patterns.

Since 1989 Rick Bagley has become a bow hunter exclusively. He would still love to gun hunt, but, like all of us, he only has so much time to invest in hunting. He loves the archery aspects so much, especially the part about whitetails moving about in their more normal patterns, that he has decided to concentrate all his whitetail efforts toward the bow and arrow side. As already mentioned, in 1994 Bagley enjoyed some monumental success with a particularly worthy whitetail. Here's how this story unfolded.

In early September of 1994, before the onset of Kentucky's archery season, Rick was clearing brush with a chain saw. The brush was being cleared to open up a particularly thick hunting area a bit, so

Bagley might be able to see a tad better, plus the chain saw work would open up some shooting lanes. He had taken an ATV into the area, mainly due to the bulk and weight of the chain saw. He was nearly done with his work when it began raining softly. He luckily turned his head in the direction of the adjacent bean field in time to see a big buck slipping out of that field. The deer wasn't running, but there wasn't enough time for Rick to accurately gauge the size of the buck's rack. He knew the headgear was big, but not how big!

Despite the rain, Bagley took the time to circle the bean field. There were three main trails leading into it, but the buck that had just exited the field hadn't used one of them. Rick returned a week later for another look-see at the trails leading into the field. The three heavily used ones were still active, but there were no large tracks in them. The little-used path that Bagley saw the buck use in leaving the previous week showed less activity than those main trails, but the only tracks in this trail were huge in comparison to the tracks in those heavily used ones. Rick knew his hunting area well. He theorized where the three heavily used trails led (Note Sketch A), but this lone buck's trail led elsewhere. Rick decided it was a different bedding area, a thicket of less than a half acre in size. Evidently, the big buck had this little haven all to himself. Rick didn't go to that bedding area to look for more sign, fearing his presence would put the buck too much on the defensive. He theorized where it was simply because his knew his hunting area so well.

He found a tree that was 18 yards off the trail in question, downwind from the predominant breeze. (Actually, you'll note in Sketch A that the big-buck trail coming from the bean field split into two trails that led to the thicket bedding area). Working quietly, he screwed steps into the tree where necessary. When he was 25-27 feet up, a height he almost always tries to reach with his treestand, he carefully selected how and where he'd hang his stand. Where possible he prefers to shoot while sitting. He believes added accuracy results from this more stable position. He also likes to shoot toward his left, being a right-handed shooter. Gauging where the big buck would come along the trail, and where he'd be able to get his shot, Rick hung his stand securely in place. "When I say I hang my stand securely, I do mean secure. I have to be able to move in the stand, without that stand making any sound. So I sit down and move around, trying to make it squeak. If it does, I secure it even tighter. This is a very important point." Before climbing down, Bagley snipped out a very few shooting lanes.

A few days later it was October 1, 1994, the archery opening in Kentucky. His hang-on stand was approximately 80 yards back in the woods from the bean field. But why would Rick expect a big buck to come to the bean field? The bruisers aren't often seen in the open until much later, when the rut is in full swing. The answer was the mast crop. That's what deer would normally be feeding on heavily at the

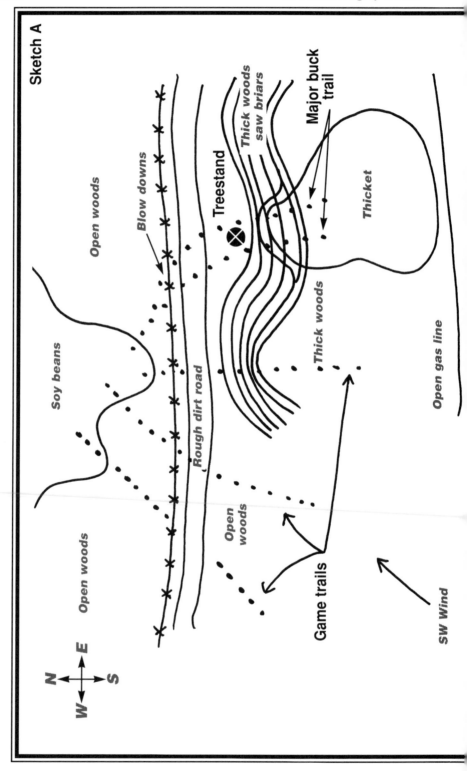

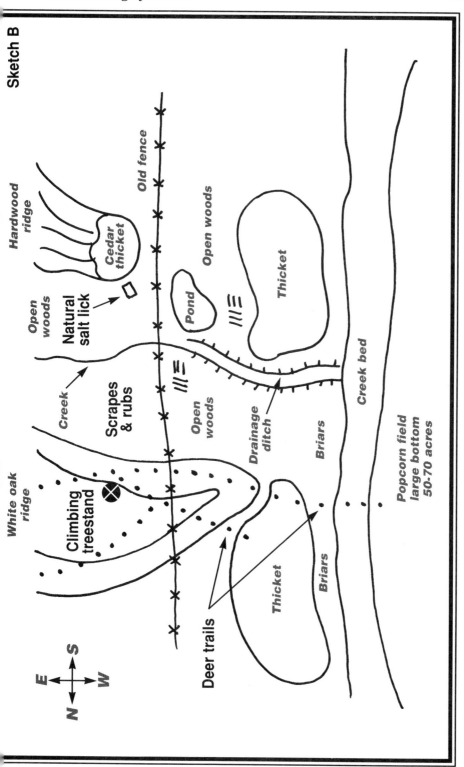

Sketch B

start of the season. However, in Bagley's bailiwick there were no acorns. The food source most readily available was the soybeans and their stalks. Rick was in his stand early that opening morning, anxious to see if his theory was going to pay off. He stayed in his stand until 11 a.m., but all he saw were does. As quietly as he possibly could, he climbed down out of his tree and went home for lunch.

It was a hot day, the high reaching 83 degrees, not the type of weather that gets most bow hunters excited. But Rick persevered that afternoon by taking another shower, then donning freshly laundered Full Foliage Mossy Oak clothing. "There was a little wind. It was out of the southwest, so if the buck did come to my stand the way I theorized, it would be a crosswind, and I could have the arrow on its way before he winded me," Rick told me. (Again, note sketch A.)

Rick began to tell his story of the eventful evening. "Legal shooting time would last until 7:25 that evening. At seven o'clock I heard something. It sounded like pebbles dropping. I tuned my ears to try and hear that noise a second time. It was 10 to 12 minutes later, but I did hear rocks again. Turned out to be the buck's hooves on limestone. Then I

Rick Bagley is a stickler for equipment, and that trait helped him bag this monster buck October 1, 1994.

saw him. He was very close, like 12 yards from the base of my tree. There was a lot of foliage due to the early part of the bow season. All I could see was the buck's right beam and one of its eyes. I had not antic- ipated the buck coming in from this direction. He was off to my right side instead of my left, so I had to turn in my stand to get in position to draw the bow on him. I slowly began turning, trusting that my stand was solid and secure and would not make a sound. My rubber-bottom boots helped me be noiseless, too. It seemed to take forever before I could get turned, but just as I finished, the buck moved a little. Now there was a tiny opening in the leaves. Looking through the peep sight, I placed the 10-yard pin on the buck's chest and touched the release.

"I heard and saw the arrow go into the deer. As he dashed away I could hear him running into stuff, and also caught a glimpse of the arrow's fletching buried almost all the way into the deer. He was still close enough that I heard him crash to earth. I waited some more. Shortly, I heard the rustling noises—those made by almost all animals as they die."

The arrow had hit the top part of the heart. He was a 12-point, but could be a 13, depending upon the scorer. Green, this buck grossed at 177, net score 165. The spread is 20-6/8, with super-tall back tines, one of them a full 14 inches. One heck of buck for a gun hunter or a bow hunter, but for an archer to take this buck at an incredible 12 yards—well, no wonder so many sportsmen have gotten so excited about archery hunting.

Twenty years previously, Rick Bagley was fortunate to take another excellent buck, this one with a muzzleloader. The year was 1974. The place was Kentucky's Land Between the Lakes, often referred to as the LBL. It was a special pioneer hunt, one of the first, if not the first deer hunt on that part of the LBL. Rick put in for the drawing and was lucky enough to draw one of the few permits. Since this area had been unhunted or minimally hunted in previous years, he figured chances were good that there would be a three or four-year-old buck that he'd have a chance at there, thus the reason for him applying for the per- mit in the first place.

Of course, this timing also centered around the period when black powder hunting was getting started nationwide. Sportsmen who became interested championed special black powder deer hunts, and these became popular in state after state. Rick Bagley was always interested in shooting of any type. He was an ardent groundhog hunter, so he loved his varmint rifles. He was even a serious benchrest rifle competitor, plus he was a shotgunner who competed regularly in trap events at that time. So it was natural for him to take up muzzle- loaders with equal zeal.

The hunt was only for two days, so several days beforehand Rick went in to scout the area he would be assigned. Several hours of slowly and silently moving through his assigned hunting tract paid

Twenty years before Bagley bagged his 1994 buck, he took this one on a special muzzleloader hunt at Kentucky's Land Between the Lakes.

off. He found a ridge with white oak hardwoods that had produced plenty of mast, then another hardwood ridge. (Note Sketch B.) There was a pond nearby, plus, important, a popcorn field to the west, and probably equally important, a lot of thick brush areas for bedding and escape cover.

Big buck activity was also discovered during this scouting venture. There were quite a number of rubbed trees, impressive in their 3 to 5 inches in diameter. Along with the concentrated rub activity were a number of very big scrapes. Finally, he found several deer trails, all of which led to the previously mentioned popcorn field. With his compass he double checked direction. Then he set up his self-climber stand downwind (prevailing) of one of the deer trails he had found. The stand was an old Baker that Rick had slightly modified. Baker was one of the few companies making deer stands in the early 1970s. The stand in place at the base of his tree, Rick left this hunting area as silently as he had entered.

Since it was only a two-day hunt, Rick decided he'd stay in the stand all day, at least the first day, so he took a lunch and thermos with him. He figured he had a good game plan due to his scouting, so rather than try to find anything else, he wanted to stick with that first game plan. Had this special pioneer LBL hunt lasted for a week or more, Bagley might not have gone with his all-day-in-one-tree venture.

Here's how he tells it. "I was on stand 30 minutes before legal shooting time. I saw several deer that morning, including a 6-point, but I passed it up, feeling I had a very good chance of seeing a much better buck. Around eleven o'clock I spotted a doe, I mean a big doe. She was easing her way along the trail I was watching, not in a hurry, but not stopping to feed either. Then, 50 to 60 yards behind her, I heard something and was pretty certain it was another deer. Shortly, I got a glimpse. Yep, it was a big buck. He wore 9-points and the tines were particularly tall.

"The buck was moving along just about like the doe. He wasn't trying to catch up or lag behind, just moving slowly but steadily. I was using open sights on a Thompson/Center .50 caliber Hawken. I set the front trigger, brought the gun up, then aligned the sights so they were just forward of the buck's chest."

The buck took off with the report of Rick's black powder gun. Gray-blue smoke encircled his treestand area, and, as with many black powder shots, Bagley wasn't certain at all that he had connected. He listened intently as the smoke dissipated, trying to hear the last sound the escaping buck made, so he'd have the best idea of where to start looking for its spoor. It was early in the day, so he waited in his tree a respectable time before climbing down. He reloaded his Hawken and took up the search. He found the buck piled up about 100 yards away. As mentioned, this one was a 9-point with nice long tines. He grossed 140-4/8, the biggest buck Rick Bagley had taken up until that time, and bigger than bucks most any of us will ever put our tags on.

Bagley is the first to admit that luck is involved in any and all successful hunting, but hunters can do a lot to balance the odds more in their favor. He's a stickler with his equipment. Not only does he want it to be the best, he also wants it to perform perfectly. In many instances that means silently. "In past years I've drawn on bucks and the only sound made was the arrow brushing lightly across the arrow rest. I could barely hear that sound inches away from it, but bucks could hear the sound from yards away—and react to it."

So every piece of equipment needs to be silent. Every archer, even the luckiest and the most successful, spends a great deal of unproductive time on stand. Opportunities to take the really big bucks come very infrequently. Anything relating to your equipment that can go wrong will go wrong unless you've had the foresight to make corrections beforehand. For example, if Rick's treestand had made even the slightest sound while Bagley had to move in it to get into shooting position, the buck would have heard it due to the 12-yard distance, and would have been gone with no shot ever taken. You know the saying in the business world about success, "Three things are so important, timing, timing, and timing." Often the big three success points with big bucks are equipment, equipment, and equipment.

Rick Bagley's Equipment

Bow - *Hoyt-Easton Super Star Fastflight*
Arrow - *Easton Mossy Oak XX75-2314*
Broadhead - *Thunderhead 100 Grain*
Latest Treestand - *Lok-On Super Spirit*
Camo - *Mossy Oak*
Muzzleloader - *Thompson/Center Hawken .50 Caliber*

OFFICIAL SCORING SYSTEM FOR NORTH AMERICAN BIG GAME TROPHIES

Records of North American
Big Game

BOONE AND CROCKETT CLUB

Old Milwaukee Depot
250 Station Drive
Missoula, MT 59801

Minimum Score:	Awards	All-time
whitetail	160	170
Coues'	100	110

TYPICAL
WHITETAIL AND COUES' DEER

Kind of Deer: WHITETAIL

DETAIL OF POINT MEASUREMENT

Abnormal Points	
Right Antler	Left Antler
	1 - Burr
	2 5/8 6-2
Subtotals	3 5/8
Total to E.	3 5/8

SEE OTHER SIDE FOR INSTRUCTIONS

					Column 1 Spread Credit	Column 2 Right Antler	Column 3 Left Antler	Column 4 Difference
A. No. Points on Right Antler	5	No. Points on Left Antler	8					
B. Tip to Tip Spread	11 1/8	C. Greatest Spread	20 1/8					
D. Inside Spread of Main Beams	18	(Credit May Equal But Not Exceed Longer Antler)		18				
E. Total of Lengths of Abnormal Points								3 5/8
F. Length of Main Beam						25 4/8	24 7/8	7/8
G-1. Length of First Point, If Present						3 7/8	5 7/8	2
G-2. Length of Second Point						12 2/8	14	1 6/8
G-3. Length of Third Point						11 1/8	12	7/8
G-4. Length of Fourth Point, If Present						6 3/8	6 7/8	4/8
G-5. Length of Fifth Point, If Present						—	1 4/8	1 4/8
G-6. Length of Sixth Point, If Present								
G-7. Length of Seventh Point, If Present								
H-1. Circumference at Smallest Place Between Burr and First Point						4 6/8	4 7/8	1/8
H-2. Circumference at Smallest Place Between First and Second Points						4 1/8	4 1/8	—
H-3. Circumference at Smallest Place Between Second and Third Points						4	4	—
H-4. Circumference at Smallest Place Between Third and Fourth Points						3 5/8	3 6/8	1/8
			TOTALS		18	75 7/8	81 7/8	11 3/8

	Column 1	18	Exact Locality Where Killed: BRECKENRIDGE CO., KENTUCKY
ADD	Column 2	75 7/8	Date Killed: 10 1 94 By Whom Killed: RICHARD P. BAGLEY
	Column 3	81 7/8	Present Owner: RICHARD P. BAGLEY
	Subtotal	175 4/8	Owner's Address: 377 GIBRALTAR DR SHEPHERDSVILLE, KY 40165
SUBTRACT Column 4		11 3/8	Guide's Name and Address: N/A
FINAL SCORE		164 3/8	Remarks: (Mention Any Abnormalities or Unique Qualities)

The Boone & Crockett scoring form for Rick Bagley's October 1994 buck.

One of Dick Kirby's beautiful 9-points. Note the good width but particularly the height of this good-scoring whitetail.

Chapter 12

A Trio Of Dick Kirby Bucks From New York, Texas, And Missouri Plus Additional Big-Buck "How-To"

Dick Kirby and his partner were scouting in late summer, no doubt several weeks prior to the opening of archery season. Timing was the early 1980s. Place was western New York. After work Dick and Bob would get together to cruise country dirt roads, the game plan to look for deer. As the sun waned in the west the whitetails would tend to come out in the open to feed on freshly cut clover, alfalfa, and other succulent, lush grasses. They kept a window mount on each side of the vehicle where they could quickly attach spotting scopes. When the vehicle was moving they trusted their eyes to pick up distant deer emerging from the woods. But often they stopped the car. Sometimes they'd stay inside and check out surrounding fields with the binoculars they carried around their necks. Of course, often they'd get out of the car for this glassing. When they found a buck worthy of closer inspection—that's when the spotting scopes on the window mounts came into play. One evening in early September they came up with two good whitetails that were running together. These were quality bucks, though not great ones, in the 130 Pope & Young class, Bob and Dick decided after carefully scrutinizing the racks in the spotting scope. What really impressed them was the body size of these whitetails.

The two decided these would be the bucks they'd concentrate on once the archery season opened. The next morning they went to scout the general area. With little difficulty they found the huge tracks of the bucks they'd viewed in the spotting scope the evening before. (Check Sketch A.) On one side of the hunting area was a significant creek which had a huge, almost sheer 300-foot drop-off to the water. This

severe drop-off formed a natural barrier that the bucks would be
forced to avoid. The cliff also helped form a natural funnel that would
help concentrate deer movements. Behind two soybean fields, a goldenrod field, a thicket of brush, and a cut corn field was a heavy thicket
which had to be the bucks' bedding area. West of that heavy thicket
was a woodlot mainly of beech, and the beech trees in those hardwoods
were producing a bumper crop of beechnuts. There was another funnel
area back near other hardwoods that led to an old apple orchard. Dick
and Bob discovered a couple of other important points about this hunting area, then they left. They didn't return, hoping their one-day
intrusion wouldn't spook the bucks they were after. Also, opening
morning was still weeks away, so hopefully the bucks would forget
about any intrusion, if, in fact, the deer did become aware of Bob and
Dick being there. This farm country was unposted and thus open to
most any other hunter, so the duo kept their mouths shut about what
they had discovered.

They did return regularly by car. They viewed the bean and goldenrod fields (See Sketch A.) repeatedly with binoculars, hoping to catch
the two 8-points out in the open, but they only saw does, fawns, and
very small bucks. Once the farmer harvested the soybeans all the deer
quit coming to those fields within two days! But it's legal to spotlight
for a few hours after dark in New York, and these two hunters did spot
the two 8-points in question again. Opening day of archery was only
days away now, so the spotting gave them renewed confidence.

Because the deer were no longer using the soybean field, Dick
decided to put his stand up in the natural funnel, the one that led from
the old apple orchard to and from the hardwoods where all the beechnuts were. (Again, note Sketch A.) This is the one he calls the Maple
Tree Blind. Also, since the area was easily accessible to other hunters,
Dick didn't go with any permanent type of stand, which would telegraph to others where he was hunting. He was younger then, just
grasped limbs and up he went. Comfort wasn't first class, for he'd just
sit in the top of the maple tree on the border of the funnel in question.

Dick did some explaining, "When I select most of my stand sights,
my first consideration is the predominant wind direction. In this area
of New York it's west northwest. Consequently, I want to be east
southeast, or close to that, from where I expect the deer to approach.
Naturally, it's wise to have other stands available that can be hunted
when the wind isn't blowing from its predominant direction."

There was no action with the two bucks from the old Apple Orchard
Area Stand, but a few nights later Dick spotted the two 8-points at
night near the cornfield. So for his next hunt he set up in the Beech
Tree Blind. (Again, note Sketch A.) From this blind Dick could look
into the heavy thicket—the route he figured the bucks would use—
coming from the bedding area to the cornfield in the afternoon. The
wind would be right in his face, assuming that predominant west

northwest breeze. The big beech tree didn't have any low limbs to grasp for climbing, so Dick quietly screwed in a couple of screw-in steps, hoping they wouldn't be noticed by any other hunters.

Next Dick waxed knowledgeably, "Deer prefer to come into a field with the wind in their faces. They depend upon their eyes, but their noses are without question their first line of defense, and what a keen, keen sense this one is for them. Many times, however, a good bedding area will be upwind from a field where they like to feed. When this happens, deer, even the does but especially the bucks, will stop inside the woods (See heavy thicket in Sketch A) without coming into the field. Most often they'll stay back in the woods several yards, looking, looking, looking. Some afternoons deer might spend 10 minutes doing this. If the sun is already down a sage buck might simply stand back there in the shadows until full dark sets in, and he might do this despite the fact that numerous does are out in the field, feeding and unconcerned about danger."

Dick's point is that it's very important where you set up in a situation like this, deer coming from a thicket, wind over their backs. You need a tree like Dick selected, the big beech with lots of branches to help hide you, but you must also be absolutely still. If not, those bucks standing back in the shadows will spot movement, and don't forget the biggest bucks might stand where you can't see them and look for seemingly interminable lengths of time.

The Beech Treestand was less than a quarter mile from the Apple Treestand. Dick didn't hunt his beech tree every evening, but he did spend three unsuccessful late afternoons in it. The fourth evening he decided to use a grunt call and a bleat call. Again, timing was the early 1980s, when calling deer was in its infancy. Even Dick knew little about it, and he headed a game call company. After he grunted and bleated for a while, a doe and a fawn came in. By their demeanor it was evident that they were responding to his calling, but once they got to the cut cornfield and started eating, they didn't pay much attention to Dick's grunts and bleats. Wanting to experiment and hopefully learn something, he kept calling, trying to gauge any response the two nearby deer would make to his efforts. He was concentrating on their behavior so hard he failed to see a 7-point. Dick finally saw that buck out of the corner of his eye when it was 70 yards off. It was early pre-rut, with minimal scrape and rub activity just started.

That 7-point came right in, so fast Dick had to hurry to drop his grunt call and grab his bow. He was ready, bow drawn, waiting for the buck to stop. The 7-point hurried to the doe. Coyly, not ready to breed, or whatever, she ran off. The buck never stopped, just kept chasing her. All three deer disappeared into the thicket before Dick finally relaxed his drawn bow. Now that he has had so much experience with calling deer, he's scolding himself for not trying to call that buck back in. That probably wouldn't have worked, since the 7-point was no doubt already enamored with his female find, but more calling would have been worth a try.

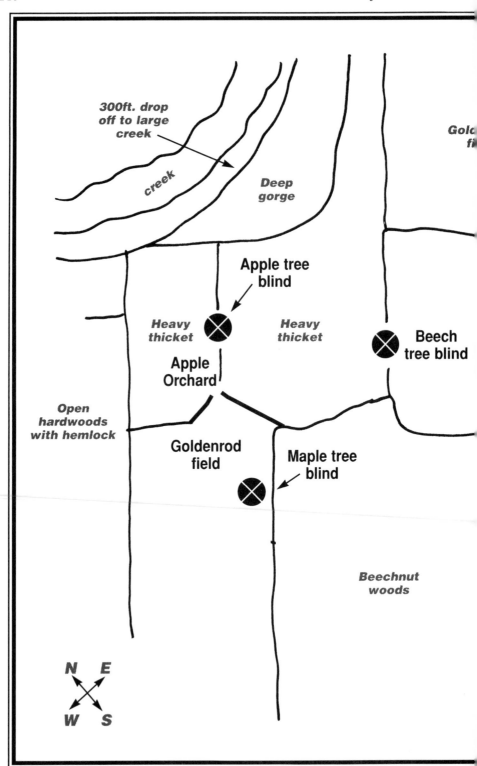

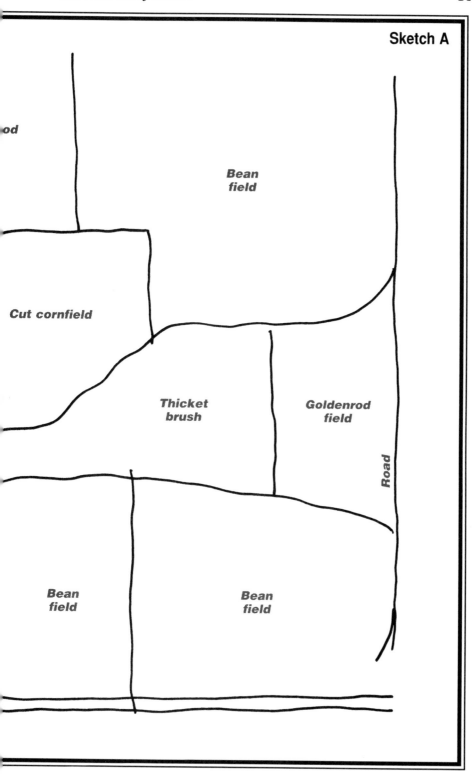

Sketch A

od

Bean
field

Cut cornfield

Thicket
brush

Goldenrod
field

Road

Bean
field

Bean
field

Dick went back to that Beech Treestand two evenings later. He offered more advice. "When going into a stand I make certain that I don't cross any deer trails as I move from the vehicle to the stand. This is seldom easy, and it almost always requires deviation in the route. If you cross a deer trail it's almost a sure thing that a deer, any deer, is going to smell where you crossed. Once that happens they're probably going to alter their route to where they were going, if not bolt out of the area entirely. Either way, your chances to see that animal, once it smells your track, are vastly diminished."

Despite his care, neither 8-point showed. But two nights later Dick was back in that same tree, this time with a set of rattling horns. "Since then I've been involved in the rattling of many, many bucks," Kirby revealed, "but at the time we're talking about I had very little knowledge. But I wanted to try it."

After tickling the horns a few times he saw movement. It was a doe. Was she responding to the rattling? She went on past, into the corn and began feeding. He rattled some more, and he noted that the doe fed on, as if she didn't even hear it. He tickled the horns together a few more times, and one of the huge-bodied 8-points showed himself! But the 8-point had already seen the doe. Without stopping for Dick to loose an arrow, the buck went right to the new female find.

"Now the deer is leaving. I'm thinking, 'I've grunted in one buck that went right to the doe I called in first, now I've rattled in another buck, and he's also going to a doe I rattled in first. I'm not going to get a shot at either one.'"

But Dick's mind started working then. He reached into his pocket and grasped his Bleat-in-Heat call. All you do with this one is turn it over and a beautiful bleat comes out. He did that. The buck, then following the doe, stopped in his tracks and turned his head back toward the sound.

"I froze while the buck looked," Kirby explained. "For long seconds he didn't move a muscle. Finally, he turned to follow the doe again. Immediately, I turned the little bleat call over in my pocket. This time he turned briefly, then walked right back in, stopped, and gave me a perfect broadside shot."

The big buck ran off, eventually disappearing into the bedding area thicket. Shortly, Dick heard a noise, but he didn't realize what it was. Now, ten-plus years of chasing whitetails a very impressive numbers of days per year later, Kirby has recognized it was the sound of a dying, gasping deer, its lungs no longer able to get oxygen. Dick waited for 20 minutes, climbed down out of his beech tree and started searching the area where the buck had been when he had shot. No blood. No hair. Now it was dark-thirty, but he had a good flashlight, so he kept looking. Finally, he spotted some blood. Later some hair. He kept working. At least 40 minutes later, and not all that far from his Beech Treestand, he glimpsed the white of the buck's belly at the edge of his light.

Here's a 10-point taken by Dick Kirby. This one has a lot of mass at the base of the antlers.

Deer prefer to come into a field with the wind in their faces. Many times, however, a good bedding area will be upwind from where they like to feed.

Hurrying forward he was rewarded with a remarkable sight. The buck's antlers were impressive at 130 Pope & Young, but it was the deer's body size that made Dick's eyes pop and his body shake. Not many deer grow this big in western New York. Field dressed, it weighed 204 pounds, and won Kirby the "big-buck contest" at a local sporting goods shop.

Dick philosophized. "I was lucky to take a wary, big buck early in my whitetail hunting career. That 8-point taught me a great deal, and everything I learned from hunting that buck I can and have incorporated into hunting whitetails everywhere I go." (Note: Dick has hunted whitetails in 12 states now. From the start of seasons in September until they end in winter elsewhere, he spends an inordinate amount of time chasing big white-tailed bucks.)

For those who don't already know, Dick Kirby is the guy who started and still runs Quaker Boy Calls out of Orchard Park, New York. His is a great American success story: a guy who had an idea (about turkey calls initially), and the intense business drive to make his idea happen.

We're going to talk about two more excellent bucks Dick has taken, but before getting into that, I asked Dick to philosophize further about his knowledge of big white-tailed bucks. He grabbed the bit without hesitation. "We read a lot about scouting and some of the things to look for. One constant is heavily-used trails. Looking for them is a good idea, but I've found that many heavily-used trails are ones deer always make at night. Consequently, sit by one of these 'night trails,' and it's likely you won't see one deer, even a doe or fawn.

"The better plan, and hunters can use heavily-used trails they find to help with this, is to try and look at the bigger picture. Deer trails are indicators of their travel patterns, and it's important for hunters to try and put the puzzle pieces together. Where are they feeding? Where are they bedding? Do the deer have more than one feeding area? More than one bedding area? What are their routes from area to area?"

Kirby broached another important subject. "Bow hunters need to be prepared with a flashlight that's capable of lasting three hours or more. Two flashlights with fresh batteries might be an even better idea. Some deer, despite how well they're hit, do not bleed much. Too many hunters think that because the blood trail is minimal to almost non-existent that they haven't made a good shot, that the buck is minimally hit, so they give up the pursuit. I've made perfect shots on some bucks and they haven't bled for a 100 yards!

"Persistence is very, very important here. Two people tracking are at least twice as effective as one, so don't hesitate to seek help. Never give up when there's the slightest hint of blood. Mark each blood sign with a piece of biodegradable ribbon, something. If necessary, keep going back to that mark and take up the vigil of looking again. If you do have a good blood trail to follow, don't be surprised if it peters out to nothing or almost nothing. I've found several bucks within a 100 yards of

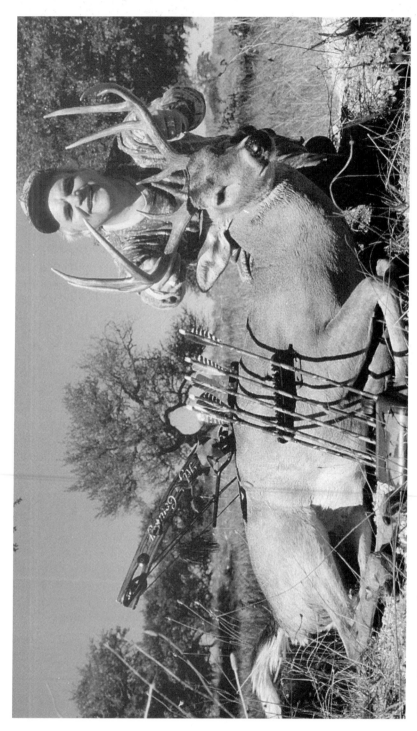

Note the extreme length to the two tines just beyond each brow tine; a great scoring bow-killed whitetail.

where good blood trails end. One tactic here is to keep circling the spot where the last blood was seen, then keep widening that circle slightly.

"I've been so dejected after spending hours tracking a buck, at night and in the daytime, half sick wondering if a great animal is going to be lost. But by being persistent I've finally found them all. The joy, the feeling of elation, when just moments before I was so down, is simply indescribable. It's worth putting all the time and effort you have, and then some, in tracking every deer."

A couple of years ago Dick was hunting the Ford Ranch in Texas. His son Scott was running the video camera, ranch manager Forrest Armke was doing the rattling, while Dick Kirby was handling his Sako in .280 Remington. Dick began, "Over several years of hunting with fellows of vast experience in rattling, like Forrest Armke, I've found these guys are very particular about where they rattle. They consistently position themselves downwind from where they think big bucks will be. That where-to knowledge comes from being very familiar with the property, where big bucks have been seen at specific times of the day and more. When a big buck does come in to rattling, they invariable try and circle to get downwind. That's why Forrest likes to position the shooter 30-40 yards off to one side of the rattler.

"Guys who have rattled in literally hundreds of bucks also feel that ground noises are just as important as horns rattling against one another. That's because when real bucks have their encounters there's a lot of hoof stomping and other noise. Top rattlers and real bucks don't keep banging horns together continually. It's more a clashing of the horns one time or a minimal number of times, then mostly the grinding of the antlers against one another. The latter are not constant noises either. The grinding noises produced by a good rattler tend to come in spurts.

"Forrest likes to start with just a tinkling, like the bucks are only jostling with one another. Remember that big bucks can intimidate the smaller ones. Then Forrest waits. If nothing happens he increases the volume of the next rattling sequence."

Forrest had called in four bucks that day for Dick, but they were all too small for the Ford Ranch's high standards. It was a bright clear day with no wind. (Forrest won't call on a windy day.) The ranch is also managed to keep the doe-to-buck ratio near 2 to 1. This not only results in a better balanced herd producing more bucks of better quality, it also makes rattling more effective. With high doe-to-buck ratios, like 5 to 1 and 6 to 1, all the bucks tend to be kept busy servicing in-heat does. They don't have time to fight, and there are not many other bucks to fight with.

Back to the Texas day in question. (Note Sketch B.) Forrest had started with his tinkling, then built up the volume of his rattling to crescendo proportions. Mark, one of Forrest's guides, saw the buck first. "Here he comes Dick. It's a big buck."

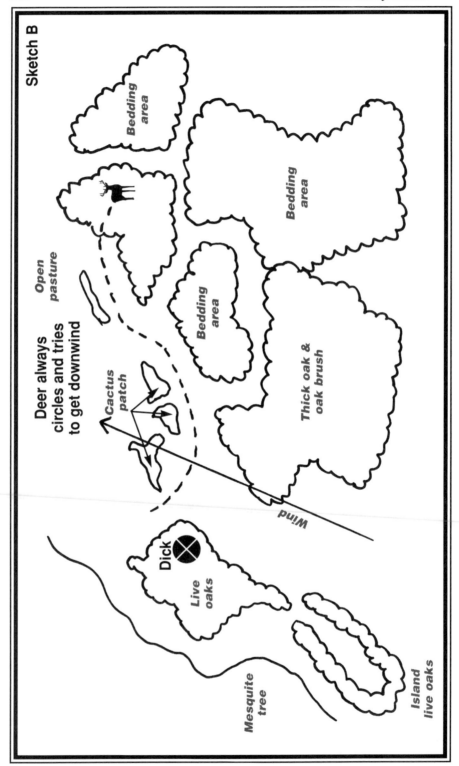

Sketch B

From Kirby's position he couldn't see him. Forrest stopped rattling. The buck stopped coming. Still Dick couldn't put an orb on him. Forrest put the antlers to work again. Immediately, the buck charged forward, and Dick soon had him in the scope. At 40 yards the buck was still coming when Dick hit the trigger and the bullet from his .280 took him in the chest, face on. This one turned out to be a 10-point of 125 B & C points.

One more Dick Kirby buck story and some interesting how-to. (See Sketch C.) In 1992 he was hunting north central Missouri near Lake Thunderhead with Dave Witt. The previous winter Dave had found several shed antlers of eye-popping size, so he kept urging Dick to come down for a hunt. Kirby arranged his stay for the last three days of bow season and the first two days of rifle season. The latter followed right on the heels of the archery stuff.

Early in the archery season Dave called Dick. Dave was sick, sick that he had arrowed a super deer and not found it, despite many long hours of looking. Kirby's and Witt's bow hunting time (last three days of the season) didn't produce, nor did the first morning of the rifle season. Next they decided to try a deer drive. There would be only two drivers, Dave and Dick's son, Scott. Lake Thunderhead was on one side of the area they would drive, always a good idea, for it eliminates 25 percent of the escape routes. (Again, see Sketch C.) The woods they would drive were about 300 yards wide, 500-600 yards long. There weren't a lot of mature trees. Predominant were scrub oaks.

One big buck did lie very tight. It didn't jump until Scott almost tramped on it. He was carrying a heavy video camera, not a gun. When he got to Dick he was excited. "Dad, what an easy shot I had at a great white-tailed buck, despite that deer running."

Dave walked up as this was going on, "Dick, didn't you see that buck?" he whispered.

Dick shook his head no. Whispering again, Dave came back. "Then there's no question that buck has doubled back. He's still in those woods we just came through. Dick, you make a big circle, downwind, then get positioned on that far hill where you'll have a good view. We'll give you plenty of time, then we'll make a drive right back where we just came through."

These drives were silent ones. No whooping and hollering, the drivers simply moving along, slowly. Once they figured Dick was in position, the drivers began going back through the woods. Dick had a great view of things from the hillside. He waited. In time he saw the orange of Dave's hat. Disappointment came with that; he figured the hunt was over. Where could the deer have gone? Several does had been spotted on the first drive, in addition to the big buck Scott had jumped.

Then Dick saw his son Scott. "It's over," he thought to himself. He kept looking. He wasn't sure but he thought he saw a flicker of movement around the one thick spot left. He kept looking intently. Soon there was another flicker of movement, but not quite in the same

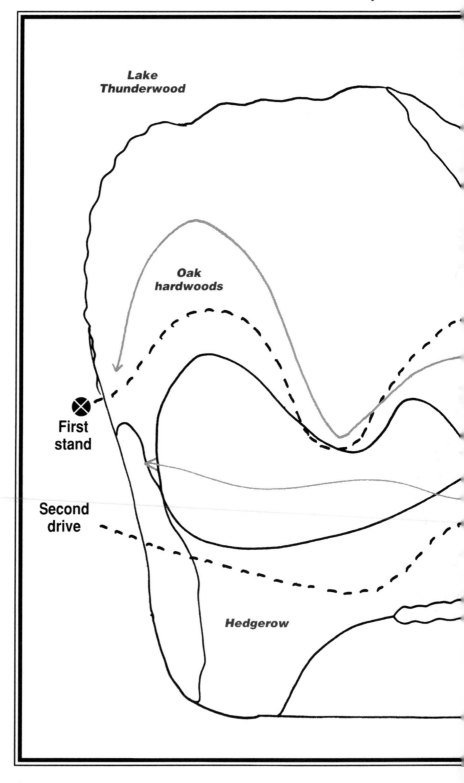

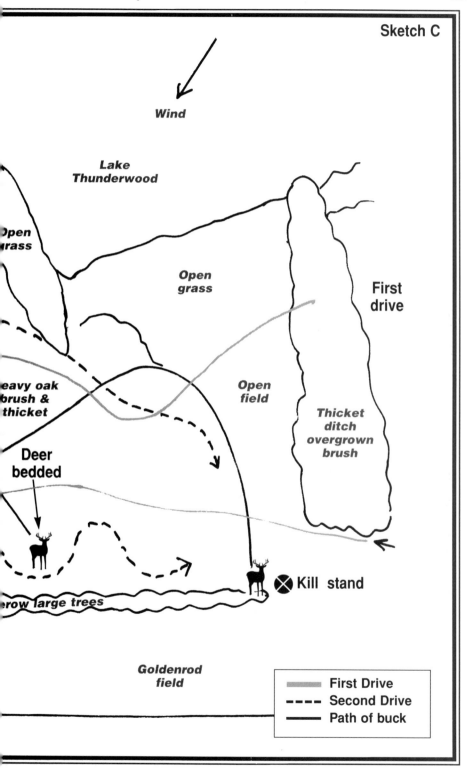

Sketch C

Wind

Lake
Thunderwood

Open
grass

Open
grass

First
drive

Open
field

Heavy oak
brush &
thicket

Thicket
ditch
overgrown
brush

Deer
bedded

row large trees

Kill stand

Goldenrod
field

	First Drive
	Second Drive
	Path of buck

The setting is Texas, the buck a beauty with remarkable spread to its antlers.

place. Dick moved to a better vantage point. Two does came through the last little patch of woods. While watching them he heard something to one side. There was the buck. Again, he was trying to sneak back through the drivers. The shot was broadside at only 60 yards, but a 4-inch tree was between, right at the chest cavity where Dick wanted to shoot. He kept the scope on the deer. When the buck took his first step Dick sent the bullet on its way. This one turned out to be a 9-point. Green he scored 144 B & C.

Scott was the first driver on the scene. In marveling over the deer he brushed his hand across its side. "Look at this, Dad." Dick bent down. It was the point of a broadhead coming out the buck's chest, and evidently causing the deer no hardship.

"I'll bet this is the buck Dave shot in archery season," Dick mused. Pretty soon Dave came up. He was fairly certain it was. In fact, he had the broken-off arrow in his truck. They later matched the broken arrow with the broken broadhead, and the fit was perfect. "Boy, am I relieved, am I glad you got this buck, Dick Kirby." It was Dave Witt doing the thanking.

Dick Kirby's Equipment

Bow - *High Country Ultra Extreme - for its lightness plus it's very fast and accurate. Dick also uses a PSE Fireflight.*

Arrow - *Easton Camo*

Broadhead - *Thunderhead 125 grain*

Rifle - *Sako .280 Remington with Leupold 4x-12x*

Calls - *Quaker Boy Old Buckster grunt call and Bleat-in-Heat are two favorites*

Clothing - *Dick suggests getting a friend to put on his favorite camo pattern. Put that person in a hunting situation, then back off 25 yards. Camo patterns should "break up" the person wearing it. You don't want too much light color or too much dark color. It's the contrast of the dark and light that helps hunters disappear to the eyes of wildlife. Dick is still a believer in down and wool when it's particularly cold.*

Boots - *He likes very light boots if he's going to be moving around, rubber for rain or wet conditions and because they leave less human scent behind.*

This is the beautiful buck Dr. Bill Cole killed with a rifle the last day of Pennsylvania's two-week buck season in 1990. While standing over this deer he decided he was going to be chasing big bucks the rest of his life.

Bill Cole's Four Year Winning Streak In Pennsylvania

Bill had only been at his stand 30 minutes. He heard the deer coming. He knew it was a buck long before he saw it because of all the noise it was making—crashing its antlers against every piece of vegetation, every limb, every tree trunk it could find. Would it be the buck Bill had scouted all summer? Would it be the biggest buck he had ever taken?

But let's back off from the end and start with Bill's beginnings. He's 35 years old and a busy chiropractor in a Pittsburgh, Pennsylvania suburb. His Dad, who has worked for Westinghouse for 30 years, got Bill and his brother, Bryan (a year younger than Bill), started in the outdoors. Dad first took the two of them hunting when they were 13 and 12, respectively.

That initial outing was for cottontails and bushytails. "I was hooked right from the start," Bill admitted. The next year Dad took the two brothers deer hunting for the first time. Bryan bagged a buck with a punkin' ball out of his 20 gauge single shot. "We youngsters were the least expected to bag a deer because there were several older men in our group. Bryan surprised all the other hunters. He has been very successful since then, too. In the last 20 years he has bagged 19 Pennsylvania bucks." (Note: It's one buck a season in this state.)

But it took Bill seven years to bag his first deer, a 7-point. Cole has enjoyed some very good success ever since, and that's the reason he has been selected for a chapter contribution in this book. He's young and very busy, as most all Doctors of Chiropractic are, which means he's pressed for time to do everything, including scouting and hunting. Somehow, he finds a way. Let's find out more about that and him.

In 1990 he took his first top-quality deer, a good 10-point with 20-inch inside spread. "Nick, I bagged that buck the last day of the two-week rifle season," Dr. Bill Cole began. "Right then and there, as I was standing over that beautiful buck, I knew I was going to be enamored with big deer for the rest of my life. But I also came to the realization then that I'd have to take up bow hunting if I was going to consistently tag big bucks in Pennsylvania where we have so much rifle season pressure. That hunting pressure keeps deer spooked and out of their normal daily patterns. By bow hunting in this state, I have a better chance of seeing deer that are into their natural movement patterns. By scouting I can see or hear about big bucks. Once I know where they're 'using,' I can then pattern their movements with further scouting."

In 1991, 1992, 1993, and 1994 Bill Cole tagged some enviable bucks. The last one would easily make Pope & Young, but Cole is another contributor to this book who does not wish to have his trophies measured. One important way he scouts is by never getting out of his necktie or his street shoes. He spends as much time as he can talking with farmers, for they're the ones who are on the land, who have the best chance of seeing bucks in the open, especially in late summer.

One farmer told Bill of two very good 8-points. More questioning pinpointed what cornfield they were seen in and approximately where these bucks were entering that field. A few days later, in mid-September, a couple of weeks prior to the archery opening, Bill had his tie off and his Florsheims exchanged for hiking boots. He carefully walked the edge of the cornfield until he discovered the heavily-used trail where he suspected the deer were entering that feed plot. Next he walked the side of the trail back in, locating a thick area where it seemed obvious these bucks were bedding down. (Note Sketch A.) He set up his stand downwind from the field, approximately 50 yards from for the bedding area, 25 yards off the trail. He talked a little about a whitetail's sense of smell. "You can do some pretty stupid things with deer if the wind is in your favor—and get away with it."

The first time he had a chance to hunt the stand in question, with a Baker self-climber, he struck out. Nothing. He wasn't disappointed with the lack of doe sightings, for the farmer had seen no does traveling with this duo of bucks. A couple days later, at midweek, he tried the stand again. Score another zero for Bill against the two bucks. A few days later, another Saturday, he was in his self-climber again, by now wondering if he had somehow spooked his quarry. Or maybe they had taken up with some does elsewhere, as the rut was slowly approaching. He decided this third hunt in this stand would be his last. By the way, this hunting area was over an hour from where he lived and worked.

Luckily, he was in the stand very early for that third and final try. At first light he sensed the deer had gotten a late start coming from the cornfield. It was not light enough to see they were bucks, but they moved slowly, allowing the day to brighten somewhat. Soon he knew they were bucks because he heard them thrashing their horns against grapevines and other vegetation as they moved closer. Cole had his

In 1991 Bill took this beauty—his first great buck with bow and arrow.

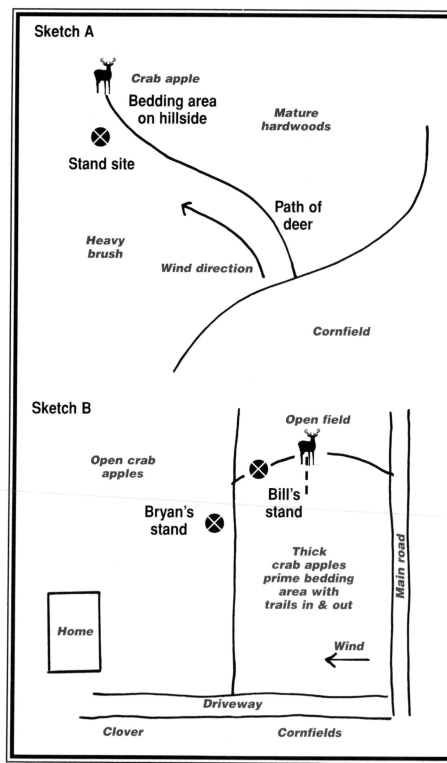

Sketch A

Crab apple

Bedding area
on hillside

Mature
hardwoods

Stand site

Path of
deer

Heavy
brush

Wind direction

Cornfield

Sketch B

Open field

Open crab
apples

Bill's
stand

Bryan's
stand

Thick
crab apples
prime bedding
area with
trails in & out

Main road

Home

Wind

Driveway

Clover   Cornfields

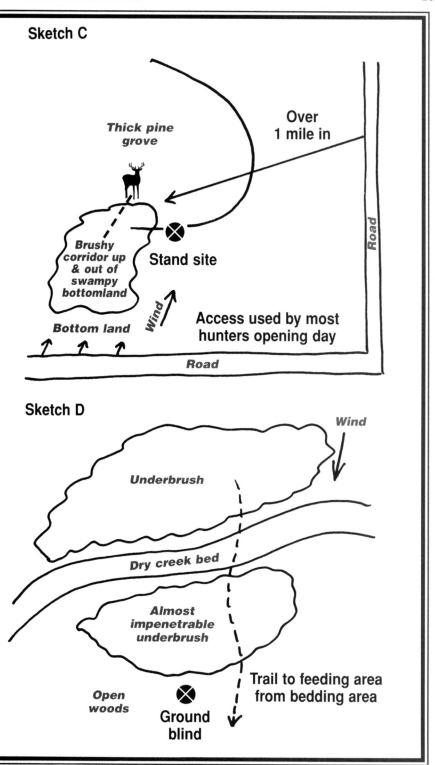

Sketch C

Thick pine grove

Over 1 mile in

Road

Stand site

Brushy corridor up & out of swampy bottomland

Wind

Access used by most hunters opening day

Bottom land

Road

Sketch D

Wind

Underbrush

Dry creek bed

Almost impenetrable underbrush

Open woods

Ground blind

Trail to feeding area from bedding area

bow ready. He loosed the arrow when the first buck was 24 yards from the base of his tree (Bill later paced it off). The buck turned and ran down the hill. Soon Bill heard him crash to the ground. He had gone no more than 60 yards. He was an 8-point with an 18-inch spread. (Note photo on page 157.)

In 1992, Bill hunted his own property. The tract was only 18 acres, mostly wooded, but right at his house. This latter fact would give him more scouting time, as well as less travel time to and from work or the house and a stand. Bill knew a big buck was using his property, but, despite a great deal of scouting and spotlighting at night, Bill never did see that buck, only the sign it left behind.

He hunted out of several stands on his property earlier in the season. Bill saw more than one buck, but he passed these up, knowing a much better one had to be close by. At mid-season, on a Saturday, brother Bryan arrived at Bill's house, and he spooked the big buck as his headlights turned into Bill's driveway. Bryan ran into the house to tell Bill. The buck had been coming from a nearby cornfield, and they reasoned that it was headed for a crab apple thicket on the opposite side of the driveway from the corn. (Note Sketch B.) But Bryan's headlights had sent the buck scurrying back toward the cornfield feed area. The two brothers reasoned that the buck wanted to reach the crab apple thicket for safety's sake, so they grabbed their self-climber treestands and headed for the crabs.

Obviously, this was turning into an impromptu hunt, not what they had planned for the day, but now it looked like the driveway experience had given them an even better game plan. They located some bigger trees at the edge of the crab thicket. Bryan took up his stand on one edge of the crabs, Bill on the other. (Again, note Sketch B.)

But they never saw a thing. Evidently, Bryan left earlier. Bill, though he expected the buck to make its move and cross to the bedding area very early that morning, stayed in his stand until noon. House and lunch were only a stone's throw away, but he got down out of the tree silently. Once on the ground he figured, "Maybe there's one last chance with this buck."

He grunted several times into his tube. Bill was down on one knee, his bow ready. "I'll never figure out how that buck got from the cornfield side of my driveway to the crab apple thicket side, but there he was coming, head down through the crabs, ready to do battle with the intruding buck I was imitating."

The shot was broadside at a mere 20 yards. He has very high tines, an 8-point whose rack is bleached extremely white (Note photo on page 161). The inside spread is only 14-inches, but note the unusual bulges on his antler tines. Cole had this buck aged at a check station: 3-1/2 years.

Now to 1993. Though Bill took another buck that year with a bow, he wanted to talk about the 8-point he shot in Maryland. The hunting area is some distance off from where he lives, so scouting couldn't be

This is Cole's 1992 buck. Bagged with a bow, the spread isn't wide, but the tines are high.

given top priority. He took the Friday off after Thanksgiving and spent that day in Maryland, one day of scouting, for the rifle season opened Saturday. He'd probably only be able to hunt one day.

The weatherman was a key factor in what Dr. Cole looked for during the Friday scouting. Although it wasn't raining that Friday, heavy rains were predicted for that night and through Saturday. Consequently, Bill looked for the heaviest, most secure cover he could find. What he did discover turned out to be perfect. I'll let him describe it. "I found some unusually thick pines, pines not only of the right thickness, they were of the right height. I figured deer would gravitate to pines like this if the predicted rains were particularly heavy. Even better, I found a super-thick finger of brush that ran from those pines to a swampy bottomland. I reasoned that the swampy bottomland would be the deer's normal bedding grounds, but if it rained like they were predicting, that swamp would not offer as much protection from the ele-

This is Bill's Maryland buck, shot in a deluge of rain the open-
ing day of the season.

ments as the pines. Next morning I was downwind of that thick finger that led from the swamp to the pines in question." (Note Sketch C.)

At the very first light the buck came, just as Bill had predicted, from the swamp to the pines, via the thick-growth finger. The shot was only 60 yards, easy with a rifle. He was a nice 8-point with an 18-1/2-inch spread.

"Was it raining as predicted?" I asked.

"Nick, it was a deluge," he came back. "It was pouring so hard you couldn't hear anything but the rain drumming down. It was the opening day of rifle season in Maryland, and my brother stayed out all day. He only heard two shots, mine and that of one other hunter." On a normal Maryland opener one might hear scores, even hundreds of shots.

Now to 1994—and the buck scenario we opened this chapter with. Bill and Bryan had secured permission to hunt 56 heavily-posted acres for the '94 season. It's a cover that might be doomed for 1995 or some season shortly thereafter. Surrounded by housing developments on every side, the cover (Note Sketch D) is supported by agricultural fields that act as feed plots for the deer, coupled with the bedding cover that's a mixture of hardwoods, mostly oak. There's an old clear cut too, where the cover is thick but not super thick.

He and his brother had spotlighted in mid-September and discovered two bucks, very good bucks that were using the area in question. At night they were able to accurately gauge rack size on both of them. Bill told Bryan, "If either of us bags the bigger of those two bucks, that's the winner of the Big Buck Contest at Nelson Arrows."

The first time Bill was able to hunt this spot was on a Tuesday, after the opening Saturday. He watched a few does, but no buck was seen. Two days later he got to his stand at three o'clock. He wanted to arrive earlier, but his patients had kept him busy at the office. "I was only at my stand sight for about 30 minutes when I heard the noisy crashing of this obviously mad but approaching buck. (Now do you recall how this chapter started?) There was no tree suitable for climbing where I wanted to set up for this buck, so I was crouching behind the best vegetation I could find. This deer was making so much noise with his thrashing; he must have been in a lousy mood."

Bill shot him head-on at 20 yards. The arrow grazed the bottom of his chest and lodged in one hind leg. Amazingly, the deer didn't bolt. Slowly it took three steps, as if it was still trying to figure out what was going on. That gave Bill the moments he needed to knock another arrow. The second shot was perfect. "I was really lucky to get the opportunity for that second shot," Bill admitted. The best buck Bill has taken yet, this one turned out to be a 12-point with 21-inch spread. This buck measures 7 inches around the base of the antlers.

Interestingly, his brother Bryan bagged this buck's cohort three Saturdays later, from a treestand on the opposite side of the woodlot where Bill had been successful. That buck was following a doe and very interested, so the rut was beginning to come on. This one was a

Bill's best whitetail yet: wide spread, 7 inches around the antler bases, and 12 points.

10-point with a remarkable 24-inch outside spread.

Some of the bucks featured in this chapter may not match the Boone & Crockett proportions of other whitetails covered in this book. But I thought it was significant for a hunter like Bill Cole to have taken some very good bucks, year in and year out, and very close to home. Further, because he's young and busy developing a chiropractic practice, he has severe time constraints. Sort of like all of us. Bill's a shining example that you don't have to travel all that far from home, or have untold hours to be able to scout, to still be successful with some very bragging-size white-tailed bucks.

Bill had a couple more important tips he wanted me to pass on to you whitetail enthusiasts. When selecting a treestand, try to pick a tree with two or three others adjacent to it. The close-by trees help to better break up your outline. Both Bill and Bryan Cole climb as high as possible when it's safe to do so. They regularly get 25 and 30 feet up in their trees. Both feel that the higher in a tree they are, the more they're able to make mistakes, especially with their movements, and get away with it. This philosophy no doubt helps with minimizing their scent to the deer as well. Further, not so many years back, deer, even big whitetails, seldom if ever, looked up. These days practically all whitetails will look upward for danger, especially the trophy bucks.

Bill Cole wrapped up, "Be aware of the terrain you're hunting, especially when scouting. Edges are keys. So are natural funnels and bottlenecks."

Dr. Bill Cole's Equipment

Bow - *Martin M44 Firecat*
Arrow - *Easton 2217 Camo*
Broadhead - *Muzzy 125 Grain*
Treestand - *Loggy Bayou Self-Climber*
Camo - *Mixes darker green camo early in the season with lighter gray camo shades later in the season. Bill is adamant about the need to keep the face and hands covered, even when he's 25-30 feet up in a treestand.*

One glance should tell you it's a big buck.

Jim Massett's Tracking Tips For Big Bucks

These days most every big white-tailed buck is taken from a stand, especially the bucks covered in this book. The knowledgeable stand hunter puts a great deal of effort into deciding where the perfect place is for his hideout. Most often it's a treestand. A few of the big bucks covered in this book have fallen to a method of old tradition—the deer drive. These drives have been what I'll call mini affairs, only a couple of drivers, one or two standers. The push is usually through known bedding grounds of big bucks. No noise is made, no whistling, shouting, clanging of metal—just a silent-as-possible sneak through, usually with the wind on the back of the driver's necks.

Earlier in this century, stand hunting was hardly heard of. Sportsmen always stayed on the move, still hunting, conducting drives, or tracking their buck! These days tracking a deer is not only a lost art, almost every modern-day hunter doesn't consider tracking an effective way of taking any buck, let alone a brute with lots of savvy. But Jim Massett, who lives in Chittenango, New York, and has hunted the fabled Adirondack Mountains all his life, has almost always relied solely upon tracking for his successes.

As the photos with this chapter attest, Jim has taken some exceptional white-tailed bucks. Further, this guy has been consistently successful with his tracking tactics. He bagged his first buck in 1952, then went 21 years straight before failing to fill his tag. He missed in 1971 and 1973, when previous winters had taken a brutal toll on the Adirondack deer population. Massett has yet another great string going now, having filled his tag in the Adirondacks every year from 1974 through 1994. Again, most of these bucks have been taken through tracking.

In this chapter he has supplied us with some wonderful how-to on tracking, sex identification, deer sizing from tracks, even sizing a

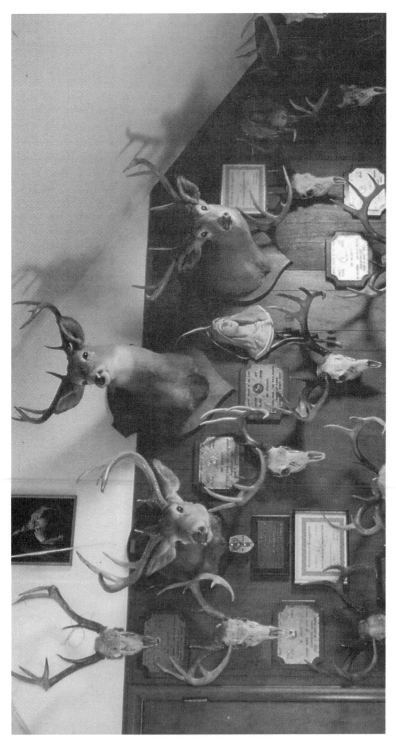

Part of Massett's trophy room at home. All of the bucks shown here were taken by tracking or still hunting in the Adirondacks.

buck's antlers, including width of spread, number of points, and beam length. If you're now skeptical that no one in the 1990s could be capable of doing all this, save perhaps a soothsayer, don't close the pages on this chapter. Keep reading. Your eyes are going to widen as you proceed, and you're going to learn that what you once thought impossible isn't so complicated at all.

Massett was born in 1937. He began hunting when he was 14. His father, plus some relatives and friends, belonged to a remote hunting camp in the Moose River Plains Area of the Adirondacks. As already mentioned, Jim has only missed taking a New York buck twice since his success started in 1952. However, Massett told me, "Many of those seasons I hunted very hard, and in several years I didn't shoot a buck until very late in the season."

The Adirondacks are unique. This is a vast track with relatively few hard roads, and these mountains are extremely rugged, so getting around in them is not for the physically faint of heart. The Adirondacks also receive significant snow falls, in some years some very significant snow falls. This latter factor can make the hunting conditions much different than they are elsewhere across the nation, plus extradeep winter snows can have a devastating effect on the overall whitetail population.

I asked Jim to talk about his beloved hunting country. "The best deer hunting occurred in the 1930s. This was when the mountains had been or were being logged. As the early stages of timber re-emerged, ideal conditions for whitetails helped the explosion. Some of the biggest Adirondack bucks were taken in those years. In 1950, Hurricane Hazel ripped through the Adirondacks, folding mature trees like matchsticks over countless acres. For four years portions of the Adirondacks were closed to hunting because the fear of fire was so great—all those dried-out toppled tree tops. From 1955 through most of the 1960s deer hunting was very good. Starting with 1969 we experienced three successive devastating winters; cold, cold temperatures coupled with lots and lots of snow. There were significant whitetail die-offs. I didn't fill my tag in 1971 or 1973. In 1970 I found one old logging road with 40 scrapes, each of the 40 about 100 yards apart. I reasoned that these scrapes were made by several very frustrated bucks, all anxious to breed, but there wasn't a doe around to accommodate them. Low deer populations like this can also mean trophy deer. I guess the few who survive are the biggest and the strongest. Anyway, my brother killed the biggest buck in the state during the 1974 season, an 11-point that scored 152-6/8. The hunting improved in the Adirondacks again from the mid-1970s through to the last two years. The 1993 and 1994 seasons in the Adirondacks have been very poor. Two cold winters and deep snows have again taken a heavy toll on these whitetails. One forester I talked with felt that 70 percent of the whitetails in the Adirondacks died last winter."

Blending in.

10-point, November 20, 1992. Notice antler hook up and hole dug by front feet in attempt to get free.

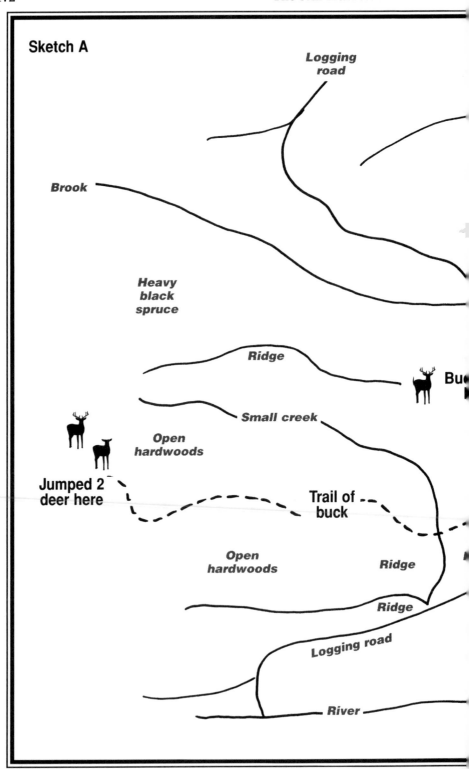

Sketch A

Logging road

Brook

Heavy black spruce

Ridge

Bu

Small creek

Open hardwoods

Jumped 2 deer here

Trail of buck

Open hardwoods

Ridge

Ridge

Logging road

River

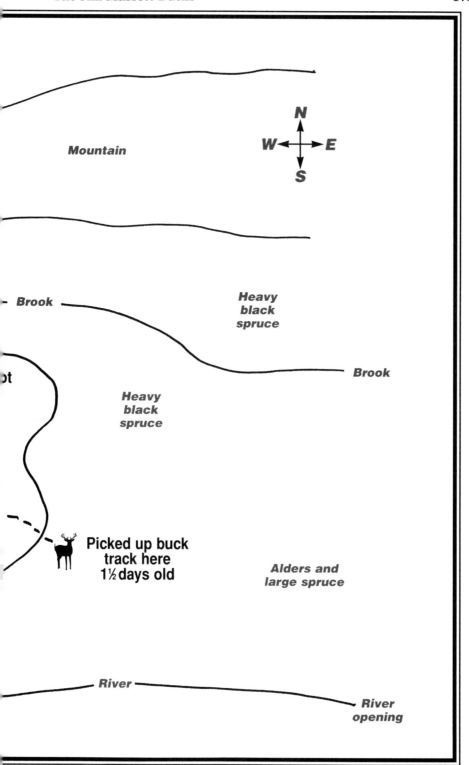

So now you have some background. What about the biggest buck Jim has ever taken? (Note Sketch A.) The date was November 20, 1992. The rut was still on, but winding down. The temperature was 10 degrees with three inches of snow on the ground and a clear sky. The area was again the Moose River Plains. Hunting with his brother, Tom, Jim's game plan for the day was to take an old logging road that led to a river. Massett would then parallel the river until he found a worthy track, i.e. a big one. Whenever possible he likes to look for the trail of a deer along a river because the sound of the water helps drown out sounds Jim might make as he moves along.

About one-third of a mile down that logging road Jim crossed the track of a big buck. Upon inspecting it he determined the track was a day and a half old. How did he know this? There was some vehicular travel on the old road, and some of the tire tracks obliterated the buck's tracks. The tire tracks had been made the previous day. Jim knew it had last snowed two nights before, and it had snowed in the tracks to some extent.

Massett gave up his game plan of looking for a track along the river. He followed the trail of the big hoof prints he found that went up over a significant ridge. How did he know it was a buck track? The average Adirondack doe will weigh less than 140 pounds. A big buck will heft over 180, so size of the track alone is one factor. In the snow it's easy to see where a deer urinates. Both sexes squat to do this. With a doe the yellow snow will be between or just behind her rear foot tracks. With a buck that yellow snow will usually be just forward of its rear foot tracks. Also, Jim offered, "A buck tends to move out in a straight line. A doe tends to meander a good bit. The width of the track can also help tell the tracker whether he's following a doe or a buck. A doe's track is much more narrow, a big buck's track much wider between the two front feet and the two rear feet. Also, a bigger chest and longer legs make for a longer stride and a more staggered track."

Jim found all this as he moved along the big buck's trail. Again, the track went right over the top of a significant ridge. That's when he came across the first scrape the buck made one and a half days previously—so more confirmation.

"Deer love to feed on mushrooms," Massett asserted. "I saw where this buck stopped to munch some mushrooms growing out of an old stump. But there were some unusual markings made by the antlers in the snow that I couldn't figure out. I saw this one more time as I moved along the trail. I decided that the buck must have torn off a branch as he was hooking various vegetation, and that the branch was still clinging to his horns. Within a short distance of postulating about that, I found the very branch."

Jim diverted a bit from the pursuit of this buck. "I remember in 1970 we had 5-6 inches of snow. It was warm, 45-50 degrees and I was on the trail of a good buck. I saw where this one fed on mushrooms, too,

Notice length of stride and stager (side to side).

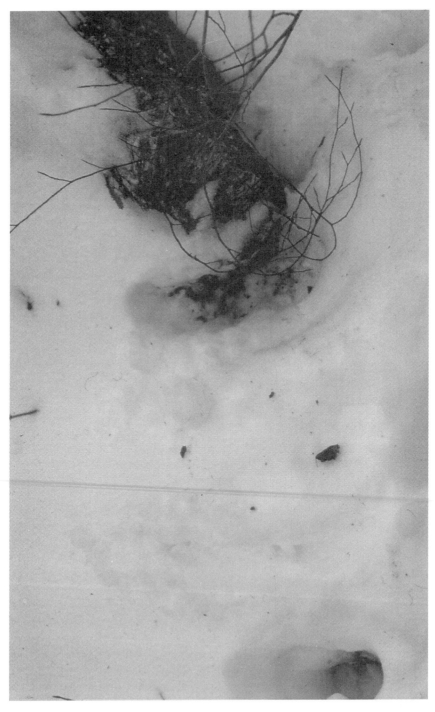

*Antler imprint from buck feeding on mushroom. Notice the
wide spread, short beams.*

this time mushrooms growing in an old blowdown. But the deer had to put its antlers into the snow to reach the mushrooms on a horizontal log. In the snow he left the imprint of one side of his antlers. It couldn't have been more obvious if the deer had drawn a picture. It was easy to see in the snow how wide he was from nose to the outside of his one antler. It was also obvious where each of the antler points had entered the snow. There was even some evidence of tine length there. Ever since then, I've made it a point to carefully scrutinize the snow where a buck puts his head down."

Jim went on to tell me that Adirondack whitetails feed a lot on fiddlehead ferns, especially during the hunting season. These are very low growing eats that require bucks to put their racks well into the snow. So this is another means Jim Massett relies upon to judge antler spread and number of points as he's tracking a buck.

Jim supplied more great input about judging antler spread. "Nick, every buck knows— within a fraction of an inch—how wide his antlers are, how high they are. Consequently, they have the perfect feel for the narrow places they can get through, under or between. I know how long the barrels are on each of the two rifles I use for whitetails. I match rifle barrel length to narrow spots where the buck I'm tracking does or does not pass through. Many times I've been tracking a big buck and discovered that his rack size wasn't of the quality I'm seeking simply by using this method. So I've quit on that track and looked for another."

Back to the 1992 buck Jim was tracking that had just tossed off the branch that had been clinging to its antlers. Maybe 100 yards farther Jim was alerted to the sounds of deer running. First he saw the doe, then he glimpsed a brute buck moving after her, perhaps 175 yards off, through mature hardwoods. They stopped. He brought up his rifle. Through the scope he could make out something reddish, but was it the buck? There wasn't a hint of movement. For a long time Jim kept the scope on the red spot. The buck finally moved, very quickly, disappearing from sight within two bounds. The doe was still there. Jim started to move toward where the buck had disappeared. The snow was a bit crusted under the surface that morning, resulting in a significant crunching sound from Jim's footsteps. Massett winced at the noise.

Waiting briefly, Jim thought about what to do next. After the doe left he started grunting into his call, then began walking. Instead of the steady step of a hunter, Massett took his steps like a deer would, shuffling, stopping, whatever. He did more grunting, then he heard deer running again. Jim himself ran after them for maybe 150 yards. He checked their tracks. They were both bounding, but Jim found it easy to tell the buck. His tracks were not only larger, his bounds were longer. Jim took up the trail once again. For the second time he tried to walk with the cadence of a deer, and he kept using the grunt tube.

Antler imprint from buck feeding on beech nuts. Notice good spread with long beam length.

*10-point, November 20, 1992. B&C 152-6/8; 4-1/2 years old;
dressed weight 167 lbs.*

The doe came to his call, walking to within 60 yards. Massett sensed the buck was in the vicinity. The doe eased off again. Jim chose a windfall for the softer walking, so he'd make less noise as he eased forward. He grunted some more. The doe came right back in. She stood there for four to five minutes. All this while Jim kept looking, looking, looking, trying to spot the buck that he sensed was there. Finally, he caught a flicker of movement behind her. Eventually he saw an eye, an ear, part of an antler. He held for what he knew would be the neck. The doe didn't bound off. Soon Jim heard a continuous clack, clack, clack, clack sound, so he rushed toward it. The neck-shot buck's legs and antlers were making their final movements clanging against a nearby spruce.

That buck was Jim's best yet, a 10-point measuring 152-6/8 B&C. He spent three and a half hours at the spot, doing the field dressing and taking photos, and the curious doe never left.

For the 1986 season Jim had joined a hunting club in the Higher Peaks Area of the Adirondacks. He had missed a buck estimated to be around 140 B&C on the opening day of the northern New York season. But now it was November 25, so the end of the season wasn't far off. There were 5-6 inches of snow. It was warm at around 30 degrees. He began in open hardwoods, mature maples where he could see as far as 300-400 yards. (Note Sketch B.)

He came across one good track that came off a mountain laden with a thick stand of spruce. After he had been on the track for some distance, he came to a spot where the buck had eaten some mushrooms from an old log. He clearly saw it was a very wide rack, about 24 inches, but he also saw there was not much beam length. So Massett gave up on that buck and went looking for something better.

Now is a good time to point out that Jim often runs on a buck track, especially one that's not fresh. Even at age 57, he logged over 94 miles during the 1994 season. In many previous seasons he has covered over 200 miles!! Running on an old track helps him, of course, more quickly narrow the distance between him and his quarry. On that November 25, 1986 day he came across two big tracks, bucks that were traveling together. While on their tracks he soon came to a 5-inch tree one of them had rubbed several hours previously.

Snow from a spruce had fallen off its branches, maybe melted in the sun, but as Jim stepped on that snow he made a loud crunching noise. That snow had obviously re-frozen. He saw a big, big buck right then. He had a quick shot at about 70 yards—at a 10-point. It was 11:08 a.m. He hurried forward to find that buck piled up. It hadn't gone far. Dressed, that buck weighed 145 pounds (weighed two weeks later) and measured 137-5/8 Boone & Crockett.

Every time Jim Massett bags a buck he makes it a point to go back to where he first jumped the deer in question. He wants to discover what the deer had been doing. When he backtracked the two bucks on

10-Point buck shot on November 25, 1986: B&C 137-5/8; 6-1/2 years old.

Same buck as previous photo. This deer was in a run down condition, but still had a dressed weight of 145 lbs. two weeks after kill.

Packing back to camp.

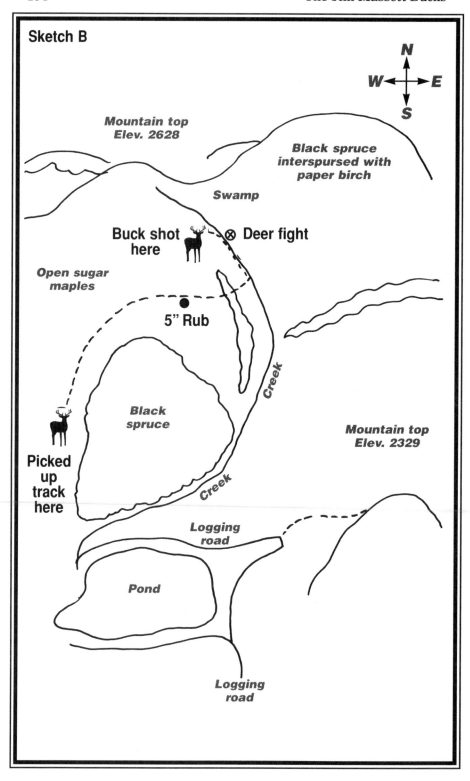

Sketch B

N
W E
S

Mountain top
Elev. 2628

Black spruce
interspursed with
paper birch

Swamp

Buck shot
here

⊗ Deer fight

Open sugar
maples

5" Rub

Creek

Black
spruce

Mountain top
Elev. 2329

Picked
up
track
here

Creek

Logging
road

Pond

Logging
road

November 25, 1986, he discovered where one had been bedded in some thick spruce, but he also found the spot where the two had been fighting. Jim believes that the deer he killed had won the skirmish, and was thus the dominant of the two.

Massett wanted to talk about one more of his buck encounters, this one of those that got away! Timing was 1981, November 7. The place was again the Moose River Plains Area of the Adirondacks. It was a warm day, and Jim began by crossing the river he and his Dad were camped along. There was no snow, but it was raining. Despite traveling 27 miles that day he had trouble picking up tracks. Finally, he spotted a mid-size deer, and when he got a glimpse of the rack it was a 7-point. He passed. Kept looking for a new track to take up. At dark he found himself what he figured was four miles from camp. While he normally carries two flashlights or extra batteries, or both, he didn't that November day. His batteries gave out soon after he turned for camp at dark-thirty.

But Jim always carries two or three compasses. "Many times I've doubted that one compass was pointing north, but when two or three of them point in the same northerly direction, a fellow better take his key from them, huh!"

One of the compasses he always carries can be held up to the sky to look through, and still be able to see the north-pointing needle inside. That was the compass he had to rely on to help him back to distant camp that night. At one point he had to navigate through some extremely thick spruce. "I had to 'feel' my way through for a long while," Jim explained.

He finally got back to the river he had crossed earlier that morning to find it considerably swollen due to the day-long rain. He forged ahead without disrobing. Many times in the past Jim has taken off his boots and pants to cross a river. The rifle he had carried that day was a bolt action, and it had been through a lot of rain. That night he made the mistake of not dismantling it, and he placed it not very far from the camp stove, as he was concerned and wanted to dry it out. As luck would have it, the night turned clear and the bottom fell out of the thermometer. Further, it snowed almost a foot! Because of this significant weather change, he and his father decided to hunt another area.

From camp they hiked out four miles in the dark, then drove for another mile. As they arrived at their intended new hunting area, it was just breaking day. Jim wanted to walk a log road at this new location until he cut a big buck track. But he never crossed one. After traveling four to five miles, he came upon an extensive tract of black spruce. (See Sketch C.) These trees provided the type of overstory that deer like to bed in during and after a heavy snowfall like the Adirondacks had just experienced. Now Jim was five miles from the vehicle. The temperature was down to 18 and the wind was howling.

Around the thick black spruce stand, Massett found an old buck

Remote tent site, 1993 season.

A small buck would have to stand on his hind legs to rub this high.

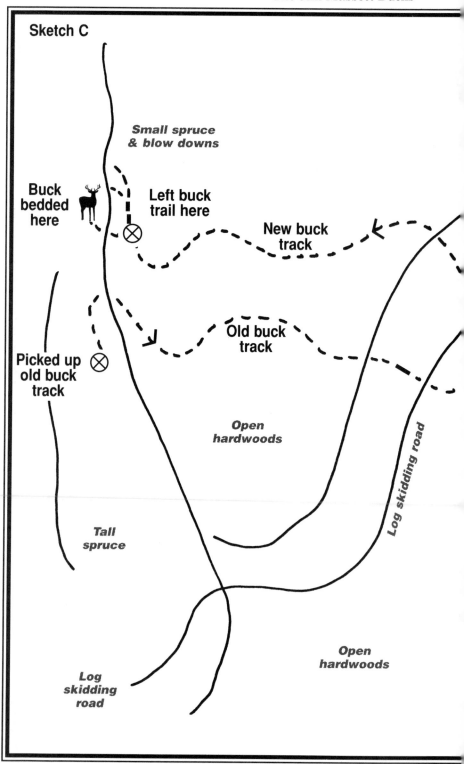

Sketch C

Small spruce
& blow downs

Buck
bedded
here

Left buck
trail here

New buck
track

Old buck
track

Picked up
old buck
track

Open
hardwoods

Log skidding road

Tall
spruce

Log
skidding
road

Open
hardwoods

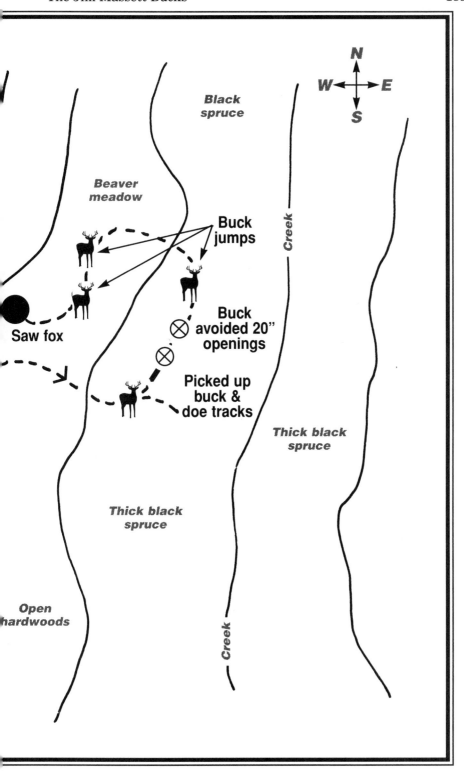

track. This was just after it had started snowing again. He took after that track, which went back through the black spruce thicket. After 150-200 yards he encountered two more deer tracks, and they had been coming toward him. These turned to Jim's left, and they had no snow in them, indicating they were very fresh. One of the tracks was made by a doe; the other by a buck. Massett was still tracking through the black spruce stuff. The doe's track went through a narrow opening of 20 inches or so. Jim measured that with his rifle barrel. The buck's track circumvented this tight spot, so Jim's pulse quickened, the obvious indication that the buck's antler spread was wider than 20!

Fifty yards farther he saw the same travel pattern of the doe and buck again, the buck circumventing a thick spot of less than 20 inches. Forty yards farther he jumped a deer. Also, he heard antlers crashing against spruce boughs. Jim knew the sound as a buck running. So Jim began running, too. (Would it ever occur to you to do that? Me neither, so we're both learning something, huh?) He came to an open beaver meadow. It was 200 yards across. But he saw nothing. Jim ran as fast as he could across this meadow. But then he spotted the two deer on the edge of the far thicket. They spooked. Massett offered, "You can spook a good buck once or twice in my experience, but after that you have very little chance of putting your eyes on that deer again unless you can outfox him."

Within 200 yards Jim came to the duo of whitetails, and they spooked away from him yet the third time. But that's when the doe broke off, heading for a thicket area, while the buck went off at a tangent, entering some mature hardwoods. One would have thought this pair might have angled off just the opposite: the buck toward the thicket, the doe toward the more open hardwoods. But Jim jumped in. "I believe the buck avoided the thick spruce stand because of the significant width of his antlers!"

Shortly, Jim spotted a fox, that critter having come from where the buck had just gone. He didn't shoot, though he was tempted. For the next 10 minutes Jim wrinkled his brow and thought. He thought some more, trying to figure what the buck was up to and what he should do next. The buck went to the top of a nearby mountain. The temperature turned colder yet, to about 15 degrees, and the wind was whipping to 20 and 25 mph.

Massett took the tracks to the top of the ridge. Then he stopped. "This deer will probably want to bed down this time of day, especially if he thinks I've quit his trail. But he's not going to bed down on this side of the mountain. It's right in the teeth of the wind. He's going to bed down on the other side, then watch his back trail."

So Jim decided now was the time to leave the track. He swung 90 degrees. (See Sketch C, top left.) Massett thus approached this buck from a 90 degree angle to the trail, going around the mountain in a new direction. Now the buck was watching his backtrail with the wind

Same buck's rub as in photo on page 187 on the same day but different tree. He rubbed this same tree three years in a row. Notice old rub by rifle scope.

Jim Massett and his cousin Roy packing out two 10-pointers they killed in 1988.

in his nose. But Jim was coming in from a new direction, not on the trail that the deer expected.

Most of you know how important it is to use extra caution when you come near the top of a rise. We should peek over the top, almost no movement, our eyes doing the work, looking, looking, looking. And that's just what Jim Massett did. The first thing he glimpsed was movement. It didn't take him a half second to put the scenario of what was happening together. The buck stood up at his bed at 40 yards. "Nick, his spread was over 24 inches. The tines were long. And even!"

Jim brought the rifle up easy. The crosshairs immediately went to the perfect spot. Instantly, Massett pulled the trigger, at the previous instant knowing he had his prize. A "click" was the answer to his trigger pull. The previous day's rain had been the culprit, freezing the bolt's firing pin in position.

Daunted only until he was able to free the frozen bolt, Massett took up the trail of this giant buck again. "That buck was then positive I was after him. I stayed on the trail until dark. He walked in other deer's tracks. He walked in more than one creek for many, many yards before emerging to the bank, all these efforts trying to shed the pursuer in his tracks—me. I never saw him again. But now I knew where he lived. For three more years I pursued that great deer, all unsuccessfully. I never saw his track again!"

Jim Massett's Equipment

Rifles - Jim relies on both a Ruger .44 Magnum with Redfield 2x-7x and a Ruger 77 .308 bolt with Bausch & Lomb 2-1/2x-8x.

Boots - 17-inch rubber for crossing streams, although he often takes off boots, socks, and pants for stream crossing.

Clothing - He relies a lot on wool since it can become wet and still offer warmth.

Camo - Snow Realtree.

Compass - Jim carries two or three, one that he can hold up to the night sky and still see the needle.

Flashlight - Two or three, or spare batteries.

Other gear - Matches in waterproof container; two pieces of rope to tie the buck he bags into a pack for carrying, or to hang it. Finally, a rosary—to help him get back to civilization!!

Jim Strelec with his 10-point whitetail, it of the magnificent spread.

Big Kentucky Buck Falls For Jim Strelec's Grunt Calls

Jim Strelec gives whitetail seminars nationwide. Whether these mini deer schools take place at major sport shows, small sportsmen's clubs or about any group situation in between, the crowds are always captured by Strelec's knowledge and his delivery. But of all Jim's considerable wisdom when it comes to deer hunting, one of his prime specialties is with deer calling. He comes by that know-how quite naturally, since he's National Sales Manager for Knight & Hale Game Calls in Cadiz, Kentucky. Harold Knight and David Hale have been in the game call business since 1972. Their first innovation was the introduction of the tube-type turkey call. Since then the company has come out with numerous unique and highly effective calls, such as the Fightin' Purr (imitates two gobblers fighting), and the Double Cluck Goose Call (produces the high and low pitch goose sounds at the same time, resulting in realistic goose talk previous calls couldn't produce). The company was also the first to produce a highly successful deer grunt-type call. Actually, Jim Strelec was working with a new prototype grunt call during the western Kentucky buck rut of 1994 when that call helped him put his scope's crosshairs on the buck pictured with this chapter. But, as usual, I'm getting a bit ahead of my story.

First a little more background on Jim Strelec. He was born in New Jersey. His Dad was an avid hunter, mainly for rabbits and ringnecks, and he got Jim started at a tender age. However, Jim's Dad died when he was quite young. Strelec's uncles took up where Jim's Dad left off. One of the things they taught him was bow shooting. "With my Dad gone, my uncles wanted to keep me off the streets and headed in the right direction. Shooting a bow really captivated my interest," he told me.

After high school Jim wanted to do something with his life. He also told me that New Jersey had too much asphalt to suit him. So he joined the Army. The year was 1964. Viet Nam was red hot, and Jim

figured that's where he was headed when he enlisted. Instead the
Army sent him to Germany for a three-year tour. There he learned the
language, saw some of the country's unique deer and their wild boar,
but he was not able to hunt. Very few are able to hunt in Germany. He
did sample the trout fishing. To finish up his tour of duty, the Army
sent him to Fort Campbell in western Kentucky.

"I fell in love with the place. Grew roots. Just love it here. Lake Bar-
kley had just been flooded. The fishing was fabulous. The Land
Between the Lakes was opening, all that public land, really owned by
the Tennessee Valley Authority (TVA). There were turkeys reported
there. Of course, the area had very few turkeys then, compared to
today. Along the way (as the years passed) I met Harold and David. I
learned about turkeys and deer in Harold's barber shop," Jim beamed.

In those days hunters were a lot more closemouthed about what
they knew regarding bucks and gobblers. But by paying attention
around the potbelly stove in Harold Knight's barber shop, Strelec
learned to separate the wheat from the chaff of those conversations.
The talk was replete with tobacco chewing, pipe smoking, and Repub-
lican bashing. Jim also got on the good side of the local people because
he was already such a good archer and was anxious to share what he
knew with others. "I started many of the locals in archery—before
shooting with a bow became popular. One of my innovations was to
use a toothpick for a bow sight, the toothpick taped in place with black
electrical tape."

Jim started to work for Knight & Hale around 1980. Prior to that he
had been the Senior Recreation Director for the Kentucky State Park
System. These duties involved mainly recreation with families. He
was also Campground Director for the Land Between the Lakes.

But what about Jim's buck that's pictured here, and the how-to he
used to bag it? I thought you'd never ask! Here goes. Like many of us,
Jim has to work full-time, so his pre-season scouting was limited to
late afternoons. He couldn't leave work until about 3:30, and he wasn't
able to hunt every day. Once the rut started, Jim came across six huge
scrapes. (Note accompanying sketch.) There were two scrapes at each
of three locations, the two on the ends over 200 yards apart.

Through archery season, Strelec eventually found out that three really
good bucks were working this small area in the sketch, and he was confident he'd score on an excellent one. One evening late in the archery season, Jim got a bit of a look at the biggest buck of the trio. Its rack was
excellent, but Jim wasn't able to see it long enough in the open to make
an accurate judgment. Two evenings before the archery season would
close, Jim made his afternoon vigil in that same stand again. This time
he was lucky enough to see the biggest of the three, plus able to make a
good guesstimate of rack size. It was a dandy 10-point, with an extra-
wide spread being the most significant aspect of this fine trophy. That
wide spread is what jumps out at you in the photo (see page 194).

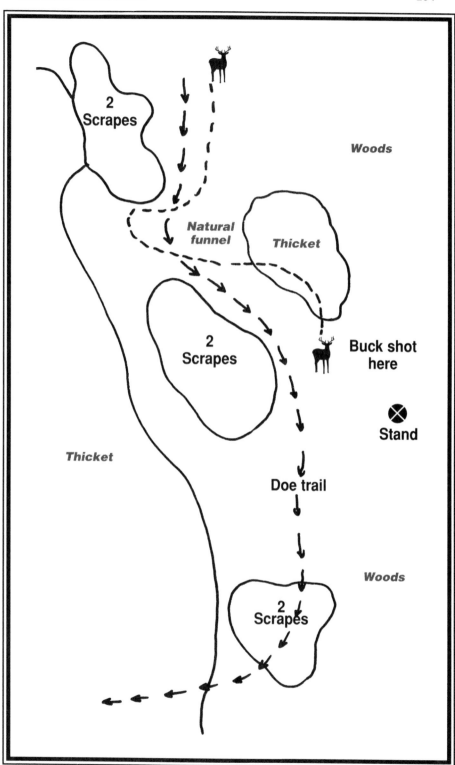

2
Scrapes

Woods

Natural
funnel

Thicket

2
Scrapes

Buck shot
here

⊗
Stand

Thicket

Doe trail

Woods

2
Scrapes

Jim Strelec was making these observations with a drawn bow that late afternoon. The buck was 45 yards away, and this transplanted New Jersey-ite was tempted to take the shot. After all, he has long been an excellent shot with a bow, even at the considerable distance of 45 yards. Jim's positive about the yardage because the buck was standing just 5 yards inside his 50 yard marker. Let him walk? Or release the arrow? If the rifle season had not been starting two mornings hence, the arrow might have been sent on its way. It wasn't!

But Jim told me, "This buck was too good a deer. I didn't want to take the chance of wounding him. I knew I was in a good place. The bucks were using this trail regularly. The rut was in full swing. They'd be chasing any doe in estrus, probably even does that hadn't come in. So I decided to bide my time that night and relaxed the drawn bow."

The opening morning of gun season Jim was in this same stand. "I was hoping very much that I'd see a doe in estrus early that morning. I figured if that happened, my chances of scoring on this big buck with the wide spread would be vastly increased."

The bucks had cleaned up the six scrapes shown in the sketch, widening them appreciably, so it was evident the deer were anxious to meet up with does that were ready. (Check the natural funnel area also noted on the accompanying sketch.) Jim Strelec is another of the many contributors to this book who's adamant about locating such natural funnels and using them to your advantage. I (we) call them natural funnels, maybe the term connoting that they're easy to find. Not so. Well, maybe some are. In most instances, however, how nature or the surrounding habitat forces deer (other game, too) to move through relatively confined areas (usually for short periods of time; often for only a few yards) can be subtle. You must be an interested, keen, and observant hunter to recognize them. Consequently, one way you might significantly increase your success with big bucks is to begin looking for these natural funnels a lot more than you have in the past.

Because Jim was anxious to see a doe early that morning, especially an estrus doe, shortly after sunrise he began to use the company's Ez-Deer Bleat Call. Bleat calling, most experts agree, tends to be more effective at calling does. Bleats are no doubt a regular means of communication between a doe and her fawn(s), for instance.

When Jim uses the bleat call he likes to come out with one series of four short calls, then, shortly after, repeat the same or nearly the same sequence. "Before calling again I prefer to wait 20-30 minutes," Strelec instructed.

It didn't take long. Jim looked for the signs of her being in estrus, the tail twitching, the tail off to one side, the doe sniffing in one or more of the scrapes, or urinating in them. She didn't pay a bit of attention to the scrapes. Her tail did nothing unusual, had the appearance of a doe's tail in August. She went through the thicket (Again, note sketch), passed the second set of scrapes, then kept on going.

Jim was disappointed that the doe had shown no interest in the scrapes. He figured that it was his bleat calling that maybe got her moving through his area in the first place. Had she urinated in one or more of those scrapes, his confidence in the day would have undoubtedly soared. But he didn't get down on his luck. The day was still going well. He didn't think about changing stand locations, as too many of us are prone to do when what we're expecting, what we're hoping for, fails to happen.

Instead Jim stayed alert. Kept looking. His eyes probed all around, but he concentrated most of his vision efforts toward the area where the doe had first appeared. Would a buck take up her trail?

The first thing he saw was a flash of antlers at about 135 yards. The direction was near where the doe had first showed. The buck began moving, went straight to the first set of scrapes and vigorously reworked one of them. Now the distance was about 120. Jim could have taken his shot then, but there was plenty of thick cover around the deer so the bullet could have been deflected by any one of many branches.

Further, Strelec didn't want to rush the pace. Things seemed to be unfolding nicely. It was natural to assume the buck would stay right on the path that had been made between these three sets of dual scrapes. Just as the doe had done, the buck would hopefully pass within 60 yards or closer, through an area that was much more open for shooting.

But shortly after reworking one of those two first scrapes, the buck angled off the trail a bit. An intervening thicket shielded Jim's view for awhile. Then, worse yet, the buck entered the thicket, avoiding the natural funnel area. Did he suspect danger lurked ahead? Maybe so. Or would that buck have stayed on the trail if the doe we've been talking about here had been in estrus?

Slowly and silently, Jim reached for that prototype *Ex-Tend-A-Tone* grunt call I mentioned so many paragraphs ago. "I made what deer biologists are calling a 'contact grunt,'" Strelec revealed. This is a grunt of short duration. Jim wanted to lure the buck out of the thicket and back on the trail the doe had taken. He made the three short grunts, these of the "contact" variety and not of the tone that might suggest a big buck was out there wanting to do battle. Instead, maybe these grunts were being made by a doe, an estrous doe, or simply any other deer. That's what Jim wanted to suggest to his quarry.

Jim saw the buck stop in the dense thicket. He didn't do anything for a short time. There was still no shot. Too thick. "I was waiting for some subtle message from the buck, feeling that his next action might telegraph what I should do." Good, sensible input.

The buck then started toward him. The range was narrowed to 80 yards, but the deer was still within the throes of the thicket in the sketch, and no shot was yet possible. "I had him interested though," Jim was almost smiling through the phone lines.

Then Jim couldn't see a bit of the deer, even any movement. There was no sound. It was obvious the buck was stopped again. What to do next? Jim's brain was thinking. "Give him something else to think about. A new twist. This buck isn't spooked. A different type of grunt, a grunt with a new pitch, which is exactly what this call is made for, seems in order now."

So Strelec pulled the extension portion of the new call out as far as it would go (Note photo below). He gave one short grunt. This one was more guttural in nature. Immediately, the buck came running out of the thicket. The call had obviously made him react like he was on Jim's string. He stopped only a few yards closer to Strelec than where the doe had taken the trail along the scrape route.

Anti-climactic now. The shot was only 60 yards, the big buck standing broadside, easy work for Jim's .270. It didn't take long for Jim to send a 130 grain Remington *Bronze Point* on its way. The buck pictured is in the 150 class. He has 10 points, with one broken tine, and an inside spread of 23-3/4, a handsome, handsome trophy.

The call in question, Knight & Hale's *Ex-Tend-A-Tone*, was introduced at the 1995 S.H.O.T. Show in Las Vegas, yet another feather in the cap of a company that has become renowned for unique new products that work so well in the field.

This is the first mention of the Remington *Bronze Point* in this book. This is a bullet both Jim Strelec and I have used with great success for years. Its praises haven't been sung much in the pages of the outdoor gun journals, mostly, I think, because so few have used it. But the *Bronze Point* is exceptionally efficient and effective at

Jim Strelec demonstrates use of the new Ex-Tend-A-Tone grunt call, which Knight & Hale introduced at the 1995 S.H.O.T. Show.

close, medium, and long ranges. Mysteriously, Remington has only ever offered it in the 130 grain .270 Winchester and the .30-06 150 and 180 grain. The design is a hard bronze point at the bullet tip that weighs only a few grains. Upon impact this hard point drives back into the copper jacketed lead core for extreme expansion. This is not a bullet that mushrooms and holds together for deep penetration. Slip it just behind the shoulder of any animal the size of a whitetail, however, and it's like a grenade going off in the deer's chest cavity. Awesome.

Sometime in the 1980s Remington discontinued offering their *Bronze Point* bullets to reloaders. I bought up about 500 130 grain .270 calibers and 500 150 grain .308 calibers. Strelec and I have been friends for years. When he told me how fond he was of the Remington *Bronze Point* in .270, within the same sentence lamenting that Remington had discontinued supplying these bullets to reloaders, I told him, "Jim, no problem. When they took them off the market, I bought a lifetime supply. I'll send you a box of 100 in the morning." So it was one of my 130 grain *Bronze Points* that helped Jim bag this magnificent buck. In the early 1990s Remington had the good sense to begin supplying all their bullets to reloaders again, so the *Bronze Point* is back, still available in .270 130 grain, .308 caliber 150 and 180 grain.

Jim Strelec's Equipment

Rifle - *Browning A-Bolt with B.O.S.S. System in .270 Winchester*
Scope - *Pentax 2x-7x Lightseeker*
Bullet - *130 grain Remington Bronze Point*
Camo - *Realtree all purpose*
Treestand - *Summit*
Call - *Knight & Hale Ex-Tend-A-Tone grunt call and EZ Deer bleat call*

It's been a while, 1983, but the spread and heaviness of the beams are awesome. Wouldn't it be something to have a similar buck mounted on the wall in your study?

Don Warren Bucks: When The Rut Is On—You Want To Be Out There—Regardless Of The Weather!

Don Warren wanted a better whitetail rifle, better than what he had been using for years. He's been a somewhat serious gun collector for most of his life, a licensed gun dealer for more than 20 years, and he had already taken more than his share of big bucks. Consequently, he had a firm base from which to make decisions about how a special whitetail rifle, one specifically suited to his purposes, should shape up.

First, Don, from Savona, New York, hunts mostly from a stand. Light weight was thus unnecessary. He wanted the rifle to be chambered for a flat shooting cartridge, for he knew at times conditions would require that he would have to make long shots. Also, for this type of shooting, he wanted the gun to be very accurate. Warren was also well familiar with the difference between a huge buck and the average one, and how the former can take a well-placed bullet and keep going, a hit that would put the average buck down within 50 yards, probably less. So he wanted his new special deer rifle to be plenty powerful.

Don Warren decided on a Ruger 77 action—in stainless steel. He had the Hart Barrel Company in LaFayete, New York put on one of their super accurate stainless barrels, then this special barreled action was bedded into a McMillan fiberglass stock. The stock's finish was given an Arctic camo paint job. Oh yes, the rifle was chambered for the .300 Winchester Magnum cartridge. Some might say this cartridge is too powerful for a whitetail rifle, but it's hard to argue with Don's successes, and I've already mentioned the super bucks' penchant for taking the full brunt of a killing bullet and be able to travel some unbelievable distances before dying. He topped the rig with a Leupold 3.5x-10x 50mm scope. Not satisfied with the reticule the scope came with, he returned it to the company's Beaverton, Oregon plant where they replaced it with tapered crosshairs. Total weight is over 10 pounds, so this is not a rifle to carry while sneak hunting or driving. But when hunting from a stand the heft adds to Don's steady hold. It keeps five 180 grain Nosler Ballistic Tips in a 1/2-inch or less at 100 yards.

Don Warren's specialized big whitetail rifle. While it weighs 10 pounds, Don's a stand hunter so the extra heft is no problem. In fact, the added weight is appreciated to aid with a steadier hold, as well as to dampen the recoil of this .300 Winchester Magnum. It's a Ruger 77 stainless action coupled to a Hart stainless barrel, fitted into a McMillan fiberglass stock that's decked in an Arctic camo finish for snow hunting. Topped with a Leupold 3.5x-10x 50mm scope, this IS very specialized whitetail ordnance.

Don's first gun was a 12th birthday present, a Remington model 512 .22 rimfire single shot. His Dad, an avid hunter, started him hunting in Florida, with squirrel and bobwhite quail, though Warren was born in New York. His first shotgun was another Remington, an 870 slide action. His whitetail hunting start-ed in New York when Don was 16. In addition to three of the bragging-size whitetails Don will talk about in this chapter, he took a 10-foot 2-inch brown bear on the Alas-kan Peninsula while hunting in the spring with Greg Hayes and Chignik Outfitters. Also, while hunting at the Dia-mond A Ranch in New Mexico, he took a great antelope that qualifies for the Boone & Crockett record book. Length is 16-3/4-inches. The antelope nets 82-6/8.

It was at the Diamond A Ranch in New Mexico that he met Ron Nem-echeck, a guide from Edmonton, Alberta. Don Warren became one of Ron's first customers. He drove from New

York to Alberta for that hunt in 1983. A New York-based friend, Jack Shappee, accompanied him. They drove right through Alberta, on into British Columbia. There Don took a nice mule deer with a 26-inch spread. There was some additional hunting on this trip, a remarkable 30 days in a row. In 1983 Alberta probably hadn't yet emerged as a mecca for whitetail trophy hunters. This Canadian province was, however, long famous for its stone and bighorn sheep, its elk, and several other big game species.

Ron Nemecheck had his hunting area well scouted. (Note sketch A.) He figured the best way to get his clients a shot was to set up a deer drive, a type of hunting we see little written about these days (though it's highly popular in my home state of Pennsylvania and elsewhere). So Ron spotted Don Warren and Jack Shappee forward of himself and another driver. (Again, note Sketch A.) Don eventually took up his stand position along the shore of a lake, Jack Shappee along a field edge. Don Warren did some describing, "The hunting area was east of Edmonton. The strip of land to be driven was brushy and broken by stands of poplar and red willow. It was in these woodlands the whitetails would hide by day, then pig out on the agricultural leftovers come nightfall."

Nemecheck and his guide cohort had their work cut out for themselves. Once Jack and Don were in their stand positions, the drivers still had a lot of terrain to cover. One reason this area was selected for the drive was the lake. The idea was to move the deer slowly from the standers to the drivers, keep any big bucks from slipping out to the drivers' left, as well as keep any good buck from sneaking back, in the direction the drivers had just come from. This would be no easy task given the mile-long length of the drive. Also, Nemecheck hadn't made this drive the first day of the hunt. He waited until wind direction was perfect, blowing from the drivers to the standers.

Note in Sketch A the terrain where our two standers were, and how the cover "necked down." Deer on the move naturally gravitate to such places in the terrain. Nemecheck knew that, and his drive plan was predicated on getting any deer they jumped to move through this natural funnel in the landscape. One last important point: Ron knew there was more than one bragging-size buck that called these scattered fields, poplar, and willows home.

"Nick, it was a two-deer area. The drive that Ron and his guides made for us took some time to develop, but it was perfect. The first two deer to come out of the willows and poplar in front of me were excellent bucks. They were moving very much ahead of the rest of the deer that the drivers eventually put out, indicating the wariness of those big bucks. I shot them both. The biggest grosses 160 plus, nets 150 B&C points. This buck has very heavy beams, but short points (note photo on page 202). Of course, had this buck sported tines of even average length he'd have scored much, much higher."

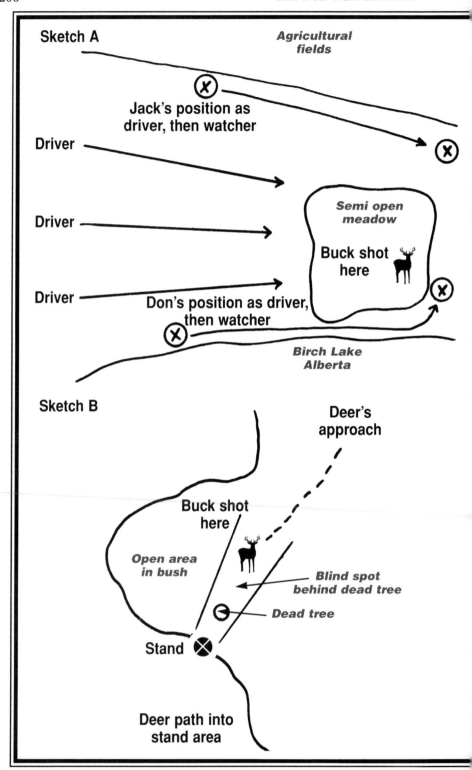

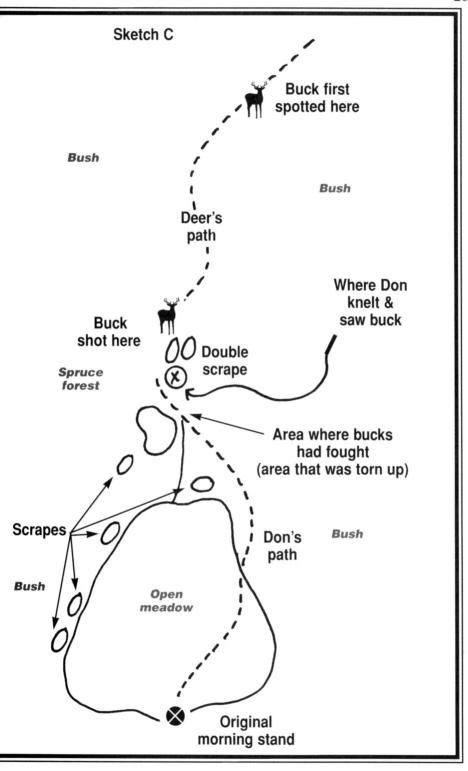

Sketch C

Buck first
spotted here

Bush

Bush

Deer's
path

Where Don
knelt &
saw buck

Buck
shot here

Double
scrape

*Spruce
forest*

Area where bucks
had fought
(area that was torn up)

Scrapes

Don's
path

Bush

Bush

*Open
meadow*

Original
morning stand

From Alberta Don went to hunt in Montana for more whitetail excitement. The last seven years or so he has been hunting around Ekalaka, Montana. It was there that he met a new friend, Alfred Carter. When Carter heard about Warren's intense interest in brute whitetails, Al started telling Don about Bently Brown in Saskatchewan. Brown, a professional guide and outfitter in that Canadian province, catered solely to moose hunters. But Al Carter told Warren, "Brown and his cohorts consistently jump some huge whitetails on their moose ventures. These guys don't even shoot at the deer since moose meat is the only thing on their minds."

"I've been hunting with Bently Brown for seven years now," Warren revealed. "I found the whitetail hunting so good early on that I convinced Brown to go into the whitetail guiding business. He now takes five groups of six hunters each year."

Don Warren always books the third week of the Saskatchewan season with Bently. "This is during the peak of the rut. I've found that the rut in this area of the province consistently takes place somewhere around the 13th to the 19th of November. Most of the hunting is strictly out of stands at Brown's insistence, but because I've been hunting there so long and know the area so well, Bently gives me what I'll call 'creative license' to move around and scout a bit. By doing that I can usually help our entire group a little, as well as myself."

During the 1993 season he discovered a big open area the first day he hunted, and it was surrounded on all sides by thick Canadian bush. However, the bush cover was thinnest on one side. This was the area that got Don's attention. It was marked by a number of huge scrapes, plus there was a rub area where it appeared the buck who did the damage went berserk. It didn't take much inspecting of this sign for Don to decide that a massive buck was responsible for this.

"The problem was the weather," Don began. "It had turned unbelievably cold there, with sunup temperatures hovering at 25 below zero, and I'm not talking wind chill either. The key to my hunting success with this buck was being able to physically be out there. I had to play mental games with myself and the cold, but more about that shortly. I screwed in steps to get into the tree I wanted, then laid a platform for sitting. After discovering that incredible scrape and rub area, I decided I was going to spend my entire seven days, dark to dark, in that tree, despite the temps.

"I was wearing no less than four thicknesses of clothing, plus I snuggled into a special sleeping bag. (See Special Clothing Sidebar, page 213.) Further, I was using up plenty of those chemical heat bags. I had them in my hat, in my gloves, over my feet in the sleeping bag. No one else in camp was even hunting, it was that cold."

Many claim, however, that severe cold weather during the rut can trigger bucks into becoming even more active. This isn't the only chapter in this book where you've read that you should be out there hunt-

From 1993, another Turtle Lake brute buck. Note the long tines and the stickers.

ing when cold weather arrives and the rut is on. Of course, the cold weather Don Warren encountered in Saskatchewan went far beyond what most of us ever experience, or are willing to experience.

Some of the mental games he used to keep himself hunting included counting birds, but while he was counting he would not move. After counting 10 birds he would allow himself the luxury of a muscle flex. He also played mental games with his watch. If, as an example, he looked and found it was 23 minutes to ten, he would allow himself to stand up as a reward at ten o'clock, but never before.

Day after day Don's patience was unrelenting, but so was the horrible cold. One entire day in his stand passed without incident. Committed, he was back in the stand the second day. Dark to dark he stayed and stayed. Nothing. More mental games. Day three. Just as cold. More mental stuff. At dark-thirty he climbed down and returned to Bently Brown's camp. Day four. "I remember playing the mental game with my watch that morning. Though brutally cold, I wouldn't allow myself the reward of standing up until ten o'clock. Before moving, I slowly scanned all around me, a full 360 degrees. Obviously, I didn't want my stand-up movements to spook the buck I was after.

"There was a large dead tree 10-15 yards in front of my stand. I couldn't see the area that was five to eight yards behind that dead tree when I was sitting. As I stood up, I leaned around slightly to scan that area. (See Sketch B.) The buck was looking me right in the eye! Very, very slowly I leaned back to where I couldn't see the buck. Again working slowly, I mounted the rifle, then cautiously leaned back out. He was still there."

Anticlimactic, but a 180 grain Nosler Ballistic Tip from his .300 Winchester Magnum was shortly on its way to destiny. Note photo of the 1993 buck on page 209. This one is a 13-point, with 8 points on one side, 5 on the other. He grosses 175, nets 160. The 8 by 5 configuration results in considerable deductions. Had this buck been a 7 by 6, he'd have scored a lot better. Regardless, what a beautiful buck, and what a test of cold weather endurance for Don.

But in 1994 Don Warren was back hunting with Bently Brown in Saskatchewan. Commonplace for this part of Canada in November, it was plenty cold again. "Temperatures were 15 degrees, which is absolutely cold," Don declared, "but nothing like the 25 below zero I had hunted in the previous year."

The day before, he had found the browse line to be about four feet high. While "still" hunting he came across a torn-up area of rubs and scrapes. Looking around, he decided there were no trees suitable for a treestand. Consequently, Warren determined he'd hunt that spot the next day via a combination of a ground blind and still hunting. He had not hunted this part of Brown's territory previously. Before daybreak he was in the ground blind he had made the previous afternoon, and it was downwind from the big scrape and rub concentration. By design, Don hadn't dressed with extra-heavy clothing, for he did plan on still hunting part of that day.

"I stayed in the blind until 10:30 that morning, and I passed up two nice bucks, both 4 x 4 8-points, each in the 125 to 135 B&C point category," Warren told me. "Interestingly, I wasn't up and on the move for 10 minutes before I came across two more very wide scrapes. I knelt down to further inspect these two side-by-side buck scrapes, shaking my head a little in amazement at their size. I looked up to see the high licking branches above both, and that's when I saw a good buck coming right toward me. It didn't register with my first glance, but in time it became obvious that this buck was on his way to right where I was. He was checking out his scrape line.

"That buck was 100 yards away then. Though I saw good antler size, most of his headgear was up above the four-foot browse line. As he walked toward me, those antlers would go in and out of the tree limbs, so it wasn't possible to make a good guesstimate initially. This buck wasn't tarrying though. A good brisk walking pace. I cranked the scope down to 3.5x when I realized he was coming closer and closer. I put the gun to my shoulder and easily watched him come on in the scope with its low-power setting.

Warren's 1994 Turtle Lake, Saskatchewan buck.

A better view of Warren's 1994 Saskatchewan whitetail, better showing its spread and heavy thickness at the antler base. It scores over 160.

"I kept figuring he'd turn off the trail, that move giving me a broadside shot, much the preferable, but he never did. He never stopped until he was 20 yards away. But then I already had the crosshairs in the middle of his chest. The 180 grain took him as he faced me. Maybe this one was overkill for a .300 Win. Mag! He was a 14-point and a perfect 7 by 7, grosses 164, nets green at 152. He'd have scored better if the middle point off the main beam was a single instead of a double. This is a deduction. (See photo of 1994 buck.) After I shot him I marveled at the moss that was all over his antlers. This moss hangs from both the spruce and the poplars in this part of Saskatchewan, so I'm guessing he had created yet another massive rub and scrape area earlier that morning."

Don Warren's Equipment

Rifle - *Custom Ruger 77 bolt action in stainless steel with Hart stainless barrel.*

Benchrest*-Quality barrel in .300 Winchester Magnum, stock McMillan fiberglass, painted Arctic camo.*

Scope - *Leupold 3.5x -10x 50mm with special tapered crosshair.*

Ever since Don has been hunting mid-November way up in Saskatchewan, he says he's been "....honing my equipment, especially the clothing." He has worked closely with his daughter, an amateur seamstress, in coming up with the warmest gear imaginable. They bought two sleeping bags with DuPont 808 Fiberfill. Thus they already had the necessary zippers. "I look like the Michelin Tire Man when I get into this suit, but I'm toasty warm when wearing it, no matter the outside temps."

The suit weighs 20 pounds! The top zips from neck to crotch. Both pant legs have full-length zippers on the outside. His daughter then covered the sleeping bag material in white polar fleece. He wears it unzipped down to 10 degrees!

"No gloves or mittens will keep your hands warm when it really gets cold in Saskatchewan," Don informs. "You need to use a muff. Otherwise your fingers will be useless when it comes time to use gun or bow."

Accordingly, his daughter made him a muff from what was left over from those two 808 filled sleeping bags. With the muff he doesn't even wear gloves! For five years he wore the warmest boots he could find, coupled with electric socks and their batteries. But these didn't keep his feet warm enough, plus it was too much fooling around. For the last two years he's worn the socks his daughter made for him. These are huge over-the-boot socks made from those same two 808-filled sleeping bags. They zipper on and off quickly and effortlessly.

*Toxey Haas of Mossy Oak camo fame with his excellent Pope &
Young whitetail taken in 1994.*

Mossy Oak's Toxey Haas Talks Big Bucks

It was a beautiful big buck, the type that makes every archer hope and pray he'll make a quick-killing shot. Of course, all bowmen want to do that with every animal they shoot, but perhaps this desire takes on added importance when it's a true-trophy whitetail. All the pre-season work had gone into this one. Toxey Haas had this buck's daily game plan figured. He now had the bow fully drawn. The correct sight pin was placed square and steady just behind the brute's shoulder. Without hesitation Haas sent the arrow on its way via the release. But just at that critical moment of the release letting off, the buck began moving forward. The arrow was fast, but would it be fast enough? Or would the arrow strike just behind the buck's vitals? But I'm getting ahead of my story a bit. Let's back up many years with Toxey Haas.

Most every big-buck hunter covered in this book got started in the outdoors at a very young age, but Toxey perhaps got his start younger than any. His father, Fox Haas, was no doubt the reason. Mr. Fox was woods wise when very young, as well. When Mr. Fox was 14 he killed his first deer. Then, at 15, he killed his first turkey gobbler. The unique aspect about this latter trophy was that Mr. Fox made up his own mouth diaphragm call out of a prophylactic, using a piece of wire for a frame. Of course, Mr. Fox did this long before there were any commercial mouth diaphragm calls on the market.

When Toxey was only five years old, Fox Haas began taking his son to the woods. When hunting season began they'd concentrate on squirrels. Toxey chimed in, "My early squirrel-hunting lessons centered mainly around the need to find the right food sources, which is also critical to scouting successfully for deer. What my Dad taught me about squirrel food sources I was able to translate into my deer hunting a few years later."

While sneak hunting for squirrels, Toxey was taken up with all that he saw, but especially the deer and other wildlife. When he was only 8 years old he killed his first whitetail. Although he and his Father would enter the woods together, by the time Toxey was 12 he was hunting alone. In those years all their hunting was done from the ground. Most every stand Toxey took involved a mature tree that he'd sit against to break his outline. Even when very young he realized how much more effective he could become as a hunter if he could vanish into the surrounding landscape.

Although he grew up in West Point, Mississippi, he and his Dad did a lot of hunting at a club in southwestern Alabama. Actually, both of them still do a lot of their hunting there. In those early years, however, whitetail pressure was relatively low at the club. Most members were more interested in the spring gobbler aspects. Also, Alabama has long had a tradition of very liberal deer limits. It's still one buck a day over a quite long season. The result was that Toxey was able to successfully hunt a great number of deer, right from a young age. Toxey took these opportunities as a base—a base from which to learn about whitetails and their habits. As this story is being written, Toxey Haas is only 34, but his significant deer hunting experience belies that young age.

He began hunting in Mississippi when he was 18, on a hunting tract where he and his Father started to manage the deer herd in an effort to upgrade the quality of the racks. "But my deer hunting ability took a lightyear-leap forward when I started Mossy Oak in 1985," Toxey told me. That's probably because Haas now has to hunt as a part of his high-tech camo clothing business. Since 1985 he has hunted almost exclusively with the bow. Because there are centerfire rifle and black powder gun manufacturers who market their guns covered in one of his Mossy Oak camo patterns, he is obligated to hunt with those firearms occasionally. But obviously, archery hunts are his unquestioned favorite these days.

He recalls the period when he loved to sneak, or as he calls it, "slip" hunt, especially right after a rain. One of the guys who works with him at Mossy Oak (the company is called Haas Outdoors), Carsie Young, has taken up this type of rifle hunting very seriously and very successfully. "These days," Toxey advised, "Carsie is sitting in his truck while it's still raining. But he has heard the weather forecast, knows it's going to stop raining soon, and that's the ideal time to begin these 'slip' hunts."

But let's get to the buck in question, the one Toxey released his arrow on at the start of all this. He was hunting at his own camp in Alabama. "Nick, I had been hunting this same treestand for three years," Toxey began. "In fact, the hang-on stand I hung there three years back is still there, and it's the one I used for the 1994 hunt we're talking about. It's adjacent to a clear cut, the timbering having taken place four years ago. As with most recent clear cuts, this is a top whitetail bedding area.

"Here's how the lay of the land looked. (Note Sketch A.) There was a 400-acre pasture, and my stand was near one corner of that field. Nearby was a steep bluff. Then a gasline right-of-way ran from one stand of mature woods toward the corner of the open pasture (near his stand).

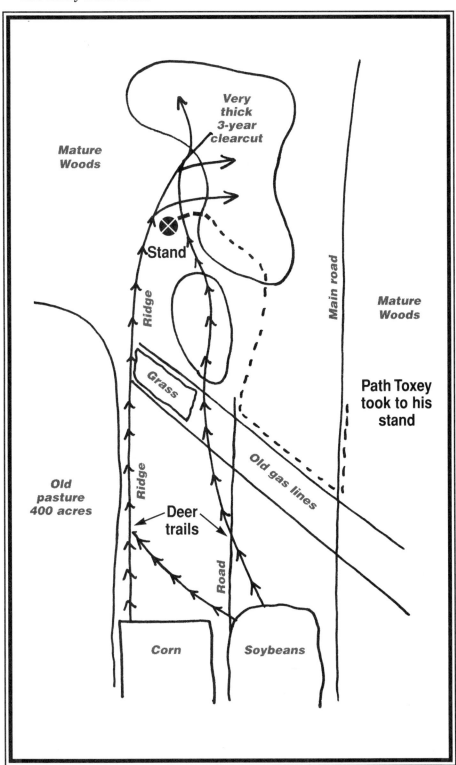

The gasline had grown up appreciably, so it was anything but cleared. Even though 1994 was the third year I would hunt this particular stand, I have never hunted it more than twice a season. In the morning, to reach that stand I had to walk about three quarters of a mile—eventually walking right through a very thick clear-cut bedding area. Naturally, the wind had to be right before I'd hunt this spot. Once I reached my treestand, I'd expect the deer to be coming from their feed area in the field. (Again, note Sketch A.) However, that I had to traipse through their bedding area meant that my scent was left on the vegetation. That would probably mean that the daily life pattern of these deer would be altered significantly, maybe for weeks. I knew this stand was an excellent one, but because I had to go through the bedding area to reach it, there was simply no way to hunt it often. If I'd hunt it and not score with a good buck, the bedding area was 'tainted,' and the deer, especially any wise, old bucks, would be spooked for who knows how long!"

The deer coming from the overnight feed area had to travel a ridge to get to their bedding grounds. Toxey's stand was located to cut them off. (Again, note Sketch A.) See the soy beans and corn? These were two other feed areas. The deer would have to cross the pipeline to reach him. Toxey reasoned that the best time to catch a good buck away from the bedding area in question revolved around two natural phenomenon. First, assuming the wind was right, select a night when the moon would come up very late. Deer wouldn't feed much prior to the moon's rise. Secondly, pick a foggy morning in conjunction with that late moon rise. With the late moon, deer would hopefully continue feeding and, because of the heavy fog, wouldn't notice daylight coming on until it was too late.

Toxey walked in to check out this area once during the second week of October 1994 during midday, and he didn't approach via the very thick clear-cut bedding area. He wasn't interested in really hunting, so he purposely avoided the pipeline and the cutover, even though he knew he'd come in via the cutover when he actually did hunt this special spot. The timing was long before the rut in that part of Alabama, but Toxey's scouting session did result in locating a large area of "licking branch" activity. There were no scrapes under these licked branches, as we all expect once even the pre-rut period gets started. But a lot of branches were broken off where a buck or bucks had chewed and licked to leave their personal calling card, and maybe they had rubbed their eye glands on these branches as well. "I remember the smell of some of those licking branches was very strong," Haas told me.

By being observant and walking for some distance, Toxey was able to determine the route this buck or these bucks were taking. "I felt strongly that one buck would not have left so much licking branch sign that early in the season," Haas commented. "I sensed there was already a rift in the pecking order. Despite the rut not ready to begin, these bucks were vying for some type of supremacy." That was on a

Saturday. Feeling quite confident he had something, Haas got out of there. He rested the spot Sunday and Monday. Monday evening he returned to this property with his Mom and Dad and his twin boys. The moon was perfect for the spot, very dark, so it wouldn't come up early. They had listened to the radio on the pickup truck ride down. The weatherman predicted heavy fog. Upon hearing that he persuaded his Mother to take care of the twins until about eight o'clock that next morning. "I'll be back to camp by then," Toxey was confident.

He showered that morning, donned his Scent-Lok carbon undergarment, then layered freshly laundered Mossy Oak camo over it. As silently as possible he made his way through the thick clear cut, then slipped up into his stand without making a sound. At 7:15 he heard coyotes. Were they running or disturbing the buck(s) he was after? Would they foul up his carefully made plans, ruin the perfect weather conditions that he had longed for and anxiously anticipated?

He heard more noises. Sounded like running deer, but maybe not. Then he saw a deer, and it was coming up the trail, the exact one he had predicted. But this deer, and he glimpsed it was a buck, was running. Was that buck running from other bucks or those coyotes he had heard? Then he saw two deer behind that first buck. His eyes ping-ponged back and forth between the single and the duo. The single, he noted, was a magnificent buck, but the two coming behind had even more mass to their antlers. The first buck stopped right at one of the licking branches Toxey had found the previous Saturday. The range was 25 yards.

"I refuse to shoot at a deer if it's beyond 30 yards. That's the maximum distance I decided upon years ago, and it's one I'll always keep," Toxey related. "I hesitated briefly about taking that magnificent buck right there in front of me. But I sensed that one or both the bucks coming up the trail were bigger. But there was that fantastic huge buck offering a perfect broadside shot. My decision made, I finalized the drawing of the bow, held low, anticipating that the deer would lower his body to jump as he heard the bow string...."

And now we're back to the opening paragraph of this Toxey Haas chapter. Remember, just as Toxey touched his release the big buck moved forward. Would the arrow strike just behind the animal's vitals? Turns out the arrow did just that. And for what ensues in these next paragraphs I salute Toxey for being candid. We all love to make perfect shots. We all love to see our trophy drop after running a minimal distance, if not sooner. But that doesn't happen, and it hasn't happened in many of the big-buck chapters of this book. Wild critters don't die immediately (nor do domestic ones), and that's a fact of life we all have to live with. Toxey's reason for being candid about the taking of this very significant whitetail will surface soon.

Because of his vast whitetail experience, Toxey was very calm. He climbed down out of his stand, but that's when he admitted to shaking, really shaking. As the buck made its dash after being hit, Haas was fairly certain that he saw the arrow's fletching. It was possible that the broadhead had cut into the vitals, but it was also possible the cutting points might be an inch too far back.

He thought briefly about what to do, but it only took him a few minutes to decide that he might need help, a special kind of help. This was too great a trophy to lose to coyotes. He went directly to Bent Creek Lodge in nearby Jakin, Alabama, and sought the help of the principals there, John Lanier and Leo Allen. Toxey's Mossy Oak PR person, Ronnie "Cuz" Strickland, had told him about a super deer tracking dog at Bent Creek.

The Bent Creek guy with the dog was Jason Armstead. According to Toxey, Jason had sort of spent his life savings on this tracking dog. It was a demo tracker, purchased from a fellow who specialized in training and selling deer tracking canines, and he used the dog that Jason bought from him to showcase the type of deer trackers he was capable of producing.

Four to five hours later, Toxey, Jason, and his male golden retriever, Rusty, were back at the shot sight. Looked like Mom would have to take charge of the twins for a lot longer than Toxey had promised. The dog picked up the scent. Methodically, the golden worked along the

Toxey Haas with Jason Armstead, "Rusty," and the super Pope & Young 11-point that the golden retriever was so instrumental in finding.

trail. Haas heard the buck snort more than once. "Nick, I could even smell that buck," Toxey almost whispered over the phone. Jason was right with the dog when the two jumped him. The dog handler couldn't believe the size of the rack. Biggest buck he'd ever seen in the woods. Blood was everywhere. "The amount of blood was spooky, Nick. A deer of ordinary size would have been out of blood. This just goes to show how much more the really great bucks have in them," Toxey was again talking softly as he related this story.

They sat down and waited. Three more hours! They began following the buck again, right behind the tracking dog, all the while marveling at how super tough a mature buck like this can be. Soon they jumped the deer again. The amount of blood left was monumental. How could a deer lose so much blood and still be able to keep on going? This is not a pretty picture we're painting here. For years Toxey's policy is this, "If I shoot a deer it has to be big enough, worthy enough of mounting. Otherwise I pass it up." A good policy for a trophy hunter.

Toxey felt he wanted to press this buck. He had lost so much blood, surely he couldn't go much farther. So they did, but slowly, probably with the tracking dog on a lead. And soon they found the trophy, an 11-point that would gross at 151 Pope & Young points. What's important here? Toxey says, "The most ethical thing an archer can do, besides having maybe a perfectly tuned bow with which he's amply familiar, is using a tracking dog."

Some states will not permit the use of dogs for anything related to deer hunting, but Toxey feels the use of a tracking dog to follow the trail of a deer that has been hit should be permitted everywhere. He thinks it's the ethical thing to do because it's the quickest way to reach the animal, end any suffering it may be experiencing. He told me one very prominent deer hunting plantation near West Point, Mississippi has had exceptional success finding bucks with their tracking dogs. Lodge management feels they never lose a buck that has been hit anywhere but superficially. The use of dogs for tracking deer that have been hit and not quickly found is a hot, controversial topic. As I said many paragraphs back, I salute Toxey Haas for being so candid on this subject.

Now that you've read about Toxey's hunting strategies, maybe you'd like to find out how he started Mossy Oak. As already mentioned, even when very young Toxey wanted to melt into the landscape better. He also hated making noise. His Dad had taught him the value of building blinds for deer, turkeys, and other game. While Toxey did his share of blind building, he always sensed that too much noise was made in constructing most of them. There had to be a better way. So why not better camouflage clothing? If a hunter's clothing allowed him to blend in perfectly with his surroundings, blind building, and the resultant noise, would be eliminated.

Toxey Haas with his 11-point buck, grossing 151 Pope & Young points.

One of the most important lessons he learned in college, as well as in his first job, centered around the phrase, "....fill a need!" So even though Toxey Haas knew nothing about the clothing industry, he saw the need for camo clothing like Mossy Oak, and soon put all his heart and soul into it.

"Because I knew so little about clothing and making garments, it took me a long time to learn," Toxey revealed.

By March 1986 he was beginning to test market his first garments. The Mossy Oak Bottomland pattern was his first. However, he told me that he already had his next three patterns drawn up in his mind before he even marketed his first. Of course, he knew it wouldn't make good business sense to bring out more than one pattern at a time. Eventually, he has come out with Mossy Oak Treestand, Mossy Oak Full Foliage, and Mossy Oak Fall Foliage.

"Consumers liked the pattern right from the start," Haas offered. "The clothing worked so well it really stacked the odds in the hunter's favor. Often there are hens in front of big trophy gobblers, does in front of big-racked trophy bucks. These hens and does are often very close to the camo-clad hunter. Here's when clothing and a back drop that merely breaks the hunter's outline isn't good enough. It pays to blend in perfectly or near perfectly, especially at very close distances."

Toxey often wears Mossy Oak Fall Foliage for his pants, but one of the other Mossy Oak patterns for his shirt or coat, if he's hunting from the ground. He theorizes that the Fall Foliage pattern blends in well with the ground where he's sitting, but he wants his shirt or coat to blend well with the vegetation just above ground level—an excellent tip.

Toxey's Equipment

Bow - *Oregon Valliant Crusader*
Arrow - *Easton Mossy Oak 2413 (Available only from Pape's Archery in Louisville, Kentucky.)*
Broadhead - *Satellite Titan 125 Grain*
Treestand - *API Baby Grand*
Clothing - *Scent-Lok Inner Layer; Early Season - Mossy Oak Full Foliage Top (Lots Of Green) - Mossy Oak Fall Foliage Pants (Lots Of Brown)*
Boots - *La Crosse Burley*

This giant buck came from Minnesota's farm country. Farm-fed, its B&C count is 192-2/8, truly the buck of a lifetime.

Chapter 18

Roger Syrstad's Tremendous 1989 Buck From Minnesota's Farm Country

This is a phenomenal whitetail, huh? No wonder. It scores a full 192-2/8 Boone & Crockett points. Typical, too, not non-typical! Roger Syrstad has worked for the Fisheries Division of the Minnesota Department of Natural Resources for 31 years. One of his responsibilities as a Natural Resource Tech is to assist with raising walleyes in a hatchery. He lives near Glenwood, Minnesota, which is west of Minneapolis. The terrain here is characterized by rolling hills with lots of farm fields. There isn't a great deal of timberland. Deer escape into brushy draws, sloughs, swamps, cattails, tall canes—that type of cover.

Roger is 59 years old and has been serious about his deer hunting for over 25 years. In the early part of his whitetail career he did most of his hunting much farther north, the big woods country of Minnesota. He still thinks about hunting there, particularly about the camaraderie of deer camp life. But for about the last 10 years he's been hunting as close to home as a fellow can get. He walks right out his back door!

Syrstad owns 60 acres near Glenwood. Twenty-five years ago there were probably a lot more deer farther north in the big woods country, relatively few in his area of Minnesota. These days deer numbers have flip-flopped, with not only more deer in the farm country of this state, but some bucks there are growing to prodigious sizes. No wonder. They're corn-fed!

Paradoxically, after the 1988 Minnesota deer season, Roger decided to become a trophy hunter. Through 1988 he had been, as he described, "....just a deer hunter." Nothing wrong with that and no negative connotation intended. But Syrstad's deer hunting philosophy had always been simple, "Shoot the first buck you see and be grateful for the venison." I used the word paradoxically at the beginning of this

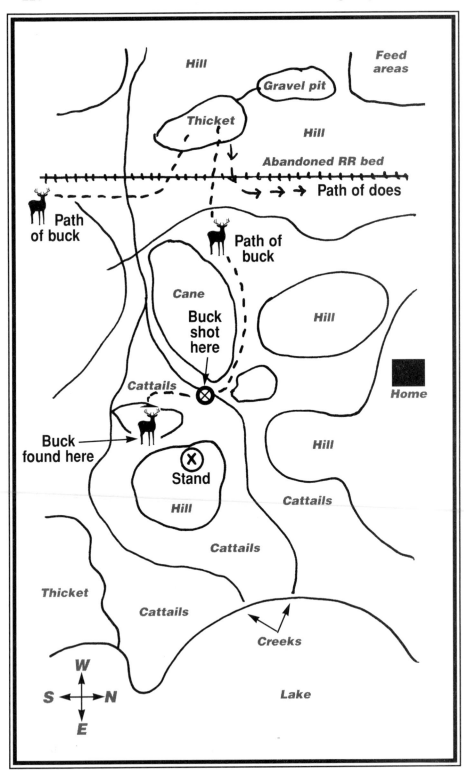

paragraph because this guy was successful with the biggest buck of a lifetime—the very first year he decided to take up trophy hunting!

Prior to the 1989 season he had heard that a few people had seen a particularly big buck not far from the area he hunted. Roger didn't pay much attention, probably figuring these were rumors. Further, he's of the opinion that bucks, particularly the biggest ones, are apt to move considerable distances during the peak of the rut. Because his favorite stands are only 300 yards from his backdoor, little pre-season scouting is necessary. He can often gauge deer movements as he's brushing his teeth and looking out the bathroom window each morning.

In 1989, Minnesota offered deer hunters a choice of either a two-day season (which took place first), or a four-day season (which took place second). You decided which of these two seasons you wanted to hunt beforehand, then applied for one or the other. Pretty short buck season, I'd say. These regulations have been liberalized now.

Syrstad applied for the second of the two, the four-day season, because he knew that it would more likely be the center of the rutting period. On opening day he made his 300 yard walk to one of his stands. Full of anticipation, he stayed out all day, but was rewarded only with doe and fawn sightings. The second day he selected a different tree and was on stand by 6:30 a.m. He sits at the tree's base, doesn't climb. It's shotgun only hunting here.

Early that morning he saw some does. (Note sketch of where they showed and went.) At 7:30 that morning he was to make his first-ever move as a trophy hunter. He passed up a medium-sized 4-point buck, something he would never have dreamed of doing in any previous year. But he was avidly reading deer magazines and learning everything he could about big whitetails, so he was determined to make this change in his hunting philosophy. The date was November 12, 1989.

After watching that 4-point come and go, Roger moved down his hill slightly to another tree where he has taken up his vigil many times before and since. (Again, note sketch.) The does were probably coming out of a bedding area—a thicket and low ground with a creek. There were lots of cattails and tall canes there, plus an old railroad bed. The 4-point walked behind Roger's stand and toward the bedding area.

The weather was overcast. The temperature was about 20 degrees. At daybreak there was a light breeze out of the southeast, but it turned calm within an hour or so. Syrstad was dressed warmly in a blaze orange coat, heavy gloves, and so forth, but even by 8:30 that morning the cold was creeping deeper. He was thinking about getting up to walk to the other side of the hill, a jaunt that would get his circulation moving enough to warm his finger and toe tips.

But he can see quite a distance from the various stands he has selected on his own 60 acres, so he hates to move around. Further, if he moved he could be more easily seen by his quarry. About nine o'clock that morning the wind quit completely. Further emphasizing the silence was the absence of any shooting. One of his favorite stand areas is near the old railroad bed, where several deer trails converge. It's high and exposed there, so Roger doesn't like that stand when it's windy, and the weatherman had forecast wind for that November 12. Just then Roger spotted the big buck we're talking about approximately 350 yards away (a tad far for his slug-shooting 870 pump), but only 30 feet away from the railroad bed stand just alluded to. Putting myself in that morning circumstance, I can hear my mutterings, cursing my luck and the mistaken prognostications of the meteorologist.

"Even at that extreme distance, without the benefit of a scope or binoculars, I could see this buck had a monster rack," Roger talked, the excitement still swelling in his voice, despite over five years having passed.

The buck followed one of the deer trails. (Again, note sketch.) The thicket beyond the railroad bed has consistently been a hotbed of doe activity. Roger is positive the deer was heading for that area, knowing that does often hang out there. At this point, the buck turned and Syrstad got a rear-end view of the prize, and that enabled him to see how far the rack extended on either side of the rump. Needless to say, Roger's eyes popped all the more.

The buck soon disappeared and Roger again mentally kicked himself for not taking that stand by the railroad bed. Maintaining his patience, he decided to sit still and see how things unfolded. There was open territory galore between him and where the deer had disappeared, so there was a good chance he'd spook his quarry if he tried to follow it.

Twenty-five minutes ticked away on his watch with agonizing slowness. He was getting antsy. He wanted to get up. He feared that this buck-of-a-lifetime was getting away from him. About then the monster reappeared 50 yards farther north. He was in a slow trot, head down, apparently sniffing a doe's trail. Yes, the buck was coming toward Roger, as all the trails funneled toward his stand. Don't underestimate the importance of that last phrase. It's a key to many correct stand selections. Obviously, a stand with a number of deer trails funneling toward it is going to be a far better producer than one that doesn't.

The deer kept coming, then disappeared in some low ground behind some canes that kept the buck from Roger's view. Roger shifted into a better shooting position just then, down on one knee, the 870 shotgun up to his shoulder and generally aimed at where the buck would reemerge. It appeared to be a long shot for his slug load.

When the buck reappeared, his head, neck, and massive set of antlers were all that Roger could see. Range was 130 yards. Some of the deer trails were still coming Roger's way. The buck again put his nose to the deer trail—a trail that turned right. Again he vanished, this time behind more canes, plus some brushy stuff, moving almost broadside to Roger. This deer trail wasn't going to bring the buck any closer. The distance would be 120 yards, which is "stretching" for a shotgun with two beads on the rib and no scope.

Roger took his first shot as carefully as he could, then, racking the action quickly, he got off two more before the buck disappeared. The third shot had been at about 100 yards. He knows he hit the buck with the first shot, but it was centered too far back from the chest. He doesn't know whether the second or third shot, which took the buck through the ribs, was the telling one. Syrstad knew his slug would be dropping 10 inches or more at the extreme range, so he had been holding significantly high. Interestingly, I shot a buck on Quebec's Anticosti Island a couple of years ago. We paced that one off at 117 steps. I had hit the buck three out of four times, but I was using a rifled barrel, Remington's new Copper Solids (very accurate), AND a scope sight. All in all, my task was a lot easier than Roger's.

The buck disappeared behind more canes. Roger sat tight. In addition to giving the buck a chance to expire on its own (actually, it already had), Syrstad had an excellent view of all the escape routes the buck had, if indeed he did try to leave from that cane-filled area where he had disappeared. While sitting there, Roger visually marked the spot where the buck had disappeared over and over in his mind. Finally, he got up. Where the buck had gone beyond his view the last time he found a good blood trail. Elation! He followed the blood trail to a creek bed. He couldn't find any blood leaving the creek. The elation was gone.

He found a deer trail going out of the creek. He followed it for over 50 yards. No blood. He returned to the creek. Found a second trail leading out of it. Fifty more yards. Nothing. Back to the creek. Third trail a charm? Nothing for 30 yards. Then, there was a spot of blood. Roger had to walk only a short distance before he found his prize—dead.

Imagine yourself standing over a monster buck like Roger was now doing. The degree of elation must be monumental. I can feel myself jabbering, shaking, not knowing what to do next. The buck was so big Syrstad would have to get help. He field dressed the buck before taking any photos, and he's scolding himself for not taking lots of photos right at the kill sight. "Such photos would have meant so much more to me," he confided.

He also told me, "I wish I had become a trophy hunter earlier in life. I didn't pass up enough bucks prior to 1989, and now I sincerely feel I could have taken at least one or two, perhaps several trophy bucks, had I simply let more bucks walk, bucks that I shot instead, indeed average bucks.

"I've also learned a lot more about hunting trophy whitetails since that 1989 success. I read every deer magazine I can get my hands on. Many of them are packed with excellent suggestions."

There are many tips that Roger Syrstad has learned, and he has asked me to pass on some of the most important ones to you. Since he hunts his own 60 acres, it's obvious that he's intimately familiar with his hunting grounds. But he stresses that all whitetail trophy hunters would do well to learn as much as they can about the area they hunt. Don't just study the area during or right before the hunting season; live with those surroundings year round.

He also likes to talk with other trophy hunters, sharing ideas. He chats with his surrounding landowners often, sharing information about deer movements, trophies that might have been spotted. He suggests hunting when the peak of the rut is on, if that's possible in your state. Large hunt parties aren't his style. The lone hunter has a better chance of encountering deer on their own terms, when they're acting and moving naturally. Areas that are relatively undisturbed by other hunters lend themselves more to natural deer movements.

Once you are hunting, be patient. Be willing to sit it out all day, having confidence in the stand sight you have carefully selected. But don't just sit there; continually be observant and alert. Your movements must be minimal. Seeing the deer before they see you should always be what you're trying to achieve. Don't smoke or chew tobacco. During the 1994 season, Roger's son lost out on an opportunity for a shot at a particularly big buck. Syrstad was watching the scenario unfold from quite a distance away. The buck was on a trail that would lead right to his son, who had carefully showered that morning and was wearing all freshly laundered clothing. But he was chewing tobacco. Roger saw the buck stop on the trail and sniff the air, and the buck wasn't even directly downwind from his son. Immediately, the buck left the trail and disappeared into a slough.

Have a plan. You should know where the deer may first appear, or at least the direction. Knowing that, select your stand so you're downwind from that area. At rug-cutting time stay cool. This is hard to do, but you can do it. Save the time for shaking when you're standing over your prize. Only by staying calm will you have a chance of properly placing your shot. When you do take that prize buck, be ready to take lots of pictures.

After taking his 1989 trophy, Roger Syrstad never fired a shot in deer season in 1990, 1991, 1992, or 1993. He held out for a trophy-type buck. But on the last day of the 1994 season, 20 minutes before sundown, two does came over the old railroad bed, with a good buck not far behind, sniffing their trail. Syrstad took his second trophy buck, a nice 8-point that scores 127 B&C—not in this same class as his 192-2/8 1989 giant, but still an outstanding trophy buck.

Roger Syrstad's Equipment

Gun - *Remington 870 12 Gauge Pump - Two Bead Sights*
Ammo - *Remington Slugger*
Clothing - *Blaze Orange Coat & Gloves-Bun Warmer*
Boots - *Rubber Insulated*

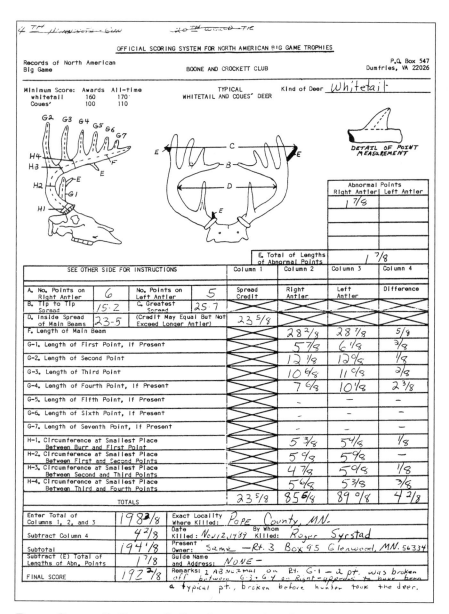

Roger Syrstad's Boone & Crockett scoring form for his 1989 buck.

Blackie Lightfoot with his Texas 6-point. Imagine how high this buck with the super wide spread would have scored if the rack had two or four more points!!

Chapter 19

Blackie Lightfoot's Encounter With A Texas 6-Point

I was listening to Harold Knight on my phone machine. "Nick, just had a call from a guy in Texas, Blackie Lightfoot." He was really excited. Lightfoot told me about the how-to of taking a 6-point in Texas, but, get this, the buck has a spread of more than 23 inches. He also told me about his unique approach to rattling and grunt-calling. Harold had told me, "He's worth phoning, for it sounds to me like he's worthy of consideration for one of your book chapters."

Harold's name has been mentioned previously in these pages. He's one of the principals in Knight & Hale Game Calls out of Cadiz, Kentucky. I've never been out with a better woodsman, and I've enjoyed the outdoors with more than my share. Like the TV ad of several years ago, "When Harold speaks, I listen."

Indeed, I found Blackie an interesting guy with whom to talk, and you're going to find his whitetail how-to both very informative and most beneficial. First a little background. He started out his job career as an engineer for an outfit called Worthington, Inc. That job required that he travel all over the country fixing turbines. Obviously, specialized stuff. He retired at an early age and opened his own turbine-fixing business. This venture went well until the bottom fell out of the Texas oil business in the early 1980s.

Since he always loved the out-of-doors, plus had devoted much of his spare time to bass fishing, he began offering his services as a bass guide on nearby Lake Conroe. He also guided his own bass fishing clients on ventures into various Mexican lakes. One day while helping Ron Phillips with his outdoor show promotion at Lake Conroe, Blackie was fishing with one of Whopper Stopper's principals. Whopper Stopper is a tackle company of considerable renown. On the first cast Blackie hooked, landed, and released a 5 pound largemouth. The rest of the day he kept boating bass after bass. Back at the dock it was dis-

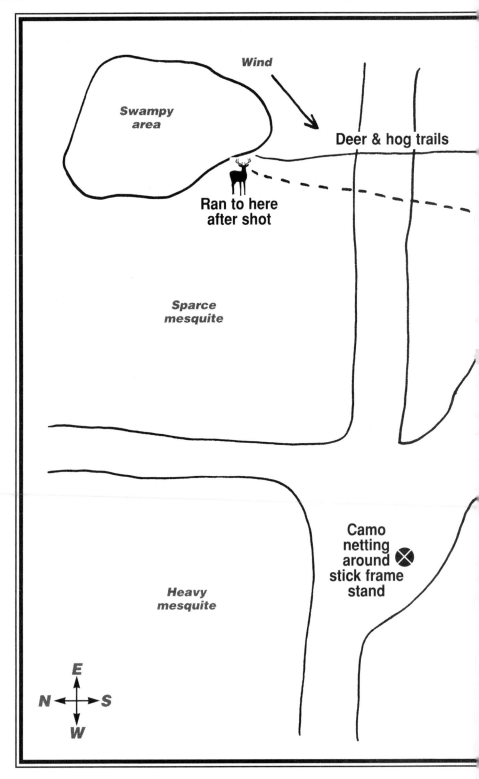

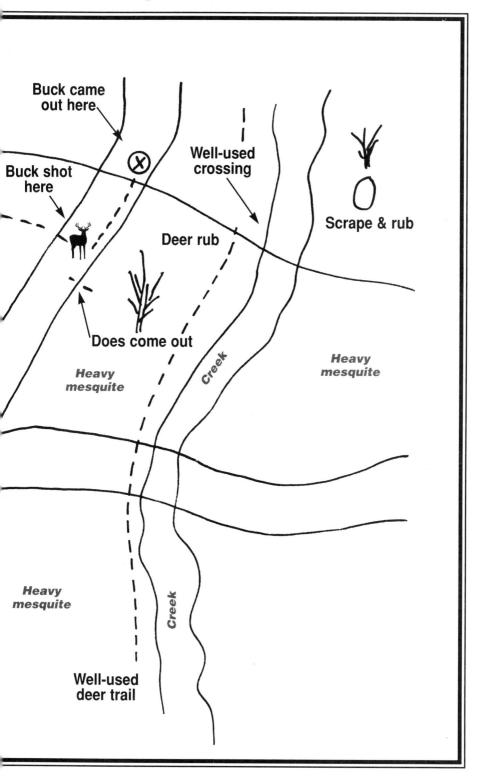

covered no one in the group, including the outdoor writers who had been invited on the outing, had caught a thing. The scribes crowded around Lightfoot, pencils pushing, tape recorders winding, as they probed him with bass how-to questions. Whopper Stopper loved it. They bought Blackie a motor home, told him to fish all around the country, and give their company some exposure. Some deal, huh!

These days Blackie is a TV host of "Honey Hole All Outdoors." Blackie and his co-host, Bob Hood, outdoor writer for the Fort Worth Star Telegraph, were supposed to film the deer hunt where Lightfoot took the major 6-point for their TV show, but Hood had to change his plans at the last minute. Blackie had arranged to hunt this area, about 1100 acres (tiny for many Texas properties), with a landowner acquaintance.

Interestingly, this particular area of Texas is not known for its big bucks, but it is known for large numbers of whitetails. Of course, other areas of Texas are well known for the out-size whitetail racks they're capable of producing consistently, but you'd better be able to mortgage the farm or have a very high limit on your major credit card if you want to hunt such a ranch.

Blackie provided more important input. "The landowner told me I could (1) take a very big buck, or (2) shoot only a spike. He didn't want any of the intermediate bucks shot, ones capable of producing prodigious racks in future years. NONE!! As you might guess, I wrote off shooting a spike. It would be a significant buck or nothing. I had one day to deer hunt!!"

But a week or so before that whitetail foray Lightfoot was invited to the ranch for a scouting session—a scouting session where he would be permitted to take one of those famous Texas wild hogs. "The ranch is absolutely overrun with wild hogs, so taking one was no problem," Blackie confided. "The opportunity to scout for whitetails and see what I could plan for our TV show was what I looked forward to most."

The one-day buck hunt took place December 28, 1994, right in the middle of the rut for that section of Texas. Weather! It was raining and miserable. A Norther had blown in off the Arctic Ice Cap. Temps were down. The wind was significant. The sendero road into this 1100 acre hunting area was hopeless. Blackie had to walk in from the hard road. The terrain is hilly, not at all like flat south Texas. Lots of mesquite though (like south Texas), plus plenty of cactus and a few oaks mixed in, the latter always important for their mast crop. As already mentioned, the ranch spread out over 1100 acres, and Lightfoot knew the boundaries.

The mesquite and cactus were very thick. Visibility was only a few yards, except down the relatively few senderos. For those not familiar with this Mexican word, it would be similar to roads in heavy brush country, mere trails where four-wheel drive vehicles can travel where there is no brush that restricts the hunter's vision. (See sketch.)

Before he even left his vehicle, Blackie had selected his stand, for he knew the wind direction, and from what he had discovered while wild hog hunting and scouting during his previous trip, he knew only one stand sight would be favorable to him. Off to the stand's right was a gully, and deer traveled that. However, from his stand he couldn't see down into the bowels of that gully. Not just the depth prevented this. It was also the extreme thickness of the mesquite and other brush. What had him most excited about hunting this restricted 1100 acres was the huge buck tracks he had found while wild hog hunting. By the way, he did kill a huge hog on that earlier venture.

Blackie Lightfoot has been rattling white-tailed bucks for many years; he started years prior to when the practice became popular. He advised, "Here in Texas it's common, when rattling, to be able to call in more than one buck at a time. Further, does sometimes come in to the rattling before any buck might. Accordingly, to rattle deer in and keep them in you have to camo in!"

He uses a camo called UV Dead. Not only does he have this camo clothing on when rattling, he also goes with complete face paint, plus he strings UV Dead mesh camo in front of him. This netting prevents the deer from seeing the movements he makes with the rattling horns and grunt tube. This netting has the short longitudinal cuts, so the wind causes minimal waving motion. "I also make up a masking scent of vanilla extract," Blackie explained. "Deer can't figure it out. Vanilla is not a scent they encounter in the wild, but the odor produced is not one that spooks them. I've found that many so-called masking scents do, in fact, spook wary bucks." In addition to this masking scent Blackie also relies upon Tink's 69.

He had some great input regarding rattling. "I start with immature buck stuff—just tickling antlers. In between the tickling I go with light grunts. This lasts for two to three minutes. After that I grunt into the call every two to three minutes. Here's where I turn the tube in different directions each time I blow. In all, I do three to four sets of this immature buck tickling and grunt calling."

But when that long scenario is over Blackie suggests that a bruiser buck has hopefully heard all this. Next he creates what is another monster coming upon the scene. He's seen this happen in true-to-life buck fight scenarios before. One of the two immatures invariably runs off. The other immature stays to do battle with the big boy, the "horse," as Lightfoot calls him. Next a big battle takes place, and that's the scene Blackie tries to play out with his rattling horns and grunt tube over the next several minutes. During the scuffle he's pounding the rattling antlers into the ground, doing everything he can to simulate a whitetail battle royale.

Guess what he does next? Nothing. Absolutely nothing. "If I've created the desired rattling scenario, here's the deal. The dominant buck has won the fight. He has established the 'territory' as his. After a significant pause I give a few light communications grunts, just tickle the antlers a tad. Now, don't look for the brute buck you're hoping to sucker to charge into the scene. Instead, look for an antler, a portion of antler, an ear, an eye."

Get the picture here? Blackie has one day to hunt. He selects his rattle-calling area carefully, most important with the wind in mind. Once on stand he camouflages himself to the utmost. Next he creates the image of two immature bucks duking it out. But then a "big boy" steps in and settles all accounts. Now the scene is complete. If a hunter has ever set up a scenario to entice a brute buck to be suckered into a man-created scene, Lightfoot has done it. However, be assured that your average one-and-a-half and two-and-a-half year old bucks would probably be spooked out of the area for days with the creation of this fake scene. Such bucks wouldn't, maybe couldn't, be persuaded to fight the dominant buck that had just been the victor. If you create this scene yourself, rest assured you'll probably drive off any decent buck within hearing.

But not a really dominant buck. And since you're reading this, we're assuming that's what you're after. Lightfoot provides more input. "While you're creating this artificial scene with the antler rattling, antler pounding, and the grunt calling, you really have to be on your toes. You must be alert, keen, eyes always probing. It's not just the dominant buck in the area that will be pulled to this scene. It's possible that every deer, especially does, will be attracted to the show. Once deer start arriving you still have to remain hidden, despite the movement you might continue to have to make with the rattling antlers and the grunt tube."

As if Lightfoot had already predicted what was going to unfold, two does were the first to appear. Were they anxious to take the proverbial ringside seat? "One of those does was huge," Blackie said. "She looked right at me, then began that side-stepping action indicating that she didn't like what she saw, but that she wasn't convinced I was all bad."

That's when he noticed that one piece of the net camo shielding him was flapping in the wind a little. As soon as the doe looked away he flicked a rock with his foot, and that held down the flapping netting. Next he went back to work, for the doe had trotted off, but her tail was not up in alarm. First he rattled very hard. Through his tube he came out with a number of communication grunts. He followed this sequence with light antler clicking. He wanted to keep her interested, keep her on the scene, hoping the brute buck was already nearby, unseen, but taking all this in.

The doe started back. When she did Blackie went back to the hard-battle scene. But not for long, stopping abruptly. The doe was looking directly at him, but his camo clothing and netting provided the perfect hide. That's when Blackie put the pièce de résistance on any buck within hearing range. He calls it the "service grunt." It's the grunt call he has heard many times while watching a buck imminently ready to service a doe in estrus. Impossible to put in words on paper, here's a try, "uunnt, uunnt, uunnt, uunnt, uunnt."

"When a buck does the service grunt, it's like he's hyperventilating," is the way Blackie puts it.

The huge 6-point, until then obviously hiding just out of sight, charged onto the scene. But Blackie already had the rifle handy. Shortly, the crosswires were where they had to be.

The rifle? It was a .300 Winchester Magnum, one that famous bass pro Randy Fite had glass bedded, then helped with fine tuning the handloads. The shot was at 175 yards. But the buck took off running. Still, Lightfoot felt he had heard the bullet hit home. He walked up, but he, mistakenly, didn't go far enough. Instinctively, he walked farther. Shortly, he saw pink, foamy blood, indicative of a lung hit, so his confidence soared. But he had to continue on the trail for another 100 yards. The big buck went that far despite the bullet taking out both lungs and the top of the heart. Again, these big fellows don't die quickly like the average buck! Blackie Lightfoot was especially excited all through the foregoing, but he forced his mind to overcome the emotions until he discovered the buck piled up in the mesquite. What a feeling. The adrenaline rush took over. A massive rack for only 6 points, plus more than 23 inches of inside spread! Imagine how high this buck would have scored with two or four more points.

Blackie Lightfoot's Equipment

Rifle - Model 70 Sporter Magnum in .300 Winchester Magnum
Scope - Leupold 4x-12x Vari-X-II
Load - Handload With Reloader 22 And 180 Grain Sierra Spitzer
Clothing - UV Dead, including netting
Call - Knight & Hale EZ-Grunt-Er-Plus

More On Blackie Lightfoot's Big Whitetail Tips

Blackie attaches pieces of fresh whitetail tarsal glands to the soles of his boots. He also adds attractor scent to his clothing and his netting material, plus adds vanilla extract as a cover scent, as well. He realizes that many whitetail trophy hunters are adamant about using rubber boots, but Lightfoot goes with leather. "I do this because I cover so much ground," he explains, "and leather boots are simply more comfortable to me when walking. However, my leather boots exude a stench of buck attractor scent and vanilla extract."

Another tip is that riflemen should sight in their rifle regularly, especially after an airline trip. They should do this themselves, not rely on someone else. Further, he recommends double and triple checking of all your equipment prior to every hunt.

David Blanton and his Mexican buck that was taken from a hill above an oat patch. The oats attracted the does. The does attracted this big-racked fellow. He's a main-frame 10-point with double brow tines that make him a 12-point.

Three Realtree Connections

How-to! How-to! How-to! That's what we're interested in here—the how-to involved in taking some big, big bucks over the years, especially recent years. You've already read about how the designer of Realtree camouflage, Bill Jordan, took three outstanding whitetails in one year—1994. (Plus he shot two others we didn't cover.) With this chapter we wanted to follow that triplicate up with yet another. For this chapter, we've selected three of Bill's Realtree-clad close friends.

So, we're going to capture a trio of significant big buck how-to's here. One is with a guy named David Blanton, a fellow I've shared many an outdoor day with and a guy you're gonna love getting to know because of his how-to stuff. Another story comes from Joe Drake, professionally a Columbus, Georgia fireman and one of the most successful and dedicated deer and gobbler hunters, and callers, the world has ever seen. The trio is completed with former Atlanta Braves catcher Greg Olson. Greg has thrown out more base stealers than trophy bucks he has seen, but he has spent an inordinate amount of time in the woods. Since his baseball retirement he's spending even more time afield after bucks with big racks. We start this trio of white-tailed buck stuff with David Blanton. Here goes!

David Blanton Heads for Mexico

David Blanton is as dedicated, sophisticated, and know-how oriented a deer and turkey hunter as you'll ever meet. To hunt with David, which I've had the privilege of doing many times, is always a learning experience, generally loaded with excitement and, most important, a pleasure. Every one of you readers would enjoy a woods outing with this guy. His perception, and especially his personal value of what the out-of-doors is all about, always shines through. He's one of the most thoughtful, concerned, never-do-it-any-way-but-the-right-way men I've shared the outback of several states with.

David has been successful as a sporting goods dealer, successful as an outdoor writer, successful in anything he does. He and Realtree's Bill Jordan hooked up several years ago. No wonder. Blanton hails from La Grange, Georgia, more than a rock-throw's distance from Jordan's home base of Columbus, Georgia, but Bill's favorite Georgia hunting grounds are smack-dab in between at Callaway Gardens. These "Gardens," by the way, are indeed the world's best hunting camp, and have some of the best hunting for long-bearded gobblers and heavy, bragging-size whitetails. This is coupled with 10-minute-away accommodations that are second to none. Further, during the mid-day slack times for long beards and big bucks, four championship golf courses await those of us who are addicted. Many a day, near Callaway Gardens, I've bagged a big buck in the fall, a bragging-size gobbler in the spring, then enjoyed 18 holes of championship golf in the afternoon. Is this a great country, or what?

But David Blanton wasn't hunting his Georgia home grounds on the days in question. He had ventured into Mexico instead. The last decade or so, Texas has been a big-buck mecca for whitetail buffs who want to bag the wall hanger to end all wall hangers. The guys and gals who have traveled to the Lone Star State during that period have been willing to pay big bucks (dollars, that is) for the opportunity of putting scope crosswires or bow pin sights on critters with eye-popping racks.

But for those few in the "whitetail-know," the Mexican provinces just across the Texas border have become the latest big-buck mecca. Why? Most importantly, the gene pool here is excellent, as these whitetails have the potential to produce progeny with one out-size rack after another. Almost as importantly, hunting pressure in this section of Mexico has been very light over the last decade. As big-buck hunting in Texas has become big, big business, landowners on the south side of the Texas border have become increasingly aware that they, too, have Boone & Crockett possibilities. Make that probabilities. So those landowners have been more jealously guarding and protecting their whitetails.

I asked David Blanton why he and Realtree's Bill Jordan had been hunting Mexico so avidly the last three years. First he gave the two above reasons, then he chimed in with a third. "In most of the United States, the prime period for whitetails in the rut is around mid-November. We're interested in filming for Realtree videos and for our Realtree Outdoors television show. We're so busy in mid-November, we can't get to one-tenth of the places we want to hunt and film big bucks in action. But in early January there aren't all that many places where the deer are typically in full rut. Even in most of Texas the peak of the rut occurs a little earlier. Where we hunt in Mexico, the rut peak takes place from about January 8-15."

For 1995, David was hunting Mexico, in the province of Coahila, a week earlier. He arrived January 3. His primary responsibility was to capture NASCAR racing star Dale Earnhart scoring on a big Mexican whitetail on video. The next morning everything fell perfectly into place; the light, the weather, Dale, and a great buck all cooperated. After the hunt, he and Earnhart did all the necessary fill-in work to finish up that part of the Realtree video. Then David was free to hunt on his own.

I'll let him describe the hunting area. "Unlike south Texas, this is brushy country with rolling hills. In south Texas, at least where I've hunted, you can never find a bluff or a hill where you can look down into a valley below. It's an advantage to be able to do that. That's no doubt why the 'Texas Tripods' have become so popular there. Also unlike Texas, the primary vegetation isn't mesquite, but black brush and cactus, a lot of prickly pear, a few palmettos. Occasionally, it's possible to find a bluff that the hunter can use to good advantage, scanning the valley or canyon below. What I found was a valley with a strip of oats planted in the bottom. We built two blinds, one on each of the ridges that looked down into the oat patch.

"The oats would offer a primary food source at this time of the winter. I figured the strip would attract does in high numbers, and that was the game plan. Several weeks earlier, when bucks were still fighting and deciding on the pecking order, rattling would have written the ticket to success. Now, with the peak of the rut only days away, pecking orders had already been decided. Big bucks weren't interested in fighting anymore. Rather, they had a one-tract mind—finding a doe that might come into her estrous period a few days early. Using a grunt call at this time was useful, but only for attracting 1-1/2- and 2-1/2-year old bucks. I wanted to find does. The more the merrier, for I knew where does concentrated, big bucks would be very close by, if not right in their midst. The strip of oats, the only food source of its type within miles, was certain to concentrate the does."

So, is there anyway you can concentrate does during this period just before the prime rut? In some sections of the country this may not be possible, but is that true where you live? Another key to David Blanton's success had to be the two blinds, one on the north ridge above the oat strip, a second on the south ridge. Now, no matter which direction the wind might blow, the hunter could select a blind where he was positioned downwind from the food source that attracted the deer.

Late in the afternoon of January 4, 1995, Blanton was in one of the blinds. "A couple of decent bucks came in, but there were tremendous numbers of does. I was confident a big buck would show soon," Blanton told me. That just didn't happen on the 4th, however.

The morning of January 5th the buck David eventually shot did come in, but David missed him. What he had failed to do when he built the blind was to create a suitable shooting rest. From both blinds it was over 200 yards to the oat stubble. During midday on the 5th he came up with two large plastic bags, the type that zip shut. He tucked one inside the other, making a double bag, then filled the inner one with sand. This would be the rest for his rifle's fore-end. At the blind he rigged a piece of 1 x 4 lumber on one side. This would be a rest for his right elbow.

"Some might wonder why I went back to the same place after missing the biggest buck in the herd. Wouldn't that deer be spooked for days, if not weeks? I was confident the deer would be back. Does were so numerous around the oat strip," David revealed.

But the buck didn't come back that afternoon of the 5th, despite does tearing up the oat strip in record numbers. But on the morning of the 6th, the brute 12-point came in at first light, and David shot him with a Remington 700 in .264 Winchester caliber.

David Blanton's Equipment

Rifle - *Remington 700 in .264 Win. Mag.*
Scope - *Redfield 3x-9x*
Binoculars - *Simmons 10 X 40*
Grunt Call - *Lohman*
Clothing - *Realtree All Purpose*

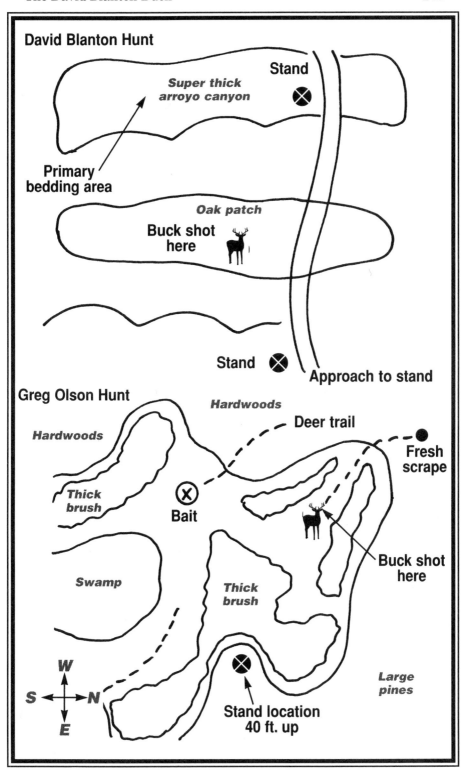

David Blanton Hunt

Super thick
arroyo canyon

Stand

Primary
bedding area

Oak patch

Buck shot
here

Stand

Approach to stand

Greg Olson Hunt

Hardwoods

Hardwoods

Deer trail

Fresh
scrape

Thick
brush

Bait

Buck shot
here

Swamp

Thick
brush

W
S ← → N
E

Stand location
40 ft. up

Large
pines

*Joe Drake and his 5 by 7 (plus stickers) from the Encinitos
Ranch in south Texas.*

Joe Drake's Texas Deer

Joe Drake is a fireman in Columbus, Georgia, but he lives turkey gobbler and big whitetail hunting. As a caller Joe has built an enviable record. A few of his turkey calling accolades include World Champion 1987, National Champion 1983 and 1993, and Southern Open Champion 1987 and 1989. He has won the Georgia State Turkey Calling Championship five times. The only deer calling contest he ever entered was the U.S. Open, where he came in 4th.

While Joe was conducting a seminar in Columbus with David Hale and Billy MacCoy in 1987, he ran into Bill Jordan. When Bill saw that Joe wasn't attired in Realtree camo, which Jordan had introduced only months before, Bill convinced Drake to join his pro staff. Since he hooked up with Jordan, Joe Drake has been guiding outdoor writers and doing a lot more deer and turkey hunting.

The buck pictured here with Joe was taken at the Encinitos Ranch in December of 1994, but Joe wanted to go back to 1991, when he was running a video camera at Encinitos for Bill Jordan. They were hunting right at the peak of the rut. Deer were not coming to the feeders, and rattling wasn't working on its own. This duo, however, finally started enticing some nice bucks with Joe working a grunt tube and Bill working the rattling horns.

Joe did the filming of Bill taking a good buck, so the next few days they used the technique to try to sucker in a bruiser for Drake. Finally a good buck came in with a doe. The buck was really mad, his rack smashing vegetation every few steps. He even created a scrape while Joe and Bill were watching. Joe wanted to shoot, but Bill told him to wait just a bit so they could observe the big buck some more, maybe learn something that would help in their future hunting efforts.

The buck and doe melted back into the mesquite without a shot being fired. But Bill said they could bring the deer back, and by grunting and rattling, the buck was convinced to return. Joe took the buck this time. Surprisingly, the 11-point only weighed 110 pounds, so the rut had taken a heavy toll on its body weight. Further, both brow tines were broken off, and its face was so scarred and torn up from fighting that Joe couldn't use the skin for a taxidermy mount. But as for technique, try going out with a buddy in the peak of the rut, one of you with a grunt tube, the other with the rattling horns!

In 1992, Joe Drake took a 15-point that grossed 168 B&C at the Perlitz Ranch. In 1993 he was back at Encinitos. A few days into the hunt, the video camera that Joe was operating broke. They sent out for parts. Meanwhile, Bill Whitfield, the guy who leases the hunting rights at Encinitos, took Joe to a new 2500-acre pasture, one that had never been hunted before. That's when they walked up a tremendous buck. There was time to shoot, only four or five seconds. Joe had his gun, but never brought it up. "There was no video camera, and this deer definitely deserved being taken on video, if that would ever be possible. The reason I was there was to film or hunt while the camera was whirring," Joe explained.

"Nick, as that buck ran off his rack was sticking out at least 6 inches on both sides of his butt. We moved tripods to that area late in the 1993 season." David Blanton was videotaping a celebrity to start the hunt, but Blanton and Drake got together for the next day, and Joe got the giant buck in his sights—only to shoot over him!! He had rechecked his rifle's zero upon arrival in Texas, but a scope mount had come loose while riding around the ranch's rough sendero roads. For the 1994 season, Joe bought a Remington 700 Sendero bolt action in 7mm Rem Mag., topped it with a Nikon 3.5x-10x 50mm scope. He had previously had the opportunity to shoot Texas bucks at extreme distances, and he had turned them down. With this new rifle, designed specifically for Texas long shots, Joe had practiced and felt confident to 400 yards.

Just when he was rigged for extra long range shooting, a buck came in that could have been taken with a shotgun. Blanton was running the camera; Joe that Sendero rifle. Despite being legal shooting time that morning, there wasn't enough light for the video camera. Drake remembers the buck standing between two does, his regal rack with 12 points—7 points on one side, 5 points on the other—plus lots of stickers, and not being able to shoot because of the derned video thing. While they waited for the light to brighten the buck ran at one of the does. The does fed toward the right. If they kept feeding in that direction it wouldn't be possible to shoot, for the deer would be in the throes of a mesquite thicket and gone. Before enough light materialized, that's exactly what happened. Joe's heart sank. But he and David kept watching. Now the light was getting better. More watching.

Suddenly, a doe flashed in an opening. Why was she running? Joe got his long range rifle into position. More watching. Then the buck stepped into view, a whopping 55 steps away. Joe's 7mm Mag bullet took him just under the chin as the deer faced the hunters head on. This 12-point grosses 163, but there are big deductions since the buck has 5 points on one side, 7 on the other.

Joe Drake's Equipment

Rifle - *Remington 700 Sendero Model in 7mm Rem. Mag.*
Scope - *Nikon 3.5x-10x 50mm*
Bullet - *Federal Hi-Shok*
Calls - *HS Strut Super Quad Grunt Call*
Rattling Bag - *HS Strut*
Clothing - *Realtree All Purpose*
Seat - *HS Strut Bun-Saver (Air Cushion Strap-On Type)*

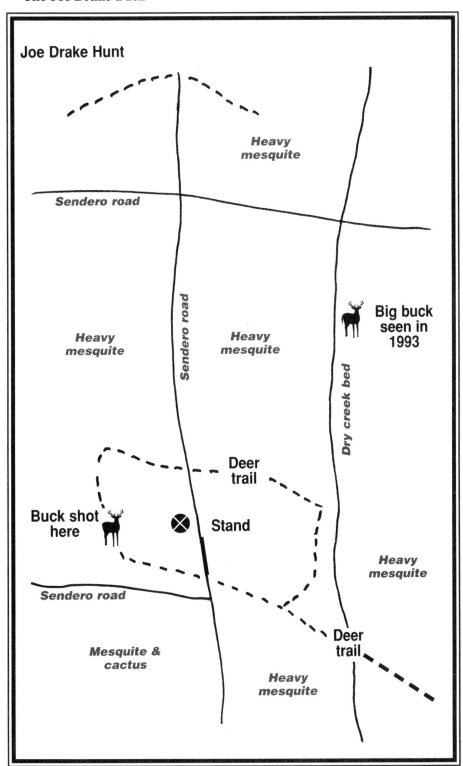

Joe Drake Hunt

Heavy mesquite

Sendero road

Heavy mesquite

Sendero road

Heavy mesquite

Big buck seen in 1993

Dry creek bed

Deer trail

Buck shot here

Stand

Heavy mesquite

Sendero road

Mesquite & cactus

Heavy mesquite

Deer trail

Saskatchewan has a lot of high-scoring whitetails, but you'd better be prepared for cold weather hunting if you go there. Of course, cold weather can occur in any state with whitetails. Prepared hunters are still able to hunt, and maybe score like Greg Olson did with this trophy.

Greg Olson's Buck - Third of the Realtree Trio

Greg Olson was born and raised around Edina, Minnesota. He loved hunting and fishing and was known as the "Tom Sawyer" of Minnehaha Creek. He caught more carp than anyone. But Greg was also interested in sports. He attended the University of Minnesota, then went into professional baseball. For seven and a half years he toiled in the minor leagues. But he learned his trade well. In 1990 he was the National League's All-Star Catcher. In 1991 and 1992 he and the Atlanta Braves won the World Series. He met Bill Jordan once he got to play with the Braves, since both have such intense interest in the outdoors. Greg has retired from playing baseball, but he hunts and fishes every chance he gets, plus manages a minor league team, the Minnesota Loons.

In mid-November of 1994, Greg Olson went to Saskatoon, Saskatchewan with Bill Jordan. They then drove three hours northwest, into what the locals call "the bush country." The timing should have meant the rut would be at its peak, but Greg said it appeared the height was 10 to 15 days behind schedule. They were in a new hunting camp, one that had never been hunted out of before. It was warm, at least for that far north in Saskatchewan, so the mild weather might have had something to do with the rut running late. Temps were about 15 degrees in the morning, 25 degrees at midday. They saw a few young bucks chasing does, but for the first several days deer simply were not moving much.

The territory was huge. Moving around in such an expanse, especially where so much looks the same, can be futile as far as whitetail success. But baiting is legal in Saskatchewan, so this is when getting into a treestand, then staying there all day, can be especially effective. When it's 15 degrees in the morning, only warms up to 25, plus there's even a little wind, staying in a stand all day is very tough to do, both physically and mentally. Of course, Saskatchewan is known for holding some tremendous big bucks, and that thought helps. Remember, the temperatures mentioned were abnormal. Greg Olson was expecting even colder weather, so he came prepared.

Greg reaffirmed this. "The toughest thing to do is to make yourself stay in that stand. If you ever get cold, it's impossible to keep seated. Also, I know there's a lot of deer movement in this part of Canada from say eleven in the morning to one in the afternoon. This is when most hunters are programmed to leave their stands, go have lunch and warm up. Believe me, it's tempting."

Greg goes with the "layer" system. That means he wears minimal clothing during the vehicle ride to his dropoff point, and while walking into the stand. Once he arrives, then he starts adding those "layers."

"If a stand hunter's hands or feet get cold, the party's over," Olson mused. "That's why I rely on Ice Breaker Booties and an Ice Breaker Muff. The company makes both these in Realtree camo. They're just the ticket for stand hunting in the coldest weather. They give a guy the staying power he needs to stick it out all day."

Greg augments the booties (these fit over the top of your warm, heavily insulated boots) and the big muff with handwarmers. Using the largest size of disposable handwarmers, Olson finds they last all day. He puts one in each bootie and one in the muff, so he needs three for each hunting day. These are real keys to his success with the buck pictured here.

Each night he'd come back to camp. Kelly, one of the guides, kept encouraging him. "Greg, stay in that stand. I've been scouting your area for weeks. There's a big buck that stays nearby."

They told him he wouldn't see any spike bucks, that there weren't any in that area. But the first day he saw a spike, plus a fair moose. The second day he watched two spikes, so he jabbed at the guides at camp that evening about his findings. The third day he saw a deer with one side of its rack already gone, probably from fighting. The side remaining had 4 points. So, 10 points total in three days with four bucks. Tough to keep your confidence up in that same treestand, in that tough weather.

The fourth day would be even more difficult because a video cameraman was with Greg. Well into the day he glimpsed a huge-bodied deer at the side of a bog. The deer moved a little. Now it was facing Greg. All he could see was neck and horns. Plenty of the latter as the accompanying photo attests. Carefully, Greg turned his eyes to the cameraman to see if the video was running. That guy was looking in the opposite direction. Greg waited, willing the cameraman's attention, which didn't work. Finally he whistled. Now the buck was really alerted. But the video was soon cranking.

Greg was 40 feet up in a cedar tree. There was a little wind, so the treetop was swaying a bit. Anticipating that a steady hold might be a problem, Olson had rigged two shooting sticks that he now had up in the tree with him. Using those shooting sticks Greg had the deer in the scope for about 40 seconds before the cameraman told him to shoot. The shooter and the videoman can whisper back and forth via wireless microphones and earphones. This electronic equipment is turned on only after a deer arrives. It's too tough on batteries to keep the microphones and earphones turned on all the time. The deer, looking straight on, lifted its head and Olson slid the bullet in just under its chin. Dead in its tracks, the big 11-point hit the ground, never moving an inch after that. In addition to the 11 points, the buck had two 1-1/4-inch stickers on each main. He grosses at 160.

Greg Olson's Equipment

Rifle - *Browning A-Bolt Stainless Stalker in 7mm Rem. Mag.*
Scope - *Leupold 3x-9x*
Bullet - *Federal Premium 140 Grain*
Camo - *Realtree All Purpose*
Over -*Boot Socks And Muff by Icebreaker*